Empowering Your Life with

WICCA

EMPOWERING YOUR LIFE WITH
WICCA

Sirona Knight

ALPHA

Penguin Group (USA) Inc.

This book is dedicated to Michael, my husband; and Skylor, our son.

International Standard Book Number: 0-02-864437-9
Library of Congress Catalog Card Number: 2003102272

05   04   03   8   7   6   5   4   3   2   1

Interpretation of the printing code: The rightmost number of the first series of numbers is the year of the book's printing; the rightmost number of the second series of numbers is the number of the book's printing. For example, a printing code of 03-1 shows that the first printing occurred in 2003.

Printed in the United States of America

Most Alpha books are available at special quantity discounts for bulk purchases for sales promotions, premiums, fund-raising, or educational use. Special books, or book excerpts, can also be created to fit specific needs.

For details, write: Special Markets; Alpha Books, 375 Hudson Street, New York, New York 10014.

Publisher: Marie Butler-Knight
Product Manager: Phil Kitchel
Senior Managing Editor: Jennifer Chisholm
Senior Acquisitions Editor: Randy Ladenheim-Gil
Development Editor: Lynn Northrup
Senior Production Editor: Katherin Bidwell
Copy Editor: Christina Smith
Cover Designer: Doug Wilkins
Book Designer: Trina Wurst
Creative Director: Robin Lasek
Indexer: Julie Bess
Layout/Proofreading: Angela Calvert, Mary Hunt

Contents

Introduction

A few years ago, my 95-year-old grandmother passed on. Initially I was very sad, but I knew she had lived a long and full life, so it didn't seem to hit me as deeply. A few months later, I realized the impact she had on my life particularly as an anchor. When it finally hit me, I found myself in a time of crisis. Suddenly everything seemed to be crumbling all around me. It felt like I was hitting rock bottom. As an eternal optimist, I found hope in the possibility that things certainly couldn't get any worse.

I began looking around for ways to empower my life. I had been raised Catholic and also had practiced Celtic Druidism and Wicca, so I looked for a way that included a strong spiritual base, much like the roots of a plant. It was at this time that I began to use meditation, prayer, and affirmation as ways to uplift my spirits. I discovered that meditation, prayer, and affirmation were powerful vehicles for turning my life around in a positive direction.

Empowering Your Life with Wicca is a chronicle of the steps I took in order to move my life onward and upward. I began reading books on self-esteem, setting priorities, and attaining goals. I listened to meditation tapes and CDs and to positive thinking tapes. I did rituals and dream magic to increase my connection with the divine and oneness. Through these power steps, plus my practice of New Age Wicca, I started to make positive forward movement in my life. I found the steps I was taking toward empowerment were beginning to influence my life in beneficial ways. I was beginning to feel positive about myself again, and the feeling was empowering.

Around the same time I was undergoing these changes, I did an interview for *Magical Blend* magazine with author Mark Victor Hansen of *Chicken Soup for the Soul* fame. He talked about success in business being related to keeping your focus on what you want and not letting it waver. To me, this seemed identical to the idea in Wicca of having a clear intention and expectation when doing magic. In both methods, you use focus, intention, and expectation to draw energy together so that it can be directed toward useful and positive objectives or goals.

As a result of my own experiences, this book coalesces many themes together into one to come up with a practical and unique way for empowering your life using New Age Wiccan practices. The ideas and techniques include positive thinking, goal setting, gardening, New Age practices and philosophies, as well as the spiritual concepts and practices of many Wiccan traditions.

There have been times in my empowerment process when I wanted to give up and chuck it all, but a force inside of me, like a divine hand, kept moving me forward. As I started formulating my empowerment goals and plans, the events of my life started flowing more smoothly. My relationships, my health, and my writing career became more positive and brighter. I was beginning to believe in myself and I found the idea empowering. At the time it was just what I needed to get my life into perspective.

I began to see my life and what I wanted in life in terms of a garden and how it progresses through the seasons, which is the essence and foundation of Wicca. I realized I needed to plan, prepare, plant, nurture, eventually harvest the fruits of my labors, and then gather the seeds to begin a new empowering generation.

One of the beautiful things about empowerment is that it flows in cycles like the seasons. Because of this, goals are like stepping stones to other goals that can lead you further along your chosen path in life. As your expectations change so do your goals, meaning that you then empower yourself in different ways.

New Age Wicca is an accumulation of ideas that are both ancient and modern. This book melds the New Age, science, and mystical traditions together to offer an approach to empowerment that is inclusive rather than exclusive. With divine help, positive intention, focused expectation, effort, and a little magic, you can give your life new direction. With goals and plans, you can follow the path that you have created toward an enriching and empowering life.

How to Use This Book

The 12 chapters or empowerment steps of *Empowering Your Life with Wicca* follow the analogy of a garden. Chapters 1, 2, and 3 relate to planning your empowerment goals, while Chapters 4, 5, and 6 correspond with planting your empowerment goals. Chapters 7, 8, and 9 relate to nurturing your empowerment goals, and Chapters 10, 11, and 12 correspond to harvesting your empowerment goals and evolving the process into the future.

This practical, hands-on book is filled with empowering stories of people like yourself. These stories come from my personal experiences as well as popular culture. In addition to the personal stories, each chapter describes what the empowerment step is about in terms of both the empowerment process and the practical aspects of your life. Then the second part of the chapter is divided into three sections of love, health, and prosperity. These sections include guided meditations, affirmations, prayers, how to set up sacred spaces, step-by-step instructions for rituals, and magical oracles.

No matter where you find yourself in life, I'm certain that you will discover something useful in this book as the ideas are positive, universal, and empowering. The empowerment process is enjoyable, and often times inspiring. The rewarding fruits of your efforts that you reap when you complete the steps of your empowerment plan and manifest your goals make it all worthwhile. So go ahead and create an enriching life more in harmony with what you envision for yourself.

Always remember that empowerment is something you can share with others. When you become empowered, you can then help those around you to also become empowered. This will empower you even more! It is also a way to help the world become more positive, changing it step by step, until the whole world is empowered. Then, we can hopefully live together as one, with the divine blessings of the Goddess and God, in peace, love, and harmony.

Acknowledgments

I would like to gratefully acknowledge one of the most empowering women I know, Randy Ladenheim-Gil, Senior Acquisitions Editor at Alpha Books. Thank you Randy for your encouragement and enthusiasm. Many heartfelt thanks to Lynn Northrup, my Development Editor, for her fine efforts and for making this book even better! I would also like to respectfully thank my Publisher, Marie Butler-Knight, for the opportunity to write this book. Any many sincere thanks to Jennifer Chisholm, Christina Smith, Katherin Bidwell, Phil Kitchel, Robin Lasek, and everyone at Alpha Books for their time and splendid work. In addition, I would like to thank my family and friends, as well as each and every person who reads this book and uses the methods within it to empower her or his life in a positive way.

Chapter One

The First Empowering Step: Setting Your Empowerment Goals

One of the most empowering things you can do is to realize who you truly are and exactly what you want in life. Go ahead and dare to dream, to imagine exactly what you want to do and where you want to be. Get in touch with the magician or sorceress within and explore all of those little nooks and crannies in your mind that you never knew existed. Once you allow your imagination to expand, you can determine your true self-empowerment goals and chart a course of action for attaining them. That's when you begin to make headway and take that First Empowering Step.

Most of us would like to be healthier and have more love, prosperity, and spiritual fulfillment in our lives. Knowing who you are, what you want to do in life, and where you want to do it, is vital for attaining these things. Take some time to think about who you are. What are your personal values, your likes and dislikes? Exactly where and how would you like to find yourself in 1 year, 5 years, 10 years, and 20 years?

A basic concept in Wicca is that if you can imagine it, you can manifest it. Your mind is the cauldron of creation.

I invite you to stir the cauldron of your mind and apply the hands-on New Age Wicca techniques you find in this book to breathe life into your dreams and manifest your empowerment goals. There are magical meditations, affirmations, prayers, practical rituals, spells, and oracles. You will discover ways to live joyously and make each day sacred. You will also learn ways to manage day-to-day stress, spice up your love life, and build more positive relationships, as well as shed a few pounds and bring more beauty and harmony into your daily life.

Expanding Your Awareness

Life and its many aspects can be viewed from many vantage points, each perception giving new insight and understanding into the overall meaning of life. In this way, life and its essential aspects such as love, health, and prosperity, can be perceived in many different ways. For example, a rose with an exquisite fragrance also has thorns that can painfully pierce your skin. From these differing perspectives, life becomes a series of paths from which you must choose the course of your life, each one leading to a different place. Nowhere are these differing perceptions more evident than in the area of literary fiction.

In the classic story *Siddhartha* by Hermann Hesse, the main character comes to understand life in terms of the river and the ferryman, who helps him on his way. Like an apprentice, he comes to know the ways of the river, and in doing so becomes the ferryman, helping others to cross by passing along the knowledge he has gained from his experience. This is the essence of life. From this experience Siddhartha offers the following insights:

> *I will no longer study Yoga Veda, Atharva Veda, or asceticism, or any other teachings. I will learn from myself, be my own pupil; I will learn from myself the secret of Siddhartha.*

He then looked at his surroundings in a new way. Suddenly, it was as if he were seeing the world for the very first time. Everything was mysterious and beautiful. He saw the colors of green, blue, and yellow in the land around him, and the colors seemed fresh and alive with new light and beauty. He looked anew at the sky, woods, mountains, and river. All was enchanting, strange, and beautiful. It was in this awakening that he found his true self.

The wisdom of Wicca is very much the same way. You can be initiated and learn a magical tradition from others, but the main thrust of energy has to come from you. Once you reach a certain point in your training and development, you can only continue expanding your knowledge through your own relationship and rapport with the divine (Goddess, God, Oneness, whatever name you prefer). The experiences and advice of others can be helpful when learning, but to take it to the next step, you have to make your own choices and go your own way, depending on your situation and the times.

To expand your awareness means to become more aware of what's around you. The divine vortex where everything meshes together into one entity is that point called Oneness. It is that point where time, space, breadth, length, and location are irrelevant because it's a concept that moves beyond limited boundaries to a boundlessness that connects everything together into the web of Oneness.

In Hesse's *Siddhartha*, the main character uses the perception of the river to gain an enlightened rapport with the divine. The process leads him to realize the full extent of the web of Oneness. The river essentially empowers Siddhartha when it becomes a symbol that helps him to understand the meaning of life.

The easiest way to use the meditations in this book is to read them to yourself, one sentence at a time. Take time to understand the meaning of each sentence, and then move to the next, and the next, and so on, until you complete the process. You can read one sentence at a time, close your eyes, and imagine it in your mind's eye.

Another way to use the meditations found here is to record the meditation in your own voice. In a quiet location, turn on some soft, mellow music such as New Age music and read the meditation slowly into the tape recorder, pausing between sentences and paragraphs. Play the taped meditation back as often as you find useful.

It's important to focus all your attention on both your breathing and the content of the meditation itself when you are meditating. Do not do anything else when you are meditating such as driving a car, watching television, working, riding a bike, or talking on the phone. You need to focus your complete awareness on the meditation process.

The First Empowering Step: Garden Meditation

Sit and watch a garden as it is seeded, sprouts, grows, and withers through the seasons. It provides a symbolic key to the ageless wisdom of life. Because of our love for the earth and her plants and creatures, most New Age Wiccans have flower, vegetable, herb, rock, nut, or fruit tree gardens. Whether large or small, outdoors or indoors, your garden is a magical place where you can get in touch with the nature of your inner self and the divine essence of Oneness.

Begin this meditation by sitting or reclining comfortably. Although you don't have to close your eyes to do the meditation, closing them can help you to visualize more effectively. Take a few deep breaths. As you breathe in, imagine breathing in pure white light. As you exhale, let go of all the tensions you may be feeling. Do this three times. Now in your mind's eye, imagine sitting or reclining in a secret and secluded spot where you can watch a beautiful garden as it grows each day. Make this spot your own. Perhaps it's a soft, velvet-cushioned daybed surrounded by roses or apple trees in the corner of your imaginary garden. Or perhaps your spot is under an old redwood or gnarled oak tree in the center of your imaginary garden. As you watch from your secret and secluded spot in your imaginary garden, you notice that the garden is covered in snow and ice. All the plants seem lifeless, as if caught in suspended animation.

With each passing day the sun shines a little longer, and before your eyes, the ice melts and bright green shoots spring up from the earth as the garden comes to life. It is springtime in your imaginary garden, when day and night become equal. As if by magic, everything springs to life. Sown seeds sprout life and grow steadily with nurturing care to florescence. Trees and bushes bud out, leaf, and blossom. By Midsummer's Eve, the garden is brimming with beauty and full of life.

From your secret spot, you notice the weather turning warmer. You watch the roses, mums, lilies, and gladiolus bloom in a vast array of color, spreading their fragrances throughout the garden. The petals of the flowers, like rare jewels, paint the landscape like a colorful melody. You see the apple, peach, and pear trees bear their fruit. You watch the corn, bean, and squash plants become full with their bountiful produce. This is harvest time, a time of celebration and giving of thanks to divine creation.

You continue to watch as autumn approaches the beautiful garden. The leaves in the trees begin to turn gold, rust, and red, and the garden enters the time when the veil between this world and magical worlds is the thinnest. You see winged faeries, divine Goddesses and Gods, and other magical beings, all come to visit the garden on Hallow's Eve.

As winter approaches, the garden turns brown and gray and wilts. Within the wilting flowers and pods reside the seeds for next year's garden. The garden becomes a temporary wasteland whose frozen parts hold life in suspended animation until the next spring, when the garden once again comes to life and ultimate florescence.

As you continue to imagine watching the garden, year after year, you begin to understand its basic nature. You realize that the garden, like yourself, has an immortal, divine, and everlasting quality. The plants in the garden, like yourself, are driven by the forces of creation, destruction, and rebirth. The garden has a definite structure and pattern just as your life has a definite pattern.

Now take a few deep and complete breaths, breathing in pure white light, and breathing out any residual tension. Clap your hands three times to bring yourself back to the present moment. Now take a few minutes to think about how you and the imaginary garden are alike. Think about your divine qualities, your eternal spirit. Think about the stages of your life; your birth, life, death, and rebirth. Also think about the pattern of your life and how you would like to pattern it in the future.

The Wisdom of Wicca

Wicca or Wicce means "wise one," and refers to a person who is in harmony and synchronicity with the natural cycles of life. Within Wicca, the earth and the Goddess are symbolically the same, meaning the earth is a living, conscious being. The seasons of the year are perceived as the divine cycle of the Goddess, also called the Wheel of the Year.

As the seasons turn, the changes are celebrated on Great Days, also called Sabbats. These are the quarter and cross-quarter days commonly referred to by Wiccans as Yule, Imbolc, Ostara, Beltane, Midsummer's Eve, Lughnassad, Mabon, and Samhain. In addition to being magical times, the Sabbats pay homage to the idea that the earth and the Goddess are immortal and everlasting. The Sabbats are times of celebrating the never-ending cycle of life.

All of nature is reborn. Fire, flood, and disease can sometimes ravage nature and send her on the run, but in time everything heals and becomes transformed. Like the mythical Benu or Phoenix, life is born again and again out of the ashes of what came before. Within the Celtic spiritual traditions, the physical body and spirit of one's ancestors are given back to the land at the time of their death. In this way, the ancestral energy, the sacred spirit of each person, literally resides within the land, waiting to be called upon in rituals and spells.

The fear of death is one of the aspects of life that can often be distressing. In Hesse's story, Siddhartha came from a wealthy family. He was insulated from the harsh realities of old age, disease, and death. When he realized these aspects exist, he began a journey that led him to the river. From this vantage point, he understood that life goes on beyond the seeming finiteness of death.

From the vantage point of the garden, life is born, lives, recedes (reseeds), and dies within any given year. Within terms of the immortal whole, it is a progression that is reborn year after year. Each generation of life is genetically, energetically, and spiritually connected to every generation before it.

In Wicca, different qualities of life such as birth, love, fertility, war, creativity, death, and rebirth are ascribed to various Goddesses. For example, the Celtic Goddess Coventina and her sacred well symbolize fertility and birth, the Celtic Goddess Kerridwen has her magical cauldron that symbolizes creation, and the Norse Goddess Frigga has her magical distaff that she uses to weave the thread that the Three Fates spin into each and every person's destiny.

The Mother Goddess embodies Oneness. From her stem the many other Goddesses and Gods, who represent the different aspects or faces of the Mother Goddess. The three primary faces of the triple Goddess are the maid, mother, and crone, the names alluding to the progressive stages of life. Goddess examples of these faces are:

- Maiden: Freya, Bridget, and Persephone
- Mother: Frigga, Anu, and Demeter
- Crone: Skuld, Morganna, and Hecate

All of the Goddesses and Gods from the many magical traditions such as Celtic, Greek, Roman, Egyptian, Norse, and Italian have unique aspects, yet they all share a commonality. They are all aspects of Oneness, just as you and I are.

In Wicca, all things are considered to be one infinite and eternal connected energy web. This means absolutely everything is connected and influences everything else, whether animate or inanimate. The practice of Wicca is essentially becoming aware of and understanding this inherent Oneness of all things. It offers methods for planting positive seeds in the energy web, cultivating loving, healthy, and prosperous life patterns, and consequently achieving your ultimate dreams and goals.

The First Empowering Step: Oneness Meditation

Each and every one of us are incarnations of the divine. You can tap into the divine powers of the Goddesses and Gods because of this shared spiritual kinship. By understanding both the unique and common qualities of the divine, you can better understand your own divine nature. You are a unique person, yet you share a common thread with everyone and everything else in the universe. You are an integral part of the whole, balanced, connected, boundless, and one with all. Use the following meditation to better understand the unique yet common thread of the web of life.

Begin by sitting or reclining comfortably. Next, take a few deep and complete breaths. Imagine breathing in white light, and breathing out any tension you may be feeling. Do this for a minute or two. Now imagine becoming one with everything around you that you can see. Then imagine becoming one with everything around you for 10 miles, 100 miles, 1,000 miles, with everything on the planet Earth, everything in our solar system, with the sun, with the universe, the cosmos, and beyond. Keep expanding your awareness as you continue to become one with everything. Do this for a couple of minutes.

Next, imagine becoming one with nothing. Become one with the abyss, with nothingness, with emptiness, with nothing at all. Keep contracting your awareness as you become nothing at all. Do this for a couple of minutes. Then imagine becoming more than nothing, becoming everything once again, and then take a giant leap and imagine becoming boundless. Move your awareness beyond everything and nothing all at the same moment. Take another deep and complete breath and imagine flying free through the skies, heavens, and universe. Do this for a few minutes. When you are done, clap your hands three times to bring you back to the present space and time.

Choice and Action

Everything is energy. Meditation, ritual, and spellcrafting are all ways of raising and directing energy to a higher level where it can empower you and help you attain your fondest dreams. In a practical and symbolic sense, setting your empowerment goals is similar to deciding what you want to plant in your flower and vegetable garden. You make the choice and take the action. Your actions are a result of choices you make. Your cumulative choices and actions are called your life pattern. To be empowered is to realize that the choices you make and the actions you take are yours.

Choice always figures into everything, especially when crafting your magical patterns and goals. More than anything, Wicca is a method and a way for learning to make the best choices possible for yourself and for achieving what you want in life. People can influence your choices in life, but they can't make them for you, unless you let them. If you allow this to happen, you are giving away your personal power. Instead of giving away your Goddess- and God-given power, be bold and dare to empower yourself, right now! Learn to make the best possible choices you can make. Begin to take the necessary steps you need to guide your life in the direction you truly desire. When you understand the choices and patterns of life, it's the first step in learning to pattern energy and influence the direction of your life.

Begin your empowering adventure by thinking about your self-empowerment goals and the steps you need to take to manifest them. Be practical. Remember to go with the flow and build on your own natural proclivities. For example, if you love being around animals, you might select a career as a vet, breed registered dogs, or become an elephant trainer. Also, always remember to plant the things that you appreciate and enjoy in your life, just like your garden. Grow the things and culti-vate the patterns in your life that you desire. The choice is yours, and yours alone!

A Story of Empowerment

With every step that Karen took, she felt a shooting pain moving from her spine down her thighs, down her legs, into her ankles until her legs felt numb with pain. Because walking had become so hard, Karen found herself walking less and less, and as a result she gained weight. She be-gan to have other medical ailments, such as digestive problems, growths on her lymph glands, and even more problems with her spine. Some days the pain became so great that all Karen could do was cry and scream at everyone around her. She was becoming an unpleasant person, not only to herself, but to her loved ones as well.

After Karen read a meditation book that stressed merging into the eternal now, her perspective slowly started changing. She started meditating with white light, and she read a few Wicca books. The books helped her to renew her connection to the earth and helped her look at her medical problems from a new perspective. Suddenly, Karen's attitude improved, and she became more optimistic. One night, everything seemed to come together, and she found herself actually merging with the eternal now, with Oneness. Miraculously, as she merged deeper and deeper with Oneness, her pain began to subside. The next day Karen realized that she had experienced a spiritual awakening that not only awakened something within her spirit, but her body felt better, lighter, than it had in years. She began to set simple goals for herself such as swimming for exercise and changing her diet. Soon her life and health experienced a 180-degree shift. She empowered herself, and the results were magical!

Each time you set a goal and achieve it, the process empowers you physically, mentally, and spiritually. Every time you have a difficult problem that you overcome and learn from, it empowers you. Empowerment is about understanding and using the personal power that is already part of you. It is the deeply personal process that enables you to realize and attain your full potential.

The Spiritual Path of Wicca

When the young Wart pulls the sword from the stone in the story *The Sword in the Stone* by T. H. White, he becomes empowered, thus realizing his destiny and becoming King Arthur of the Round Table. Many historical personages have experienced a moment of empowerment that subsequently changed the course of their lives. Both Mahatma Gandhi and Albert Einstein talked about empowering dreams they had. Joan of Arc spoke of a vision that propelled her as a woman to lead the French against the English in ways that moved beyond her known physical abilities. Each of these people were able to transcend their present condition by being empowered through a process of seeing their true purposes in life.

The First Empowering Step is about helping you to better understand your purpose in life, even if your path is one that's less traveled than other paths. Wicca is both old and new, and growing at extraordinary speed, due in part to its popularity in current books, movies, and television programs. In terms of the "old," it has to do with traditions that have been passed down and refined since the time when humans first started communicating with one another. Technology has changed, but spirituality has remained fairly constant. Whether female or male, humans have worshipped and relied on a divine force that maintains the eternal pattern.

The way of Wicca is about following a spiritual path that has consistent and time-tested methods for personal empowerment. These methods include creating sacred spaces and using meditation, affirmation, prayer, rituals, and spells, combined with magical tools and focals, to direct and influence energy for the purpose of setting up patterns to achieve your goals. Within the context of magic comes the process for creating a sacred space, setting up an altar, and drawing a magic circle. In addition, rituals are a way to establish your relationship with the divine, which in terms of modern Wicca is "Oneness," a concept that includes everyone.

Creating Your Sacred Space

The first thing you need to do is create a sacred space in which to do magic. This should be a place that is private and personal. It can be large or small, indoors or outdoors. Select and set up a sacred space that is conducive to doing your empowerment meditations, affirmations, prayers, spells, and rituals.

Once you have created your sacred space, you need to clean it of any unwanted energies before you begin. Using a lit smudge stick (usually made of cedar and sage), walk clockwise around the area while repeating the following incantation:

Let all negative energies be gone from this space,
In the name of the divine Lady who protects this place.
So be it! Blessed be!

Afterwards breathe in slowly, and as you exhale, imagine the space around you being washed out with a bright cobalt-blue light. Do this a total of three times. You have now purified your sacred space. To empower the space, say:

I empower this sacred space with divine light.
So be it! Blessed be!

Next, set up your altar in your sacred space. A dining room or coffee table, bookshelf, bureau top, fireplace mantle, or sturdy box can all be used as altars. Traditionally, the altar is known as the "Lady's Table." It serves as a focal point when doing magic. It is a sacred connecting place between the mortal and the divine worlds. The altar holds your magical tools and is arranged in way that is consistent with the Goddess and the God, with the left half of the altar being the Goddess side and the right half the God side.

The most common locations for your altar are in the north, east, or center quadrant of your sacred space. An altar set in the north honors the earth and the ancestors. An altar set in the east honors the sun and new beginnings. An altar set in the center of your sacred space connects the directions and elements together into one. Please refer to the Sacred Space sections under Love, Health, and Prosperity throughout the 12 chapters of this book for specific altar layouts.

It's customary to cover the altar with a cloth to protect it from melting wax and incense ashes. The cloth can be any color, fabric, or size. Be creative and feel free to change the color of your cloth to match the seasons, or decorate your altar cloth by painting magic symbols on it such as stars and moons.

Magical Tools and Focals

Wands, swords, chalices, candles, incense, crystals, and scented oils are all magical tools and focals that can be used to enhance and embellish your magic making. Symbolically they represent the powers of the elements, divine powers that can help you achieve your goals, and thus empower you.

Focals add a sensuous touch to your magic making. Whether visual, auditory, kinesthetic, olfactory, or gustatory, they trigger your senses and help you focus more intently on your magical goals. They also add a sense of pleasure and fun to magic.

Music is one of the most powerful focals in magic making. Use melody, rhythm, and song whenever possible when practicing the empowering techniques provided in this book. The rhythm, melody, and cadence of the music adds power to your magic making. Match your musical selection to the meditation, affirmation, spell, or ritual you are doing.

Magical tools such as wands are imprinted with your energy signature by consecrating and using them. They are, in a sense, energetically alive. The basic tools for practicing Wicca include a wand, athame (a double-edged, dulled knife), candle holder, incense burner, cauldron or bowl, and a chalice. For a detailed list of Wiccan tools and their uses, please refer to Appendix C.

Empowering Your Magical Tools

To empower your magical tools, first clean them by smudging them with cedar and sage smoke. This cleanses them of unwanted energies. If you prefer, use sandalwood incense to purify your tools. You can make your own smudge and incense sticks, or you can buy them at health food, New Age, and Wicca shops or through catalogs and over the Internet.

Next, empower your magical tools by blessing them with the elements of earth (salt or soil), air (incense), fire (flame), water, and spirit (scented oil). For example, to consecrate your wand, hold it in your receiving hand (left if you are right-handed). Face north, sprinkle your wand with salt or soil from the bowl, and say:

I empower this magical tool with the element of earth.

Then move in a clockwise direction, face east, pass the wand through incense or smudge smoke, and say:

I empower this magical tool with the element of air.

Now turn clockwise and face south. Pass the wand quickly through the flame of a lit candle and say:

I empower this magical tool with the element of fire.

Face west, sprinkle the wand with water from your chalice, and say:

I empower this magical tool with the element of water.

Face your altar, apply a few drops of scented oil to your wand, and say:

I empower this magical tool with divine spiritual power.
As I will, so shall it be! Blessed be!

Your wand is now empowered with the elements and divine spirit. Do the same thing with your other tools to empower them for magic making.

The Magic Circle

You can cast a magic circle when you do magic spells and rituals. The circle is a vortex of energy that creates a portal for you to commune with the divine. You are also protected from unwanted energies in the magic circle.

To draw a magic circle, begin by taking your athame, wand, or power hand (your dominant hand; the right hand if you're right-handed) and drawing a circle of light energy. Start at the north point of your circle, usually the place where your altar is located. Point your athame tip outward and slowly spin clockwise from east, south, west, and back to the north point. As you spin around, imagine a brilliant blue-white light coming from the tip of your athame. Imagine the light connecting the directions of the circle into one, a circle symbolic of the connection of all things, of Oneness, and say:

I empower this magic circle
With the divine powers of Oneness.
So be it! Blessed be!

To enhance your magic circle, outline it with fresh flowers, seeds, pinecones, or herbs, or lay crystals and gemstones around the circle. If you like, you can sprinkle water or scented oils around the inside of the circle.

Empowering Your Circle

Empower your magic circle by calling on the elements. The elemental powers stand guard at the four directions while you make magic. You release them when you are done. Begin by facing north. Stretch your arms upward and become one with the earth element. Say:

I call upon the generous powers of earth
To protect and empower this circle.

Next, turn clockwise and face east. Say:

I call upon the generous powers of Air
To protect and empower this circle.

Then, turn clockwise and face south. Say:

I call upon the generous powers of Fire
To protect and empower this circle.

Now turn clockwise and face west. Become one with the element of water, and say:

I call up on the generous powers of Water
To protect and empower this circle.

Now face your altar and become one with the divine. Say:

I call upon the divine spirit of the Goddess and God
To protect and empower this circle.
So be it! Blessed be!

Closing the Magic Circle

Once your magic work is complete, close the circle by bidding farewell to the elements and pulling up the circle of blue-white light. Use your athame, wand, or power hand to do so. Begin by facing north with your athame pointed toward the north point of the circle. Slowly spin counterclockwise and imagine the circle being drawn into your athame. To bid farewell to the elements, face north and say:

Generous powers of earth, I bid you farewell
Depart in peace and harmony
Many thanks for your empowering presence.

Next, face east and say:

Generous powers of air, I bid you farewell
Depart in peace and harmony
Many thanks for your empowering presence.

Face south and say:

Generous powers of fire, I bid you farewell
Depart in peace and harmony
Many thanks for your empowering presence.

Then face west and say:

Generous powers of water, I bid you farewell
Depart in peace and harmony
Many thanks for your empowering presence.

Once you have bid farewell to the elements, close the circle by pulling up the circle of blue-white light.

Wiccan Rituals

Basically, rituals are a systematic way of doing things that work. They are procedures that produce results. In terms of Wicca, they relate to the Sabbats and full (high) moons, also called Esbats, that occur within the annual cycle of the garden. Wiccan rituals celebrate the path of the Goddess and God as they progress through the seasons. This path is symbolized by the eight-spoked wheel, where each spoke represents one of the eight Sabbats.

Besides being a forum for honoring the divine, rituals offer a means for directing and influencing energy, the main focus in the practice of magic. The popular myth about magic is that the results happen instantaneously, which more than anything plays into a desire for immediate gratification.

In a practical sense, magic is about making choices and initiating patterns that have both short- and long-range implications. In other words, finding a relationship that works for you, pursuing an occupation that gives substance to your life, and getting your body, mind, and spirit healthy sometimes takes longer than you would like, but the end results are well worth the wait. You need to plan, plant, nurture, and harvest the garden of life. More than anything, the planning stage requires you to make choices. Those choices form the foundation for everything else you do.

To Choose or Not to Choose

In a recent interview with Mark Victor Hansen, author of *Chicken Soup For The Soul* and *The Power of Focus*, for *Magical Blend* magazine, he reiterated the point that "Life doesn't just happen to you. It's all about choices and how you respond to every situation." That is, the choices you make in life determine the overall content of your life.

As anyone who has taken a test can conclude, if you know what you're talking about, you'll be all right, but if you are just guessing, the result is like tossing dice—sometimes you're lucky and sometimes you're not. When things are rigged, more times than not the outcome has already been decided before you even show up. In this case, you don't have much choice.

Fortunately, not all life is rigged, which is why you have lots of choices to make. These choices all have a bearing on what happens in your life, because making choices are key elements in formulating and setting up your magical patterns and self-empowerment goals.

You make choices every moment in your life. When getting up in the morning, you decide what to have for breakfast, what clothes to wear, and what you're going to do for the day. At times your obligations and agreements with others determine your choices, such as a job where you agree to show up Monday through Friday.

Keep in mind that your obligations and agreements are themselves choices. What this means is that one choice influences and determines other, future choices. This effect can either be expansive or limiting depending on the choices you make. As an example, some jobs offer you a lot of potential for making contacts and moving forward, whereas other jobs seem to take all of your time while giving you little psychological or financial reward.

The choices you make can either be active or passive. Active choices involve using conscious thought to make your decision, while passive choices are those where you take what is chosen for you, what is easiest, and what comes your way both in terms of opportunities and problems.

Although you normally don't think you are making choices when you sleep, when you dream you are making either active or passive choices about *what* you dream. Lucid dreaming is a New Age technique for making active choices in your dreams.

When you understand that choices can either be active or passive, you can begin to create a balance between the two. You cannot control all of the aspects of your life. As such you cannot actively make choices about everything. You can concentrate on aspects that are more important and make your active choices in these areas. Basically, this is what setting up your empowerment goals is all about: choosing what you want to direct your energies toward.

The First Empowering Step is the most crucial because it lays the foundation for everything else. At this point, it is very important to understand what it is you want; otherwise, you are, in a sense, gambling with your future. The idea of gambling is interesting, but most professional gamblers who win all the time play the odds or percentages. In science, it's known as probabilities. The more times an outcome can become predictable, the more it lends itself to the overall archetypical pattern, meaning it happens on multiple levels simultaneously and becomes part of the intricate fabric of human consciousness.

Goals and Patterns

At the beginning of the movie *Space Jam*, young Michael Jordan announces to his father that he wants to be a basketball player. His father responds by telling him that he should become a baseball player instead because there is more prestige in it. Both in the movie and in real life, Michael goes through much practice and determination to become one of the best players in the history of basketball. At the height of his basketball career, he decides to follow his father's suggestion and become a baseball player. After several valiant attempts to play professional baseball, Michael decides he's a mediocre baseball player, so he returns to basketball, something much more in tune with his natural proclivities and desires as a person.

Defined by Webster's Dictionary, goals are "the end toward which effort is directed." In Michael Jordan's case, that end was to become a successful basketball player, something that required all his efforts and energies. As with most goals, the degree of success that is achieved is proportional to the amount of ability you have and the effort you are willing to put forth. If goals are the "ends," patterns are the "means" for empowering yourself and getting what you want in life. In terms of sports, music, creative writing, and just about anything else, this requires preparation and practice. Practice does make perfect in terms of your life patterns. The more directed efforts you make, the more likely you are to attain your goals.

In life, it's important to move beyond the patterns of your parents. They are the ones who raised you and comforted you when you were sad, but in the end your parents' goals are not necessarily your own. If you try to make them your own, you will ultimately be miserable.

As human beings, we have no apparent control over our genetic coding. Like the script from a play, we act out our part on cue. These cues originate from many sources—from the cultural, energetic, and physical to the mental and spiritual.

Michael Jordan attempted to play out his father's goals by becoming a baseball player, and it ended in failure. In terms of self-empowerment, his own goals of playing basketball achieved fruition and success. Only when he tried to follow goals other than his own was he disappointed. Like Michael Jordan, you must follow your own path, not someone else's, no matter how well-intentioned that person seems.

In essence, your patterns are your plans for achieving your goals. Most business people will tell you that failing to plan is planning to fail. In this sense, your life patterns are essential to your success. Goals are meaningless unless you set up the patterns to achieve them. Goals need to be set in accordance with your abilities and desires, otherwise you find yourself in the predicament of forcing yourself to do what you don't want to do. When you make a poor choice, you might feel you are living a lie. In this case, achieving your goal doesn't empower you, but adds to your feelings of deceit and disappointment. You need to get in touch with who you truly are, so you can make better choices, today and for the rest of your life. In this way, you can become great at what you do!

Setting Your Empowerment Goals

Peter Townshend of the rock group the Who wrote the song "Who Are You" after meeting members of the punk band the Sex Pistols and discovering they had no idea of what they were doing. Townshend found that they had no goals, and thus no coherent patterns except that of total destruction, something that some of them and their followers had no problem achieving.

Determining who you are and what you want to do is the key to self-empowerment.[You must set your own goals in accordance to who you are. Who you are is accessed in terms of your abilities, your desires, and determination. If you know your abilities, understand your desires, and have a great deal of personal determination, your chances of self-empowerment improve accordingly. Armed with this information, you can easily determine your goals and attain them.]

[Complacency is the biggest reason for mediocrity, in that you just don't care what happens. To get what you want, you must first know what it is you want. You need to choose paths in life that are conducive and in alignment with who you are in terms of love, prosperity, and health.

[Don't be alarmed if you find your empowerment goals keep increasing in number. Having a number of goals is important. The reason is because when you achieve one goal and feel empowered, there is no period of let down because you can easily move on to the next goal.

When setting up your empowerment goals, it's helpful to keep an empowerment journal for writing down your goals. Any spiral-bound notebook will do, although you may want to buy one of the many attractive blank journals available in bookstores. The journal will help you stay focused while working on and realizing your goals. Start by entitling one page "Love Empowerment Goals," one page "Health Empowerment Goals," and one page "Prosperity Empowerment Goals."

Keep in mind that even though love, health, and prosperity are covered individually within each chapter of this book, there is some natural overlapping between the three. For example, you often feel healthier when the relationships in your life become more empowering, or you enjoy prosperity when your business relationships become more empowering.

Love

Isabel married Eduardo, a man of Cuban descent, who had the archaic, although well-intentioned, idea that women shouldn't work. At first the idea didn't bother Isabel because her husband had a good job that provided her with all the things she wanted. But soon she became bored. She started taking workshops and classes on self-improvement and empowerment, which meant that there were times when she was not home to do the domestic chores, such as cooking. After coming home from a workshop on crystal healing, she walked into the kitchen and found Eduardo sitting stoically on a chair at the dining room table. He began demanding that Isabel cook him something to eat because he had not had anything to eat since he got home from work. Isabel marched him first over to the cupboard where there were a variety of canned goods, and then picked up a can of spaghetti. She walked over to Eduardo and said, "This is a can." Moving over to the other side of the kitchen, she said, "This is a can opener." Pointing to the microwave oven, she said, "Open the can, put it in a bowl, set the timer for two minutes, and you have food." At first he was a little put off by the concept, but at the same time the wheels started turning in his brain. He finally smiled and said, "Good, I don't have go hungry anymore because I can feed myself."

In this case, empowerment happened on multiple levels for Isabel and Eduardo. One person's path to personal empowerment can initially disrupt the lives of those around them. But in the long run, those close to the person can also become empowered by the experience. This mutually empowering kind of experience is what you're looking for when you empower your love life.

Love revolves around relationships and the give-and-take you have with others. Some relationships can stifle you, while others can empower you and help you be who you want to be. The relationships that empower you are the ones you need to focus on, but this is not always so easy in practice. Because of feelings and emotions, sometimes it's hard to tell in a practical sense which relationships drain you and which ones empower you. One way to tell the different types of relationships apart is to start becoming aware of how you feel after interacting with a particular person. Are you happy? Excited? Ready to take on the world? Or are you depressed? Drained? Grouchy? Ready to scream at the next person you meet?

All relationships have their ups and downs, meaning that a relationship may not always be the same. Look for the overall and consistent nature of your relationship with a particular person. Use this simple exercise as a guide for determining the relationships in your life that empower you and move you forward:

1. Take a few deep and complete breaths to center yourself. Then close your eyes. In your mind's eye see an imaginary dressing room. You are in the dressing room, "trying on" relationships like you would try on new clothes. Focus on a person you are in a relationship with, and then try that relationship on. How does it feel? Pleasant? Too tight? Too loose? Just right? Make a note in your empowerment journal of the person's name and how the relationship feels.

2. Now try on another relationship. Imagine another person in your mind and determine how that relationship feels to you. Does the relationship make you feel brighter, lighter? Make a note in your journal of the name of the person and how the relationship feels.

3. Keep trying on relationships until you have gone through most of the people who are close to you.

In Wicca, love and the divine union is expressed as "the perfect love of the Goddess, and the perfect peace of the God." Metaphysically, it is the energetic balancing of female and male energies and how their divine union creates the Oneness, a term signifying the all-inclusive divine whole.

Anthropologists use the term "boundary culture" to refer to the relationship that members of a culture have with one another and how this relationship ties them together as a whole. In one view, you have all the separate members. In the other view, you have them coming together and forming a culture—essentially, an extension of themselves—that is an entity in and of itself. In terms of the complete cosmos and everything in it, this extension and entity is Oneness.

The idea in Wicca is to tap into and become one with or merge with Oneness as a means of setting up your goals and the magical patterns for achieving them. When you merge with Oneness, your awareness diffuses like a cloud, and you become one with everyone and everything.

Merging with Oneness and becoming one with the Goddess and God and their many aspects is a way to invoke divine power into your rituals and overall magical patterning. When you do this, you bring in an energy that knows no bounds and can make all your empowerment goals come to fruition.

Another main concept in Wicca is to love, honor, and respect the earth and nature. This is an empowering relationship that not only involves love, but also health and prosperity. Establishing a good connection with the earth and Mother Nature is an empowering experience that helps you merge further into Oneness, releasing its infinite power to create and transform. It also helps preserve the planet for future generations.

When setting up your love empowerment goals, you need to include all the various parts—your love and relationship with your primary partner, family, the earth, friends, pets, and everything else. Love comes in many forms and is expressed in a multitude of ways. Keep this in mind when doing the following love meditation.

The First Empowering Step: Love Meditation

In this empowering love meditation, you are granted a love boon or wish by the Goddess. Make an effort to choose the most empowering love wish that you possibly can. As with everything involving wishes, carefully consider the consequences of your wish. Your love wish needs to be positive, detailed, and definitive. Be specific and to the point. Repeat your love boon three times to yourself to get it clear in your mind.

Begin this meditation by turning on some soft, soothing music, and then sit or recline comfortably. Close your eyes and take a deep breath. Hold it for a three seconds, and then exhale completely. Do this at least three times to focus your energies.

Now imagine that you are deep in the woods on a warm spring morning. The peaceful forest around you is safe and inviting. You can hear the wind softly whispering through giant cedar trees, growing louder as the branches of the giant trees begin to sway above you. The breeze fades, and then returns, rolling through the forest and rolling out again. The scent of the cedar trees is carried on the rolling wind, and you breathe in the heady scent. The scent fills your senses as you walk slowly through the woods, listening to the birds singing in the tree canopy and enjoying the peacefulness and beauty of the woods.

The forest floor is damp from a recent rain shower. Covered in a cloak of moisture and shining in the morning sun, the natural greens, browns, and grays of the forest are even more vibrant. You walk slowly, careful not to slip on the wet needles as the sunlight filters through the mighty cedars, casting mysterious shadows on the damp forest floor.

You come to the edge of the woods, to a small crystal-clear lake. The wind rolls off the surface of the lake and presses against your face. You walk to lake's shore and gaze out at the water, tiny ripples stirred by the wind rolling across its surface. Suddenly, you see the image of an extraordinarily beautiful woman dressed in long white robes and spinning and dancing across the lake toward you. She looks like a Goddess, enchantingly beautiful, as she gracefully floats across the water. As she reaches the lake shore, she addresses you in a melodic and kind voice. "I am the Goddess. Tell me what your love wish is, and I will gladly grant it."

You tell the beautiful woman your wish, repeating it three times. You smile at the Goddess, empowered by her divine help and blessing, and then you thank her. She smiles in return, reaches out, and touches you on the shoulder. As she touches you, a bright white light fills you with loving, peaceful energy. Just as quickly as she appeared, the Goddess disappears. You gaze out at the lake, feeling relaxed and filled with the divine light of the Goddess.

Now take a deep breath through your mouth, hold your breath for three seconds, and exhale through your nose. Take another deep breath through your mouth, hold it for three seconds, and breathe out through your nose. Once again, take a deep breath in through your mouth, hold it for three seconds, and then breathe out through your nose. Slowly open your eyes, count to 10, and come back to the present time and place. Move your hands and feet and stretch your body like a cat.

Take a couple of minutes to jot down in your empowerment journal the insights you gained from the meditation experience. Make a note of the date of your entry and also write down your love wish three times. In addition, write down how you felt before, during, and after the meditation process.

Love Affirmation and Prayer

Affirmation and prayer can be used to bring love, health, prosperity, and harmony into your daily life. Affirmations are statements of faith that you repeat to yourself with sincere belief for the purpose of attaining your self-empowerment goals. Prayers are requests to the divine, to Oneness. They are one of the most powerful forms of communication that stem from a yearning and caring within.

To successfully use affirmation, you need to eliminate the negative, accentuate the positive, and don't mess with the in-between. To successfully use prayer, you must have a genuine need and faith in the divine power of Oneness.

Say your affirmations and prayers before meals and several times during the day for the best results. The best times to say them are as you wake up and just before you go to sleep because these are the times of the day when you are most suggestible.

Your love affirmation needs to reflect your deepest desires, phrased in a positive way. Tune in to how you feel inside when you state your love affirmation. Does it make you feel warm and joyful inside? If so, you are plugging in to your divine power source. You are on the right path. Now rethink, rephrase, and restate your affirmation until it feels absolutely blissful. An empowering love affirmation example is:

I am drawing more joyous love into my life each and every day.

Now move your awareness into the future for a minute or two and imagine your love affirmation coming true. See and sense it getting brighter and brighter. Be there in the future, feeling the empowering joy of attaining your deepest desires. Say your love affirmation at least six times a day every day for the next 28 days to empower your love life.

Like affirmation, a simple empowering love prayer can fill your life with joy. Before praying, take a few deep and complete breaths to center yourself. In your mind's eye, imagine the loving Goddess and God standing before you and pray from your heart:

Dear Lord and Lady
I pray you
Help me find love and joy
In each and every day.
Blessed be!

Sacred Love Space

Set up a simple love altar by first covering your altar surface with a red altar cloth. Next, select something that represents the Goddess to you. This can be a stone, seashell, feather, statue, plant, photograph, book, or anything that symbolizes the power of the Goddess to you. Empower the item by holding it in your hands and saying:

I dedicate this symbol to the Goddess
May she fill it with her divine, loving power.

Put the empowered item on your altar. Then put a clean red candle on the altar, along with a vase of fresh red or pink flowers. Hold the candle and flowers in your hands and say:

I dedicate this candle and these flowers to the Goddess.

For the next 28 days, keep the flowers fresh. Use the candle in your love ritual.

Love Ritual

Use this ritual to reaffirm your relationship with your beloved or to find that special someone with whom you would like to share a sacred and lasting relationship. This ritual is best done on a Friday night on or just before a full moon.

You will need lavender scented oil, a quartz crystal, paper, and a ballpoint pen. Begin by drawing a magic circle of light around your sacred love space and empower the elements. Use the pen to write down on the sheet of paper the qualities you would like your beloved to have. For example, you might write down "Caring," "Responsible," "Sexy," "Generous," and "Fun." Put the paper on your love altar where you can easily see it.

Next, use the pen to write the same words on the candle body. Cover the candle and crystal with a thin film of lavender oil. Then anoint yourself with the oil by putting a few drops on the insides of your ankles, wrists, behind your ears, and on your third eye (your forehead between your brows). Wipe the oil from your hands and light the red candle, dedicating it to your favorite love Goddess, such as Venus. (For a list of empowering Gods and Goddesses, see Appendix A.) Hold the crystal in your receiving hand as you gaze at the candlelight. Now imagine each of the qualities you desire in your beloved coming to life in the flame. Take your time and refer to your list on the paper until you imagine each of the desired qualities. Then say:

In this flame, I see my sacred love [state the love qualities on your list]. By the loving power of the Goddess So be it! Blessed be!

Continue gazing at the candlelight, all the while imagining the qualities you desire in your beloved for at least 15 minutes. When you are done, put the crystal in the center of the paper with the desired qualities. Fold the crystal into the paper, once, then twice, and finally a third time. Seal the folded paper and crystal with wax from the candle. Then hold the sealed charm in your hands and say three times:

I empower this charm with the power of the love Goddess.

Then bid farewell to the elements, thank the Goddess for her loving presence and help, and close the circle. Either snuff out the candle or allow it to safely burn down on its own (but don't leave a burning candle unattended!). Put the sealed paper and crystal under your bed to encourage the desired qualities in your beloved or to attract that special someone.

Oracle of Love

First, think of a simple question about love and write the question and date in your empowerment journal. Then find a romantic novel or a book of love poems. Hold the book in your hands and close your eyes. Take a deep breath, breathing in white light, and then exhale, letting go of your concerns and tensions for a minute. Now turn to a page in the book and take another deep breath in. As you exhale, put the index finger of your power hand on a line on the page. Open your eyes and read the sentence your finger is on. Does it answer your love question? If the answer isn't clear, turn to another page and repeat the process. Do this a total of three times to clarify the answer to your love question. Write the answer in your journal.

Health

Ann had trouble getting pregnant. She had endometriosis, which caused problems with her ovaries, and eventually she had to have one removed. When a doctor advised her to have the second one taken out, she said no. Having been given no hope from medical doctors, she began seeking alternative methods to treat her problem. After taking homeopathic drugs and doing hands-on healing, she finally had a beautiful baby boy who the delivery doctors termed a "miracle baby."

This story shows that there is more to health than what modern medical science would have you believe. There are many cases of people who miraculously get well after exhausting the resources of their traditional doctors. Many Wiccans speak of experiences where a healing circle has had more of an impact than modern prescribed drugs. This is not to take away from the benefits of modern medicine, but merely to point out that New Age Wiccan methods also have merit in terms of health. After all, the ancient Druids were renowned for their curative abilities.

What you eat, what you do, and how you think all contribute to the holistic nature of your health. What you eat has to do primarily with your physical body, what you do is associated with your physical and spiritual self, and how you think relates mainly to your mental attitude. Keep in mind that body, mind, and spirit all interrelate.

A popular New Age saying is, "What you eat is what you are." This statement points to the importance of diet with regard to health and who you are because of it. In terms of the Goddess, it's about eating the fruits and vegetables that she provides for you. Countless books proclaim the endless benefits that can be gained by eating more organic fresh fruits and vegetables. When you eat these things, you ingest the healing goodness of the earth, and thus the divine power of the Goddess.

What you do also determines how healthy you are. Exercising, playing, meditating, praying, and performing rituals are all activities that influence your health. Exercise is great for empowering the body, just as reading empowers the mind and prayer empowers the spirit. All of your activities together determine your overall health—physically, mentally, and spiritually.

As with love and making wishes, the choices you make regarding your health have consequences later in your life. Although eating healthy food may at times seem less exciting for your taste buds, the overall effect is that you will be healthier. This is why so many people, Wiccans and otherwise, are turning to a vegetarian diet, particularly in light of the hormones and chemicals used in meat, along with animal diseases and cruelty often involved in raising and butchering the animals. In the long run, you need to make healthy choices for your body if you want to get and stay in good health.

When I was growing up there was a lot of discussion as to whether a large part of illness was all in the mind. Many traditional healing techniques not only relied on the medicinal power of the herb, but also in the belief that you would get well. Numerous surveys show that people with positive attitudes overall live longer than people with negative attitudes.

In terms of Wicca, your body is part of the divine. The idea is to get in tune with your body and listen to what it tells you. This is particularly important when setting your empowerment goals for health.

The First Empowering Step: Healing Meditation

Imagine that you have just been made director and star of a video entitled "This Is Your Health." You instruct the camera person to take footage of you as you move through all of your daily routines. At the end of the day, you take all the tapes and edit them into a video that shows who you are health-wise, particularly in terms of your basic habits, with respect to eating, activities, and mental attitudes.

The first video goes over so well that you're commissioned to do a sequel to "This Is Your Health," only this time the video is going to be about who you want to be health-wise. Through the use of special effects, you make a video that portrays you in a state of optimum health, empowered by your habits with respect to eating, activities, and mental attitudes.

Imagine playing out the first video of "This Is Your Health" in your mind. Visualize your body and state of health as they are today. Play a movie of your day and notice what you are doing, what you are eating, your emotions, and your environment. Continue viewing the movie in your mind until you have a realistic view of your current habits.

Next, clear your mind by taking a few deep and complete breaths. Imagine inhaling a bright cobalt-blue light into your body and breathing out any pain or tension. Do this a few times until you feel centered and relaxed. Now play the second video of "This Is Your Health" in your mind's eye. Imagine yourself becoming healthy and full of energy as you make better choices about what to eat, how to spend your time, and what to think about. Notice some of the foods you are eating and the activities you are participating in. As you watch the movie, see yourself in excellent health, doing the things you enjoy, feeling better than ever before.

Now take another deep breath and slowly open your eyes, coming back to the present time and place. Take a few minutes to think about the meditation. In your empowerment journal, write down how you felt as the new, healthier you. Write down some of the foods and activities you imagined. Specifically describe one basic health goal you can take empowering steps toward today. For example:

I am empowering my health by drinking organic fruit juice.

Then make an effort to drink more organic fruit juice today and every day. You're on your way to a healthier you!

Healing Affirmation and Prayer

Doing successful healing affirmations requires strong intention, focused expectation, intense desire, and becoming one with the divine. Begin by taking a few deep breaths and centering your mind, body, and spirit. In your mind's eye, see your healing affirmation already happening. Imagine the specific result you desire. Then repeat your healing affirmation several times a day for at least 21 days. With sincerity, say:

Each and every day, I am empowered by the uplifting, healing light of the God and Goddess.

Continue to imagine the best possible healing result.

As with the affirmation, prayer depends on your intention, expectation, and desire, including your ability to merge with the divine. Prayer fields (energetic thought fields) are emitted by those who sincerely pray with the divine. These prayer fields can travel great distances and help heal those in need who live far away. A key to successful prayer is to have faith that your prayer will help you, that the divine, within and without, will help, guide, and protect you. When you do this, you become less angry, your blood pressure levels out, you think more clearly, and you are more able to tap into your full healing potential. Say this healing prayer before you start your day for 28 days (a moon cycle) to empower the healing energies within and without:

Dear Lord and Lady,
Father and Mother of all things
I pray you, help me grow healthier
Fill me with your healing grace
And empower the healing energies within me
I ask this in the Lord and Lady's names
Blessed be!

Sacred Healing Space

To empower your healing, place a couple photographs of loved ones and friends sharing happy times with you and your family on a small table or bookshelf in your sacred healing space. Add pictures of healing gardens and sacred sites, a white candle, a living plant, clear quartz crystals, and green-colored stones to add healing ambiance to your sacred healing space. If you like, put a tabletop fountain on your healing altar to promote healthy flowing chi (energy).

Keep in mind that your sacred love space and sacred healing space can be located in one spot. You can integrate them into one or you can set up separate altars. The advantage of integrating them is that you can use one altar, set of tools, and focals such as stones for all the rituals. Also, the divine energy of your sacred space becomes more pronounced with each magical work you do in it.

29

Healing Ritual

Perform this ritual on a Sunday, either on or just before a full moon. Gather a bowl of clean earth, a cup of water, a ballpoint pen, and cedar and sage smudge. You will also be using the white candle on your healing altar. Set all the items on your altar, draw a magic circle around your sacred healing space, and empower the elements. Inscribe your name on the candle body and inscribe the words "Divine Healing Power" on top of your name. Next, light the candle, dedicating it to your favorite Goddess of healing, such as Isis. Light the smudge, also dedicating it to the Goddess of healing. Put the smudge in a fireproof dish while it smolders. Pick up the bowl of earth, face north, and hold the bowl upward. Merge with the powers of earth and say:

Goddess of the North
Let your divine healing power
Fill my body, mind, and spirit.

Put the bowl back on the altar. Hold the smudge upward, face east, and merge with the powers of air. Say:

Goddess of the East
Let your divine healing power
Fill my body, mind, and spirit.

Put the smudge back on the altar. Carefully hold the candle upward, face south, and merge with the powers of fire. Say:

Goddess of the South
Let your divine healing power
Fill my body, mind, and spirit.

Put the candle back on the altar and pick up the chalice of water. Face west and merge with the powers of water. Say:

Goddess of the West
Let your divine healing power
Fill my body, mind, and spirit.

Now move to the center of the circle. Merge with the divine healing powers of the Goddess and say:

Great Goddess of earth, air, fire, and sea
Let your divine healing power fill me.

Gaze at the candlelight and imagine yourself growing healthier and happier with each new day. Imagine your body feeling strong and flexible, your mind clear and sharp, and your spirit filled with joy. In your mind's eye, see yourself as radiant and filled with the divine healing light of the Goddess. Do this for at least 15 minutes. When you are done, bid farewell to the elements, thank the Goddess for her healing presence, and pull up the circle. Allow the candle to safely burn down on its own.

Oracle of Health

Think of a question regarding your health. Write the date and question in your empowerment journal. Then find a book on healing and health. Hold the book in your hands, close your eyes, and take a few deep and relaxing breaths to center your awareness. Open the book and turn to any page. With your eyes still closed, put your index finger on a line. Open your eyes and read the sentence your finger is resting on. Does it shed new light on your health question? To clarify the oracle's answer, repeat the procedure a total of three times. Write the answers you receive in your journal.

Prosperity

Carla had worked in an insurance office for more than five years, starting out as a receptionist, moving to the file room, and then on to typing policies. Having always been a secretary, she was surprised when the company procured computer software that completely changed the nature of her job and the way she thought about herself.

After the computer system was installed and the training had begun, Carla began to demonstrate remarkable abilities. Suddenly she was training the account executives on how to use the new system. As the office became more automated and computerized, Carla moved from secretary to middle management and then to head of the computer department. In her case, she was lucky enough to find something she was good at that empowered her and helped her prosper.

Finding the things that you do well and determining your strong points is an important part of prosperity. Before planting a garden, you have to figure out what will grow best given the soil and climate.

Prosperity is very much the same; your abilities and environment are like the soil and climate of your garden of abundance.

In Wicca, prosperity is proportional to finding a path that empowers you physically, mentally, and spiritually. Sometimes it means taking a path that is less traveled or pushing the envelope and foraging your own path. Part of this involves being in harmony with yourself, nature, and Oneness.

The trick in life is to find things you are good at, enjoy a prosperous lifestyle, and still remain in harmony with yourself, nature, and life in general. It's easy to be spiritual when you are by yourself, merging with Oneness, but it gets harder when you have to take this spirituality out into the world, particularly when things get a little nasty out there!

It's easier to empower yourself when you place yourself in an environment that is conducive to your overall growth as a human being. To be truly empowering, prosperity must happen on all levels of body, mind, and spirit—otherwise it is out of balance and continually disappointing. This is especially important to keep in mind when setting prosperity empowerment goals. Make sure they encompass your whole being.

The First Empowering Step: Prosperity Meditation

This meditation is intended to help you find the things that you are good at, the things that are in harmony with you, nature, and Oneness. Part of this process is discovering your life pattern, which stems from the agreements that you've made with yourself and the divine through your many lifetimes. Your life pattern is your unfolding life purpose. When you discover your life pattern, you empower yourself and feel truly happy. Your personal journey unfolds with new passion, and you wake up excited. Each day suddenly has tremendous direction and meaning.

Begin this meditation by getting as comfortable as you can. In a quiet and undisturbed place, sit back or recline. Take a deep breath, breathing in the color green—the lush green of fresh grass, of trees, the pure green light of a thousand emeralds. As you exhale, breathe out any tension and concerns of the day. Now take another deep breath, breathing in the color emerald green, and breathing out any residual tension. As you take another deep breath, begin to imagine a single point of bright green light in your mind's eye. Notice the light becoming brighter and clearer as you move toward it. The light feels warm, soothing, and inviting. As you move closer, you are drawn to it.

Now imagine walking into the warm, emerald-green light. Suddenly you find yourself standing in a huge hallway carved out of a single huge emerald-colored stone. In the middle of the hallway is an enormous mirror, its massive wooden frame ornately carved with sun, stars, and moons. You take a deep breath and walk through the giant mirror as if you were walking through a doorway. You feel a slight popping as you pass through the mirror into an Otherworld of existence. In this Otherworld, you discover your life pattern, how to pursue it, and how to create prosperity and abundance in your life.

First, you ask yourself, if money were not a consideration, what would you be doing, where, and with whom? Think about what your passions and true interests are in life. What do you like to do so much that you would pay someone to do it? Think about your deepest desires and your most heartfelt goals and ask yourself why these things are dear to you. What are the qualities you truly love about them?

Now imagine stepping into the future where you are doing exactly what you want to do, exactly where, and with whom you desire to do it. Know you are living life to its fullest. Hold this image in your mind's eye and imagine that you are happily pursuing your life pattern. Imagine yourself as creative and prosperous. Make this image of yourself in the future very exciting, bright, bold, and colorful. See the image up close, in rich detail. Do this for several minutes to sharpen this prosperous image of the future.

Take another deep and complete breath, breathing in the color emerald green and breathing out completely. Take another breath and slowly open your eyes, coming back to the present time and place. Move your hands and foot and stretch your body like a cat.

Think about the meditation for a few minutes and come up with a simple sentence that describes your life pattern, your purpose in this lifetime. Write the date and the sentence in your empowerment journal.

Prosperity Affirmation and Prayer

Affirming the good things in life empowers you. When you say an affirmation, you engage your eyes, voice, and ears. By affirming the positive elements around you, you create more prosperity and abundance in your daily life. It becomes easier to get what you want. To continue with the gardening analogy, it's up to you to select the seeds of your prosperity, plant them, give them light and plenty of water, watch them grow, and harvest them.

Begin by writing an empowering prosperity affirmation on the back of your business card or an index card. For example, write:

I empower myself by drawing riches and prosperity into my life today and every day.

Feel free to personalize the affirmation in any way you like. For example, you might add:

With the help of the Goddess, each day I make the best business choices possible.

Carry the card in your pocket, wallet, or purse, and take it out and read it aloud several times during the day. Do this for 28 days. Then try it for six months, a year, and so on. The more you sincerely repeat the affirmation, the more you become one with the affirming statement on the card, and the quicker you manifest your prosperity goals.

Together with your prosperity affirmation, say this simple prayer for abundance and prosperity to get you in the proper frame of mind to enjoy your riches every moment of the day. As you pray, notice the cadence of your words. Commune with the divine and be one with the meaning of the prayer. See your prayer being answered in your mind's eye, feel the joy of it. Now take a deep breath, merge with Oneness, and pray:

Great Goddess and God of creation
Today I ask for your divine blessings
Help my garden grow abundant
From my good efforts and works
Empower me with riches and prosperity
And bestow your divine blessings
On those I care for and love.
In the Lady and Lord's names
Blessed be! Ayea!

Sacred Riches Space

Put a golden altar cloth and a green candle on your sacred riches altar. In addition, to bring you good fortune and continued prosperity, put a lucky bamboo plant (*Dracaena sanderiana*), a tropical plant available in plant shops and nurseries, on the east side of your sacred riches space. Lucky bamboo resembles bamboo; it's really a common ribbon plant and part of the agave family. As your lucky bamboo plant grows, your prosperity grows as well.

Prosperity Ritual

Do this ritual on a Wednesday or Thursday during a waxing moon, just before it becomes full. You will need the green candle from your sacred riches space, a ballpoint pen, and honeysuckle scented oil. Begin by drawing a magic circle around your sacred healing space. Then draw a circle of green light on top of the magic circle. Next, empower the elements. Then use the pen to inscribe your name on the candle body. Write the name of your favorite Goddess of prosperity and wealth, such as Lakshmi, on top of your name. Draw a large dollar sign ($) on top of the names and then draw a clockwise circle around the names and dollar sign, starting at the top. Dress the candle with a thin film of honeysuckle oil. Anoint yourself with the oil and then wipe the oil from your hands. Put the candle in the candlestick and light it, dedicating it to the Goddess of prosperity and abundance that you wrote on the candle. Merge with her divine abundance, and say three times:

Dear Goddess of abundance and plenty
Empower me with riches and prosperity.
So be it! Blessed be!

As the candle safely burns down, imagine the generous Goddess of abundance gifting you with riches, abundance, and continued prosperity, each and every day of your life. When you are done, bid farewell to the elements, thank the Goddess for her help, and close the circle.

Oracle of Wealth

Begin by thinking about a question regarding prosperity. Write the date and the question down in your empowerment journal. Next, find a book on business or finances. Take a few deep breaths to relax and center your mind. Close your eyes and turn to a page in the book. Place the index finger of your power hand a line on the page. Open your eyes and read the sentence. Does it provide any insight into your question about prosperity? If you want more information regarding your question, repeat the procedure a total of three times. Write the answers you received in your journal.

Chapter Two

The Second Empowering Step: Creating Your Empowerment Plan

Every year in the early spring, I map out where I want to plant the various inhabitants of my vegetable garden. I like to rotate my crops so everything is in a different place each year, which has the interesting effect of making each year's garden unique. In addition, each year after I till the garden and plant my seeds, something sprouts that I didn't plant. The first year it was lettuce that appeared in little places throughout the garden. The next year it was melons, and the third year it was little white pumpkins that we used to decorate our home for the harvest celebration.

Initially, I viewed these unexpected visitors as intruders, but as I reaped the benefits of their growth, I began to see them more as gifts from the Goddess. I have my plan, and she has hers. The better these plans come together, the easier things are all the way around. This year I have the Goddess's potatoes growing along with the summer squash. It should make for a divine vegetable stew!

Oftentimes when making plans, you have to allow for the divine hand. This divine manifests itself in ways that can both be anticipated and miraculous. Because of this, plans are best left flexible to allow for divine input. Allowing for this, empowerment happens one step at a time, and creating your empowerment plan is one of those steps.

I am always delighted when my garden comes alive in the spring after lying dormant all winter. Suddenly trees and bulbs bloom, and the flowers, bushes, shrubs, and vegetables sprout and grow. One of the best spots to watch nature at work is in a garden, and better yet is that you are part of it—a participant working together with nature growing wonderful things.

The garden makes the perfect analogy for empowering your life. In order to become empowered, you need to work with what's around you while influencing the general direction of events, rather than struggling with things. At times, you need to go with the flow, be flexible, and adapt to situations. Trying to plan and control absolutely everything in your life is a sure way to drive yourself and others around you crazy!

In empowering yourself, it's important to focus on your strengths and potential rather than your limitations and self-defeating habits. When you focus on your limitations and bad habits, you give them power. You make choices based on these negative tendencies. When you put the focus on your strengths, you take back the decision-making power and accept responsibility for what happens to you. As long as those choices are in alignment with who you are, you feel a sense of empowerment within the various aspects of your being. Remember, you mirror the divine, and the divine in turn mirrors you. You are one.

Seeing the Big Picture

At a tiger show, a young trainer had seven large tigers performing a variety of tricks—dancing, jumping through hoops, and doing balancing acts. I marveled at the way she seemed to work with rather than control the animals. During the performance, she revealed her training secrets. She told the audience that she always worked with each animal's natural proclivities. If a particular white tiger jumped particularly well, she would develop routines that made use of these talents and have the animal jump through hoops and in a complete circle. She was continually using each tiger's strengths as a means for successfully training the animal.

Obviously people are not tigers, but we have aspects in common—we are born, we live, we die, and we are reborn. People put on a civilized face, but each of us still has a wild, animal nature that extends into every aspect of our being. This is why we always return to the garden, our natural source of creation.

Basically, any plan consists of specific steps that you need to take to make your goal a reality. Depending on your goal, there are many types of plans; for example, financial, home, health, diet, marriage, or spiritual. Making choices and setting goals lays the foundation for planning. Viewing these choices and goals in terms of the larger picture is what gives plans definition and direction.

Plans and goals can be divided into three categories—short-term, mid-term, and long-term. Short-term plans and goals facilitate the mid-term, which in turn facilitate your long-term plans and goals. At the same time, long-term goals give meaning and perspective to short- and mid-term goals, and they give you a larger picture of your life.

Let's say that one of your long-term goals is to build your dream home. Some of your short-term goals might be accumulating money, building your credit, researching house designs, and learning what's involved in putting together a home—material costs, utilities, permit and school fees, and options for building from modular homes and kits to log cabins and custom homes. Your mid-term goals might be to find and purchase a piece of property on which to build your home, secure financing, and bulldoze a driveway into the property for access. Your long-term goals would be to actually build the house, move in, and enjoy the pleasures of living in your dream home.

Your short-term goals influence and reflect your long-term goals in that if you make more money in the short-term, then your long-term vision incorporates this change, and your vision of the house increases in scope. For example, from another view, if your long-term goal is to live on a houseboat, your short-term goals might change to learning as much as you can about boats, boat slip fees, marine navigation, and waterways. Again, there is a connected balance between the short-, mid-, and long-term elements of your plans, goals, and life.

Wicca adds a magically divine element to your plans and goals. When you make magic, you merge with the divine. The divine then helps you attain your heart's desires. In this sense, divinity becomes a powerful helpmate that empowers you toward personal fulfillment and success.

Goal Planning

Goal planning is a process that starts small, and if properly nurtured, can be one of the most empowering things you can do in life. Like a garden, once you attain your goals, they reseed themselves time and again, growing, thriving, and influencing many areas of your life in positive ways. In this sense, goals have a way of growing legs of their own once you add intelligent and directed awareness, effort, persistence, and of course, some powerful magic!

The first step in goal planning is writing down all your goals. Start by taking three sheets of paper and writing "Love Empowerment Goals" on top of one, "Health Empowerment Goals" on another, and "Prosperity Empowerment Goals" on the third sheet. (Or do the same exercise in your empowerment journal.)

Focusing on the exercises you did in Chapter One, write down your goals for love. Write down everything that comes to mind without trying to evaluate or judge it. Be in the moment and write everything that occurs to you, even if it seems far-fetched. Ideally, each sheet should have about 30 goals. Be sure to include everything short-, mid-, and long-term. If you would love to spend more time with your children, take a dream vacation with your beloved, or write a special poem for someone you love, write those things down on your list. Have fun with this process. Remember, the choice is yours and yours alone.

Making plans and attaining goals that you feel good about can help create a lifestyle that you welcome, one that empowers and fulfills you. Keep in mind that the choices must feel right to you. Otherwise you will end up being miserable because what you have created isn't in alignment with who you really are. This is why it's important to know who you are before you set your goals and make plans for attaining them.

You need to spend some time studying yourself, who you are, what you like, who you like, and things you like to do. You also need to examine those people, situations, and things you don't like. You need to become your own best friend.

In some ways, it's easier to be more charitable and less scrutinizing when it comes to another person. You may have a tendency to be hardest on yourself. This is something you learn from your parents, teachers, and peers. It's important to drop this conditional view for a while when you write down your goals. Instead, pretend that you are the explorer of uncharted waters who is just learning how to swim in the mysterious ocean of life.

Being a perfectionist is not conducive to making plans and attaining goals. At best, perfection is an elusive pursuit that provides little or no satisfaction. It is also an excuse to avoid setting goals and making plans. Since nothing can ever be really perfect, you have a ready-made excuse to give up before you even begin! On the opposite pole, being a wannabe is not helpful either. Changing your mind from day to day and pursuing one whim after another without any direction or plan won't give you a sense of fulfillment or success.

Goals must be reflective of who you are and what you hope to be. Remember these things as you are writing down your goals for love, health, and prosperity. There will probably be some overlapping of goals between the three areas. Goals such as moving into your dream home may come under the headings of love, health, and prosperity, because it reflects all three. If this is the case, list the goal under all three headers. This way the goal will be approached from different perspectives depending on your list. Overall, the goal lists are a focal point for developing a plan to achieve the things you want, and as a result, empower your life.

Becoming the Director of Your Life

Ron Howard started acting at 18 months of age. He went on to become Opie in the television show *Andy of Mayberry* and Richie Cunningham in *Happy Days*. But unlike most child actors, his goals didn't end there. When he was 15 years old, Ron decided his calling was to become a movie director, so he began making silent home movies, using everyone and everything available. Years later he would achieve his dream by directing hit movies such as *Splash*, *Apollo 13*, and *A Beautiful Mind*. The acclaim his movies have received has been one of the greatest thrills of his professional life.

Director Oliver Stone attributes magic as the underlying power that makes movies great. He knows that the best cinematographer, designer, actors, and the most creative script don't necessarily add up to a great movie. There's something more to the process, something indescribable yet ever-present. You know when the magic is there. You can feel it, and it comes across in the production.

Movies are like capsulated segments of people's lives. How they are planned out, implemented, and the magic they create determines their level of success. You can experience the same thing when you begin attaining your personal goals. You realize you are on the right path, and often the events of your life start falling into place in a positive way. Knowing what you want to create is an essential key to that success.

In the movie *Harry Potter and the Sorcerer's Stone*, first-year students go through a process in which a "sorting hat" sends them in one of four directions, depending on each student's magical proclivity. This is an apt analogy for what you must do with your goals. By sorting your goals into different groups, you organize and prioritize them. The following is a three-step process for organizing and prioritizing your empowerment goals:

1. **Take your goal lists and organize each into three subgroups.** In my case, I found my love empowerment goals combined into three groupings: "Primary Relationship," "Family Relationships," and "Friends and Other Relationships."

   I divided the page into three sections and listed these three headers. I wrote goals of achieving more romance in my life and improving my relationship with my husband under "Primary Relationship." Under "Family Relationships" I wrote goals of seeing more of my parents, particularly as they get older; and strengthening my relationship with my son. Finally, I included goals of seeing old friends more often and establishing more of a rapport with the Goddess under "Friends and Other Relationships."

   I then took my health empowerment goals and grouped them under the headings "Physical Health," "Mental Health," and "Spiritual Health." My main goal was to stay in good health as I grow older. To achieve this, I included goals such as improving my diet and securing a medical plan under "Physical Health." Having more fun, relaxing, and staying positive are some of my "Mental Health" goals; while praying, meditating, and merging with the Goddess and God are listed as my "Spiritual Health" goals.

   My prosperity empowerment goals seemed to organize under three groupings as well—"Home," "Work," and "Future and Retire-ment." I put goals such as planting a new garden and finishing the front porch under "Home." Finishing this manuscript, securing more book contracts, and presenting workshops are listed under my "Work" goals; while goals such as buying property for investment purposes and continuing to write useful and popular books are listed under "Future and Retirement."

On a practical level, the easiest way to complete stage one is to take your original love empowerment goals list and on a separate sheet paper write the headings "Primary Relationship," "Family Relationships," and "Friends and Other Relationships." (Feel free to tweak the headings to suit you.) Now go through the goals on your original list and write them under the three headings until all your goals have been transferred to the updated list of goals. One you have finished love, do the same for your health and prosperity goals.

2. **Prioritize your goals as to their relative importance to one another.** By establishing what's most important to you, you begin working on your important goals first and progress from there.

Every time you attain one of your goals, a little burst of energy goes off inside of you creating a feeling of elation. It empowers you! Suddenly you feel in sync with yourself, nature, and the universe. The whole world is singing your song.

Take a new sheet of paper and write "Love Empowerment Goals" at the top. Write the three headers or subgroups underneath it across the page. Next, get your list of "Primary Relationship Goals" and from the list select the most important goal. Write it at the top of the new list and cross it out on the old list. Now, select the most important goal to you from what's left of the list and write it under the first goal on the new list. Do this until all goals have been transferred over to the new list according to their importance to you. Now repeat the same process with your other lists of empowerment goals, until all your goals have been sorted by priority.

3. **Give each of your goals a time frame.** Will it happen in a day, week, month, year, five years, or longer? Be realistic in your assessment. Now write down a specific calendar date next to each goal. A good rule of thumb is to be generous and give yourself plenty of time to attain your goal; you will have more success attaining your goals by giving yourself ample time. This empowers you to continue setting goals and achieving them.

Now go down the list and rate each goal as to whether it's short-term, mid-term, or long-term. Short-term means a goal that happens within a year, mid-term means a goal that happens in two to five years, and long-term is five years or longer. Often short-term goals link with mid- and long-term goals, meaning one must be attained before the other can be. There is a definite pattern to setting goals, making plans, and achieving goals.

Patterns by nature are ordered, not random. At the same time, patterns need to include the possibility that random factors can occur and influence the overall outcome. Sometimes these seemingly random factors can be beneficial and almost magical, while other times they can be hindering and destructive.

Planning, Patterns, and Wicca

Rituals, spells, and magical patterns all progress out of the idea that you have an expectation or goal, and that the ritual, spell, or magical pattern is a means or plan for attaining that goal. In this sense, the foundation of Wicca is built on the idea of setting goals and using prescribed magical techniques as a plan for helping you to actualize your goals.

Magical patterns are founded on the idea of imagining the steps needed to get the results you want. These steps in the magical realm translate into intention and expectation, desire, and merging, also known as the three eyes of the Goddess.

Intention and expectation address the nature, circumstance, and overall scope of your goals. Intention is what you intend by attaining the goal, the reason behind the goal. It is also how you intend to achieve the goal, the plans you need to make for successful results. Expectation is what you set your sights on, the goal itself. You expect to set, plan, and attain your goals. Wicca stresses the idea that making a "good" choice results in finding yourself in a "good" situation.

Also under the umbrella of expectation is the plan for attaining your goal. In your mind's eye, you imagine not only what you want, but also what you need to do to manifest it. If your goal is losing 20 pounds, then you need to imagine the steps you expect to take to do just that—improving your self-image, improving your diet, and beginning an exercise program. These are all steps that will definitely help you attain your goal of weight loss.

Desire centers around the question of how strongly you want your plan and goal to become reality. If your desire is intense, then you are more motivated to follow your plan through to fruition. Your desire fuels your goal setting, planning, and attainment. You get up each morning enthusiastic and ready to move on to the next step in your empowerment plan. Desire is what drives you to push the envelope a little further, bringing more empowerment, positive change, and personal growth.

Change occurs whether you want it to or not, so you might as well have a hand in influencing its general direction. In terms of the weight loss example, your desire is reflected in your ability to follow your plan for changing your diet, self-image, and exercise habits.

Merging involves becoming one with the divine. It is the key to all magic! The stronger the merge, the stronger the magic. When you merge with the divine, you become like a cloud diffusing into Oneness. You connect with a boundless, timeless energy, with the Goddess and God, the source of all creation. When you bring this energy into your goals and life, you open yourself up to miraculous things. Life becomes divine! Everything is energy, and when you merge with the divine, you become one with the cauldron of creation that renews and makes everything whole again. In the case of weight loss, you become energetically, mentally, and physically the person you want to be with a little help from your divine friends. I invite you to stir up that cauldron and merge on!

The Pentacle: A Five-Step Magical Pattern

A Wiccan pentacle is a five-pointed star with a circle drawn around, and it is frequently used in magic. The pentacle in the twenty-first century is what the peace sign was in the 1960s. It is a primary symbol of Wicca and magic. Esoterically, the pentacle represents the powers of spirit plus the four elements of earth, air, fire, and water.

When I did my first magical pentacle (in a series of steps I'll show you in a moment), I kept it simple. My goal was to obtain a computer, something that would make my college life a little easier. Shortly after doing my pentacle, a friend called to say that I could borrow his computer for as long as I wanted, enabling me to finish several writing projects I was working on at the time.

Pentacles often work this way, where an unforeseen force has a hand in influencing the outcome of a pattern in a positive way. More often than not, magical pentacles work because of careful planning, clear intention, and expectation, as well as a strong desire and deep merge with the divine.

One couple I know made the goal of their first magical pentacle to buy a home of their own. That was what they wanted more than anything else at the time. They made a pentacle plan that involved finding a house they liked in their price range, securing financing, and coming up with the down payment. They manifested their pentacle when they kept looking at houses until they found the one they both adored, got their financing approved by the lending company, and their parents lent them the money for the down payment. They manifested their dream home by working their pentacle through to fruition. This demonstrates that pentacles do work. First you have to intend and expect to attain your pentacle goal, create your pentacle, and follow the steps of your pentacle to manifest the desired results.

When creating pentacles, it's better to start small and work up from there. The first thing you need to do is select one of the goals from your empowerment list to use in your pentacle. Then follow these five steps:

1. Write down your goal on a blank page in your empowerment journal and underneath it write out the steps that you need to take to attain your goal.

2. Use a large sheet of thick paper or poster board and draw a large pentacle (a five-pointed star) on it. The five points on the pentacle represent you (top point), your goal (upper-right point), your plan (lower-right point), your action in carrying out your plan (lower-left point), and the successful outcome and completion of your goal (upper-left point).

3. Choose a symbol that to you represents each of the five points (you, your goal, your plan, your action, and your success). Draw each symbol above the point it represents.

4. Tack the sheet with your pentacle on the wall. Take your wand and imagine white light shooting out of the tip. Now move your wand clockwise from the head of the pentacle around to the arm, leg, other leg, other arm, and finally back to the head. As you do this, imagine that you are weaving the five points of the pentacle

together into one with a thread of white light. As you move through each point, focus on the symbols and what they represent.

5. Now merge with the divine as strongly as you can. One of the easiest ways to do this is to focus all your energy on one point and diffuse it out like a cloud dispersing your awareness into Oneness, into everything and nothing at the same time. Use deep breathing, chanting, drumming, singing, dancing, or other methods to deepen your merge. In this state, you are divinely empowered and experience life from a greatly expanded awareness.

Creating Your Empowerment Plan

As human beings progressing through the stages of life, we are all endowed with an internal voice that can either help us or hinder us. This internal voice echoes the inherent polarities of energy and the universe that move back and forth like the tides. It tells us we can do things, and we achieve greatness. On the other hand, it tells us we are doomed to failure, and it becomes a self-fulfilling prophecy. Finding a balance between the polarities and using internal dialogue as a positive aspect of your life is the beginning point to creating your empowerment plan—the Second Empowering Step.

It's important that your internal dialogue be positive and encouraging to the rest of the pattern. Have the courage to imagine your success, and as such own it as yours. You made the effort. You deserve it! Keep telling yourself this until you believe it, better yet, until you know it. Owning up to your good qualities and your abilities and affirming your self worth are crucial steps in the empowerment process.

Plans become honed and fine-tuned through usage and time. As you progress through the process of setting your goals, making your plan, and attaining your goals, they will naturally evolve. The best idea is to develop plans and achieve goals that are most enriching and empowering. To do so in the course of this year, you will need to:

1. Adapt your habits so that they work for you.
2. Work from your strengths and proclivities.
3. Be realistic and generous with your timetables and your abilities to accomplish certain steps in your plan.

4. Create a basic five-step plan for each of your goals.

5. Fill in the details of each of your goals by moving from the general goal to the specific plan and steps you need to take to attain it. Then take the steps, one at a time.

Planning and organization help you take more control over the events of your life. As such, you are less likely to become a victim of random circumstances or the patterns of destruction that other people lead you into or you create yourself. Organization is the opposite of feeling out of control. The more you organize your magical patterns, the more your life will positively flow and grow.

Creating plans is about gaining more organization in your daily life. It's a way to manage your goals so you can manifest them. It's important to pace yourself and do what you can. Work at your own speed. If you do, you will have great success at attaining each and every goal you truly desire. The main idea in planning and organizing is to work within your basic means and add the divine element. Merge with, affirm, and pray for divine help, and it will be provided to you. You can count on it!

Love

The first time I saw Michael, the man who would become my husband, a giant hand seemed to come down from the heavens with the message, "He's the one." Being only 13 years old, I was hesitant, but at the same time the influence of the hand was overwhelming to my overall psyche. I knew I saw a hand, and it was pointing, and I heard a voice in my mind. I wondered what was going on as I tapped in to energies and feelings that seemed to move beyond the present moment into something that had its roots in past lives and divine intervention. I didn't know then that the meeting represented my future.

From the moment I first saw Michael, I knew I had to meet him. I developed a plan to establish a relationship with him. Being in school, I figured out where his classes were and began bumping into him in the hallways. I convinced one of his friends to introduce us at a school dance, at which point we immediately begin going together. A few year later, we went to the same college. A couple of years later, we were married, and our relationship has continued to grow deeper through the years.

Over the years, we have changed and our views of one another have expanded, and we have developed patterns that permeate our relationship. Our mid- and long-term goals have changed, producing a profound effect on our short-term goals and our relationship in every sense. Obviously, sad and difficult times have had a negative effect on our relationship, while joyful and loving times have had a positive effect.

Love is more than the good and bad times together. To work, it must hold fast and strong, impervious to the emotional ups and downs of everyday life, and to undermining people and events. Otherwise love has a tendency to become like a roller coaster ride—something that is initially exciting, but after a period of time, you begin wanting things to level off a bit and then eventually, you just want off the ride.

You need to establish a balance that moves you beyond these emotional mood swings that have a tendency to eventually break up relationships and lives. It's important to find a balance that you can live with. This helps you to continue growing as a human being.

Keeping focused on your goals and developing an empowerment plan is one of the ways for finding and keeping this balance, especially when it comes to love. When you know what you're doing and where you're going, you have a tendency to swing to extremes less, and for the most part it's easier to stay centered in your relationships. This is why it's important to write down your goals and the plans for achieving them. Seeing them and being able to refer to them everyday gives you the focus and balance you need to move toward empowering your life.

The Second Empowering Step: Love Meditation

Begin by choosing one of the items on your love empowerment goals list that you want to work on in this meditation. As with the love meditation in Chapter One, turn on some soft music, sit or lie down, and get comfortable. Close your eyes, and begin slowly breathing in and out. As you inhale, envision all of your tensions and anxieties coming together into a single breath of air, and with your exhalation, see them moving out of your body. Do this three times, each time becoming more relaxed.

Imagine yourself walking along a path that leads to a garden gate. Approaching the white, wrought-iron gate, you hear the songs of birds coming from the other side that seem to beckon to you, and you see five flat stones that lead to the gate.

Stepping onto the first stone, you immediately feel all of your dreams, hopes, and expectations come together into a ball of energy that moves throughout your body, invigorating and energizing every cell. The scent of lilac wafts through the gate. As you breath in, the sweet aroma carries you onward.

As your feet touch the second stone, you feel a sense of where you are going in life, a sense of purpose. Like being in the sky looking down, you get an overall view of everything and how it works together as a whole. Through the bars of the gate, you can see a fruit tree that has golden apples that glisten in the sun, making your mouth water with anticipation as you move forward.

On the third stone, you feel yourself resonating and becoming in harmony with divine Oneness. First, breathe in while focusing all of your energy on being a point of white light surrounded by darkness. As you breathe out, diffuse the light outward, feeling it as it permeates all the darkness until there is only light. You are now merged with Oneness. The sun shines through the latticework of the gate, creating patterns that look like mandalas on the ground before you, which leads you further on your quest.

The moment you come in contact with the fourth stone, you feel a sense of unending and limitless love that sends a warm glow throughout your entire being until you're glowing like a candle. You feel love for yourself, you feel love for others, and you feel love for the divine. The love you feel moves within you and without you. It is a love you give, and it is a love you receive. Through the gate, you momentarily glimpse the sight of your true love, who waves for you to come closer.

The fifth stone sits before the gate, and as you move onto the stone, you reach for the handle of the gate. Turning the handle, you push the gate open and move through the doorway into the garden. There to greet you is your true love, who takes your hand and leads you through the garden to a special spot where the two of you lay in each other's arms and stare into each other's eyes. You feel a sense of perfect love and peace.

Now take a deep breath in through your mouth and hold it for three seconds before exhaling out through your nose. Do this three times, open your eyes, count to 10, and come back to the present. Begin moving your body around while retaining the sensation of love you experienced in the meditation.

Take a few moments to write down in your empowerment journal some of the feelings you had during the meditation, particularly what you felt at each of the five stones, including when you saw your true love on the other side of the garden gate.

Love Affirmation and Prayer

Affirmations are the perfect way to start your day because they begin things on a positive note. Repeat the following affirmation to yourself when you first awaken in the morning as a way to affirm your connection to love and your love empowerment goals throughout your day:

Each morning when I wake up, I am empowered with love.
Each day that I am alive, I am empowered with love.
Each evening when I go to sleep, I am empowered with love.
Each night when I dream, I am empowered with love.

As with affirmations, prayers can also help you begin each day in a positive way. A prayer you can say when you awaken is to thank the Goddess for being alive and having love in your life. Praying is about communication both with yourself and the divine. Keep this mind when praying, and always remember to pray from your heart:

Thank you Lady for your gift of life
Thank you Goddess for your gift of love
Thank you Lady for your gift of family and friends
Thank you Goddess for your daily blessings
Thank you Lady for helping me attain my goals
By the loving grace of the Goddess, blessed be!

Sacred Love Space

Add a pentacle shape from nature to your sacred space. For example, you can add a couple of starfish, a sand dollar, five sticks connected together into a five-pointed star, a small pentacle traced with white pebbles or sea shells, or five-petaled pink or red flowers on your altar. Before placing the item(s) on your altar, hold them in your hands and bless them by saying:

Dear Goddess and God,
Please bless my love plan
And help me attain my love goals
By the Lady and Lord, blessed be!

Put the item(s) on your altar. Also bless five white tea or votive candles, one at a time. Then place them in the shape of a five-pointed star on your altar to symbolize the five points of your magical love pentacle—you, your love goal, your love plan, your actions in carrying out your love plan, and the successful outcome of your love goal.

Love Ritual

Use this pentacle ritual to propel your love empowerment plan into reality. It's best done on or just after a new moon on a Friday night— the night of love magic!

You will need a red gel or felt pen, two sheets of paper, rose scented oil, your wand, soft music, and the five tea or votive candles in candle holders on your sacred love altar. Candles act as excellent focals when making magic. Once lit, the flame symbolizes your highest potential, the flickering of the candle represents its voice, while the smoke carries your wishes to the divine.

Begin by selecting one love empowerment goal from your goals list. Use the gel pen to write out a five-step love plan for the goal on one of the sheets of paper and put the paper on your altar where you can easily see it. Next, turn on some soft music. Then draw a magic circle of light around your sacred love space and altar. Empower your circle by calling in the elements. Take the tea candles or votives out of their holders, anoint them with a couple drops of the rose scented oil, then place the candles back in their holders. Now anoint yourself with the oil by putting a couple drops on the inside of your wrists, ankles, and on your third eye (your forehead between your brows). Wipe the oil from your hands and light the topmost candle. Merge with the powers of fire and say:

Fires of passion and desire so bright
Empower my love plan tonight.

Continue lighting the candles, one at a time, moving clockwise around the pentacle. Each time you light a candle, repeat:

Fires of passion and desire so bright
Empower my love plan tonight.

Gaze at the candle flames for a few minutes and refer to your love empowerment plan list on your altar. Imagine following the steps on your love plan and manifesting your love goal. Imagine a bright, color-ful, joyful, and loving outcome. (You can use a mirror behind the can-dles to amplify their light. Moving your gaze from the reflection of the candle flames in the mirror and the actual flames is easier on your eyes than just staring at the flames themselves.) As you gaze into the flames, use deep breathing to deepen your merge with images and sensations of your successful love empowerment plan, action steps, and outcome.

Next, draw a large pentacle on the sheet of paper with the red gel pen. The pentacle should be large enough to put a symbol into each point. In the topmost point of the pentacle (the head), write your initials and draw a symbol that represents you. You can create your own symbols or use ones you are familiar with. Next, in the rightmost arm of the pentacle, draw a symbol that represents your love empowerment goal. In the right leg of the pentacle, draw a symbol that signifies your love empowerment plan. In the left leg of the pentacle, draw a symbol that represents your five action steps in carrying out your love plan. In the left arm of the pentacle, draw a symbol that represents the successful outcome and attainment of your love goal.

Now, tack the paper on the wall at eye level where you can easily see and reach it. Hold your wand in your power hand, a few inches from the surface of the pentacle, and trace the pentacle's shape three times. Point your wand tip at each point, beginning at the topmost (head) point and moving clockwise. Allow each symbol to flash into your mind as you do this. Continue to the leftmost arm, which signifies attaining your love empowerment goal. Then draw an energetic clockwise circle around the pentacle three times, and say:

In the name of the Lady and Lord
I pray you, empower this love pentacle
By the powers of earth, air, fire, and sea
By the powers of the Goddess and God, blessed be!

Now hold your wand between your hands and quietly gaze at the pentacle. Imagine a bright white light totally engulfing it. Merge into and become one with your love pentacle. The pentacle head becomes your head. The pentacle arms and legs become your arms and legs. Fully transform into a luminous white five-pointed star, shining brightly. Now imagine spinning your brilliant star body forward out into the divine night skies. As you do this, move your awareness into the future for a few minutes and feel the joy of attaining your love empowerment goal.

When you are done, set your wand on the altar and clap your hands together three times. Turn away from the pentacle for a few minutes until your mind returns to normal. Bid farewell to the elements, thank the Goddess and God, and close your magic circle. Allow the candles to safely burn down on their own.

Keep the sheet of paper with your love plan steps on your love altar, and keep your love empowerment pentacle on the wall in your sacred love space. Recharge your love pentacle once a day by pointing your wand at the head, arms, and legs, in a clockwise pattern, and repeating:

In the name of the Lady and Lord
I pray you, empower this love pentacle
By the powers of earth, air, fire, and sea
By the powers of the Goddess and God, blessed be!

Focus on the pentacle frequently, giving it energy and positive reinforcement until you attain your love empowerment goal.

Oracle of Love

Think of a single question about your most important love empowerment goal. Write the question and date in your empowerment journal. Go over to the television set, place your hands on the screen, and say:

May the Goddess and God bless you as a divine oracle.

Sit back with the remote control, a pen, and your journal. Take a deep, relaxing breath, and let go of any tensions you may be feeling. Now use the remote to turn on the television. Write down in your empowerment journal the first few words that you hear and pictures that you see as you turn on the television. Then take another deep, complete breath, and switch the channel. Again, write down the first few words you hear and pictures you see. Repeat this process a total of five times. When you are done, look for connections and messages about your love goal in the words and pictures. Circle the ones that are most meaningful to you.

Health

David had been experiencing a numbness that seemed to be moving down his left leg. He went to a chiropractor who did some adjustments, but the problem kept gradually getting worse until he was having trouble walking. The evening strolls with his nine-month-old son were starting to become extremely painful. David woke up every night screaming from the pain, which was making sleep an impossibility. At this point, he truly thought he was becoming crippled.

After a visit to a doctor, David was told he had a herniated disk, which could either be fixed by surgery, or as his doctor suggested, through a plan whereby for the initial period he stayed laying on his back with his feel elevated.

David didn't want surgery so he opted to lay on his back for a period of six weeks. After some of the swelling in the disk had gone down, he was able to start doing basic exercises that included laying on his stomach on the floor and elevating himself with his arms in order to restore the curve in his lower back. Gradually, as he stuck to his routine, the pain moved back up his leg. He could again walk normally, but from then on he always had to make sure he never sat for too long without stretching. When sitting, he also used a lumbar pillow to keep the curve in his back.

David's experience is a constant reminder that you have to stay positive and not give up even when in extreme pain. Pain is usually your body's way of telling you something is wrong. The idea is to make sure you listen.

Also, always check your options when it comes to healing and health. Sometimes the first option isn't the best one. In most cases, surgery is something that should only be used when there are no alternatives. When you cut into body tissue, you do things to the whole of the body that can sometimes have far reaching effects. In terms of your back, if you have one of your disks removed, your back is suddenly less mobile because your disks are what make it flexible. This does not mean you should never have surgery or turn to modern medicine for help, but you should exhaust all other options first if time allows it. And remember to apply meditation, prayer, affirmation, ritual, and oracles to help you make the wisest possible health empowerment plans you can follow and attain.

The Second Empowering Step: Healing Meditation

The meditation and techniques are intended to help you develop a plan for making your health empowerment goals a reality. A basic plan for better health should be straightforward and realistic. Be honest with yourself. Meditation leads your subconscious mind forward, and your conscious mind follows, helping you to move forward toward better health and positive well-being.

For this meditation, imagine you have just won a free vacation to the health spa of your dreams. The brochure for the place says it has a five-step plan for positive health transformation.

Begin by sitting or reclining in a comfortable place. Breathe in deeply and imagine yourself being transported to the spa in the brochure, a place that before only existed in your dreams. Breathe in again, and as you slowly exhale, imagine the place before you. Take two more deep breaths. Each time, the image of the spa becomes more defined until the front door to the place stands in front of you. Imagine knocking on the door three times. The door opens and in the doorway stands a beautiful, gentle, Goddess-like woman. She greets you and asks you to enter. She escorts you down a hallway that leads to five rooms. She stops at the doorway of the first room and motions for you to go inside.

As you walk in, a wave of warm moist air quickly surrounds your body. In the middle of the room is a luxurious bathtub surrounded by lush shrubbery and blooming flowers of every color. You get undressed and get into the relaxing warm water of the tub. Laying back, you can feel the jets streaming gently across your lower back and upward to your shoulders. You relax even more as the warm water washes away any stress and tension. They just seem to melt away into the water. After a while, the beautiful woman reappears and escorts you to the next room.

You open the door and enter the room. In the middle of the room is a bathtub filled with thick, brown-colored mud. Climbing slowly into the tub, you sink into the moist earth and feel the warm mud oozing around you. As you lay in the tub, you feel the mud absorbing the impurities and unwanted energies in your body. The nurturing mud makes your skin feel soft and supple. After the mud bath, you shower and towel off. The woman returns, leading you to the next room.

As you enter the third room, the beautiful woman gestures for you to lie face down on a soft green velvet cushioned massage table that sits in the middle of the room. Soft music plays as you feel your body begin to be massaged by divinely friendly hands and fingers that are both gentle and firm. You feel your neck and back being kneaded, releasing all the tightness that builds up because of stress and tension. Your lower back succumbs to long strokes that move all of the blocked energy down your legs, and out through the soles of your feet. You relax for a few minutes before the woman returns to take you to the next room.

The fourth room is filled with a magnificent swimming pool. You dive into the cool blue water, and you feel refreshed and invigorated to your very core. Your body, mind, and spirit become one with element of water as you move through the water like an aquatic creature of your own design. After slowly swimming for a while, you get out of the water and towel off. The gentle woman then returns to lead you into another room.

Looking like a banquet hall, the fifth room is lined with long tables that are covered with every kind of healthy, delicious food imaginable. There are tables in the middle of the room for sitting and eating. You pick up a plate and begin filling it with all the foods to make you healthy. Back at your table, you begin by feasting on a golden apple that is as sweet as any you have ever tasted. Next you bite into a fresh grape that seems to revitalize your body. Each bite of food that you take fills you with divine healing energy. After you finish eating, your body feels transformed and renewed.

Now take a deep breath in and exhale completely. Gradually move your awareness back to the present time and place. Take another deep breath and slowly open your eyes. As you gradually move back into the present moment, recall the image of the new healthy you. Move your hands and feet and stretch your body like a cat. While the meditation is fresh in your mind, write in your empowerment journal the date and your thoughts and feelings during the experience. Use these notes to help you when formulating your health empowerment plan.

Healing Affirmation and Prayer

Healing affirmation can help you stay focused on your health plans and goals. Affirmations work best when practiced with regularity so that they become a habit, like brushing your teeth or taking a shower or bath. Each time you say an affirmation, it turns your mind toward what you want. Affirmations actually change the way you think, little by little. When you turn your mind toward affirmation, you find that you can easily attain your health empowerment goals.

57

Repeat this affirmation to yourself before your morning meal. Say the affirmation until you believe it, and you manifest your goal:

Each and every day, I take one action step of my health empowerment plan until I attain my goal.

As with affirmations, healing prayers are excellent ways to stay focused while at the same time asking for the divine blessings of the Goddess:

Dear Goddess and God, I pray you
Fill me with your healing power so that I am healed
Lend me your strength so that I am strong
Please help me manifest my goals one step at a time
With the divine blessings of the Lady and Lord,
Ayea! Ayea! Ayea!

Sacred Healing Space

Add a picture of a healing spa, hot springs, or place in nature to your sacred healing space. Next add a photo to your space of you having fun. Then add a blue candle and a star symbol. One of the best symbols you can use for this purpose is the symbol of a five-pointed star with a picture of a woman or man superimposed on the star, the head lining up with the top of the star, the arms with the arms of the star, and the feet with the feet of the star. The star symbol in your sacred healing space represents the five points of your health pentacle—you, you health empowerment goal, your plan for empowering your health, the steps you will take to attain your goal, and the successful empowering outcome. Next, add a clean blue candle to your sacred healing altar. Before setting it in its holder, empower the candle by holding it between your hands and saying:

I dedicate this candle to my health empowerment plan.
In the name of the Lady and Lord empower me, blessed be!

Healing Ritual

Best done during a gibbous to full moon phase on a Sunday or Monday night, this healing ritual can help you stick to your health empowerment plan and manifest your goals.

You will need a green gel or felt pen, a sheet of paper, a strip of gold star stickers, pine-scented oil, and the blue candle from your sacred healing altar. Begin by drawing a magic circle of light around your sacred healing space and empower your circle by calling in the elements. Coat the candle with a thin film of pine-scented oil and wipe the oil from your hands. Next, light the candle, dedicating it to a favorite Goddess or God of healing. Then say:

Candle of divine healing light
Let your fire fuel my rite tonight!

Now use the pen to write your most important health empowerment goal at the top of the sheet of paper in large letters. Next to the goal, write a date by which you expect to attain your goal. Under that, list the five action steps of your health empowerment plan. Now apply the gold star stickers in a clockwise circle around your writing and lightly rub a drop of pine oil on each of the stars. Put the paper on your sacred healing altar in front of the candle where you can easily read it. Focus all your attention on your empowerment plan outlined on the paper in front of you, merge with the divine, and say:

Goddess and God, I pray you
Hear me now as I call to you.
Help me attain my healing goal
Heal my spirit and heal my soul
By earth, air, fire, and sea
So be it! Blessed be!

Gaze at the candle flame and imagine the successful outcome of your health empowerment goal by the date you indicated. In your mind's eye, see and sense yourself taking the actions you listed on the sheet of paper, one step at a time, until you manifest your goal. Do this for at least 15 minutes.

When you are done, thank the Goddess and God, bid farewell to the elements, and pull up your magic circle. Allow the candle to safely burn down. Keep the sheet of paper on your sacred healing altar. Read your goal and the five action steps of your plan out loud at least once a day to encourage its fruition. Over the next few days, begin taking those action steps you listed on the sheet of paper to manifest your health empowerment goal.

Oracle of Health

Think of a main question about your most important health empowerment goal. Write the question and date in your empowerment journal.
Now go over to the television set, place your hands on the screen, and
say:

May the Goddess and God bless you as a divine oracle.

Sit back with the remote control, a pen, and your journal. Take a
deep, relaxing breath, and let go of any tensions you may be feeling.
Use the remote to turn on the television. Write down the first few words
that you hear and pictures that you see as you turn on the television.
Then take another deep, complete breath and switch the channel. Write
down the first few words you hear and pictures you see. Repeat this
process a total of five times. When you are done, look for connections
and messages about your health empowerment goal in the words and
pictures you have written down in your journal. Circle the ones that
are most meaningful to you.

Prosperity

In the late 1980s, Michael and I found ourselves living in the San
Francisco Bay Area at a time when rent was going up and real estate
was beginning to skyrocket. We realized that we didn't want to keep
renting, and we didn't have the money or credit to buy a house at Bay
Area prices. Realizing this, we set up a basic five-step plan for acquiring
our own place in the country.

The first step involved finding areas that had properties for sale that
we could afford. Once we did that, we looked for a piece of property
that would fulfill our needs. On the Wiccan Sabbat Lughnassad, we
found the perfect piece of property through some friends of ours who
were buying property in the same area. In the second step, we decided
where we were going to position the house on the property. In the third
step, we found a manufactured home we liked that included all the modern conveniences. The fourth step revolved around getting our permits,
clearing the area for the house, and putting in a well and septic system.
The fifth and final step came when the company we bought the home
from moved the home onto the pad we had prepared and connected
everything. We then moved into our dream home!

The main thing you need to do to manifest your prosperity goals is to develop a plan and stick with it until fruition. Once you have a plan, you have the "means" for attaining your goal, which is your outcome or "end." In this sense, the end does not justify the means, but more appropriately, your goals provide a focal point and purpose for your empowerment plans.

The Second Empowering Step: Prosperity Meditation

Sit back or recline comfortably in your favorite spot. If you like, you can hold a clear quartz crystal point in your receiving hand as you meditate. Be sure to clear out your crystal before using it for the mediation.

Begin breathing slowly and deeply for a few minutes until you feel yourself flowing into a relaxed state of being. Now imagine yourself entering a "worm hole" through space. At the speed of light you are transported anywhere in the universe through this hole. As you move through the hole, you see flashes of light that flicker all around you. You discover that you are moving so fast it feels just like you are standing still.

Gradually the flashes of light begin to slow down, and you find yourself in a cave. The ceiling and sides of the cave are covered with crystal points that twinkle like a lighted Christmas tree decorated with the brilliant colors of the rainbow. In the north section of the cave, a giant mother crystal pulsates with white light, enough to light the cave with a brilliance that is only equaled by the midday sun.

A red crystal point begins blinking as if to catch your attention. Reaching for it, you easily pluck its slender shape from the wall, and you feel something that seems to stir your cauldron with a desire that ignites and excites your entire being. After drawing a circle of light around the perimeter of the cave, you point the red crystal at the mother crystal, and suddenly you see a flurry of images that move across the cave like a giant monitor, displaying all of your dreams, goals, aspirations, and expectations.

After the images begin to disappear, an orange crystal wand begins blinking. You remove it from the wall and feel a force that seems to direct the fires of your cauldron towards your dreams, aspirations, and expectations. Again draw a circle of light around the cave before you point the orange crystal point at the mother crystal. The images that stream across the cave are images of your empowerment plan and the steps you need to take to make your empowerment goals come true. The images display a map for getting from one place to another.

After the images end, a yellow crystal begins to blink. You pluck it from the wall of the cave and feel a sense of empowerment because finally you are doing what you want to do. Drawing a circle of light, you point the yellow crystal at the mother crystal, and images flash by of you actually taking the steps that you laid out as the plans for your empowerment.

Next, a green crystal begins flickering, and you move toward it. It almost glides into your hand. You feel a sense that your dreams, goals, aspirations, and expectations are crystallizing. Everything is coming to fruition and manifesting into reality. For a period of time, you can do no wrong and everything seems to be at your fingertips. The eternal question becomes, "What will you do with your 15 minutes?" This is your moment, enjoy it while it happens and make it last as long as you can. It is your moment of florescence.

The images keep building until a blue crystal begins pulsating and blinking. When you touch the blue point, you feel yourself merging into Oneness. Moving the crystal point around the room, you feel yourself step-by-step becoming one with the Goddess, God, and all things. When you reach that point, you feel a burst of empowering energy that flows throughout your being. For a moment, you feel on top of the world. Stay on the top of the world for a few minutes and enjoy the pleasurable sensations and joy.

Now take a deep and complete breath, feeling refreshed and relaxed. Breathe in white light and breathe out white light. Take another deep and complete breath. Slowly begin moving your fingers and toes, and open your eyes without focusing them on anything in particular. Now move your hands, feet, and stretch your body like a cat to come back to the present time and place.

After meditating, write down in your empowerment journal any insights you gained from the experience. Note the date, and also write down how you felt before, during, and after the meditation.

Prosperity Affirmation and Prayer

People and situations are continually testing your faith in yourself and your chosen path in life. Because of this, often you find yourself questioning your goals and everything you are doing. Sometimes the inner dialogue becomes so intense that it becomes easy to lose your focus and, in turn, your direction and desire.

Affirmations are a great way to bring things back into focus and put you back on the empowerment track. Try these examples of empowering prosperity plan affirmations:

- ✐ "Today and every day, I am on the path I want be on, doing the things I want be doing."
- ✐ "I feel the divine hands of the Goddess and God helping me follow my prosperity empowerment plan and attain my goal.
- ✐ "Each and every day, the divine love of the Lady and Lord help me move one step further on my plan toward the fruition of my prosperity goals."

Prayers ask for divine intervention and help. No matter how you view the divine, it is generally accepted that it is the totality of the whole, a Oneness that manifests itself in infinite ways. This is the intention behind the following prayer:

Oh great and mighty one,
Give your blessings to my prosperity plan,
I pray you, help me to clearly see,
The person that I really am.
By the Lady and Lord, blessed be!

Sacred Riches Space

Pentacles in tarot cards are also referred to as coins, and they represent wealth and prosperity. To empower your sacred riches space, add five coins to represent the five steps of your prosperity empowerment goal. First, clean the coins by rinsing them in cool salt water for a few minutes. Then place the coins in a five pointed star configuration on your prosperity altar. These coins represent the five points of your prosperity pentacle—you, your prosperity empowerment goal, your prosperity plan, the action steps you will take to attain your goal, and the successful outcome of your goal.

Next, add a clean gold candle to your sacred healing altar. Before setting it in its holder, empower the candle by holding it between your hands, and saying:

I dedicate this candle to my prosperity empowerment plan.
In the name of the Lady and Lord empower me, blessed be!

Prosperity Ritual

This ritual is most powerful when it is done on a new moon. This is the time when wishes are granted. You will need a gold gel or felt pen, a sheet of paper, five coins, and the gold candle from your sacred riches altar. Begin by drawing a magic circle of light around your sacred love space and empower the elements. Place the coins around the candle in a pentacle shape, starting by placing a coin on the topmost point of the pentacle and putting the coins clockwise around the candle. Now light the candle, dedicating it to a favorite Goddess or God of abundance and wealth.

Write one of your prosperity goals on the sheet of paper with the gold pen, and then write the date you expect to attain your goal. Draw eight five-pointed stars around your goal and the date. Underneath your goal, write the five action steps of your prosperity plan. Be specific and use as few words as possible. Also draw eight five-pointed stars around each of the five steps. Put the paper on your altar where you can easily read it. Then read your goal, the date, and the five action steps on the paper out loud. Focus your attention on the candle flame and coins, merge with the divine, and say:

Pentacle coins of plenty
Divine candlelight that I see
Bring my prosperity goal to me
So be it! Blessed be!

Gaze into the candlelight and imagine following the steps of your prosperity plan and attaining your prosperity goal. In your mind's eye, actually see the calendar page of the date you indicated on the sheet of paper. Feel the sensations of following your plan and manifesting your goal. Drink in the joy and happiness. Do this for at least 15 minutes.

When you are done, thank the Goddess and God, bid farewell to the elements, and pull up the circle. Allow the candle to safely burn down. Keep the pentacle coins of plenty and your health empowerment plan on your sacred healing altar. Read your plan aloud at least three times a day and take the action steps, one at a time, to manifest your prosperity empowerment goal. Once you manifest your goal, you can spend the coins, leave them on your altar to remind you of successfully attaining your goal, or use them in another ritual.

Oracle of Wealth

Think of a pressing question about your most important prosperity empowerment goal. Write the question and date in your empowerment journal. Go over to the television set, place your hands on the screen, and say:

May the Goddess and God bless you as a divine oracle.

Sit back with the remote control, a pen, and your journal. Take a deep, relaxing breath, and let go of any tensions you may be feeling. Now use the remote to turn on the television. Write down the first few words you hear and pictures you see as you turn on the television. Take another deep, complete breath, and switch the channel. Write down the first few words you hear and pictures you see. Repeat this process a total of five times. When you are done, look for connections and messages about your prosperity empowerment goal in the words and pictures you have written down in your journal. Circle the ones that are most meaningful to you.

Chapter Three

The Third Empowering Step: Preparing to Use Your Empowerment Tools

Continuing with the analogy of the garden, it's important to prepare your soil before planting your seeds. Preparation is instrumental to the whole gardening process, and tools make it that much easier. Having a good shovel, hoe, and rake can help make preparation and maintenance of your garden more manageable, enjoyable, and efficient.

As in gardening, preparation and tools are invaluable in the empowerment process. Preparation lays the groundwork for empowerment, and tools facilitate the task. In terms of Wicca, planning and crafting your magical work, gathering your tools, and setting up your altar help form the foundation for successful magic. Your altar and magical tools can be used to help you merge and become one with the divine, which is essential in all magic. Your altar and tools actually empower your magic-making process.

Anthropologists have long asserted that one of the main differences between the human animal and other animals, with regard to intelligence and evolution, is that humans use tools to improve their existence, while animals, as a general rule, do not. By definition, tools are things that are fashioned for particular uses and are kept and repeatedly reused for those purposes.

Today, tools have become extremely sophisticated and technical in their development and use. They have specific applications as to the ways that they can help improve your life. Wiccan tools are specifically designed to absorb and direct elemental and divine energies in magic. They are considered to be living tools as they are consecrated, empowered, and often given names. Also, each of your magical tools is imprinted with your energy every time you hold and use it. This is why many Wiccans choose not to have others handle their ritual tools.

Laying the Groundwork for Your Empowerment

On a Friday, Jennifer had a series of X-rays taken. They showed a large black mass in her lungs, indicating the possibility of cancer. Jennifer was terrified about the possibilities. Her doctor recommended a CAT scan to confirm the X-rays; however, the results of the scan would not be available until after the weekend. Her mind ran through every possible scenario, from the extremely bad to the extremely good, and everything in between.

Interestingly, at the same moment that Jennifer realized she might have cancer, she also realized that she had to make some overdue changes in her lifestyle. She suddenly became aware of how her fast-food, microwaved, canned, and packaged food diet and home environment were harming her overall health. She immediately began eating fresh fruits and vegetables and drinking organic fruit juice and green tea. She also began setting up a backyard garden, something she had been meaning to do for more than a year. She started making the changes in her life that she felt were essential to her survival. Fortunately in Jennifer's case, the CAT scan results did not show the dark mass. Even so, she continued to empower herself and her health.

Why is it that it often takes a major wake-up call before we start changing the things that are obviously disempowering our lives? Unfortunately, only in the midst of catastrophe do we actually sit up and take notice of what's happening around us. The outworn cliché "If it's not broke, don't fix it" is pointless in the empowerment process. It implies that we should never strive for anything other than what we already are and have.

Empowerment is about moving beyond these outworn ideas and illusionary boundaries and forging your own path within the world. It's vital to go ahead and push the envelope and move toward your dreams. If you are afraid to let your dreams be known, then there isn't much of a chance that your dreams will become reality. You need to follow the proverbial Yellow Brick Road. No matter what obstacles you encounter, stay on the path to empowerment.

Your immediate environment must be conducive to your empowerment. In a practical sense, you need to create an environment in which your goals can grow healthy and prosper. Without the proper environment, they will wilt and die on the vine. Your dreams and goals deserve more than that. You deserve more than that!

Your self-empowerment goals are like seeds that you plant. The better conditions you give them in which to grow, the more abundant and productive they become. The effort and energy that you put in is equal to what you get out. The one outside effect that has the most influence on this equation is divine intervention, whether positive or negative. For example, a late frost in the spring will kill your seedlings, and you have no control over that.

To empower yourself, you need to create an environment that uplifts and inspires you, rather than upsets and frustrates you. Unfortunately, this is a give-and-take scenario; there will always be things at home and work that you don't like and can't control. How you deal with these challenges influences your overall attitude. Your attitude has everything to do with successful love, health, and prosperity empowerment. You can either become embittered or realistic. The realistic view is that there are positive and negative elements in the world, and a lot of space in between. The embittered view creates anger and frustration that lead to disempowerment.

As many differing views of life exist as there are people. Accordingly, there are multiple choices that you can make in relation to the character and fabric or your life. You may choose several different paths on your way to empowerment. Don't worry when these excursions don't work out because exploration is part of the process.

Your understanding of the environment that nurtures your goals has a large influence on whether or not you will be successful. Reading books, listening to empowerment tapes, and watching self-help videos are all ways to expand your understanding and knowledge of your personal environment.

In terms of a garden, each goal is like a seed that you plant and care for through its many stages of development. Overall every seed needs space, sunlight, water, and nutrients to grow. Beyond that, each kind of plant has its individual needs that include exactly how much space, sunlight, water, and specific nutrients it requires.

Goals, like seeds, have specific needs in order for you to manifest them. Goals need organization, planning, preparation, and implementation. Their individual needs must be met for them to be most productive and grow to their fullest potential. Depending on what you choose as a goal, you need to prepare and create an environment where the goal will flourish and become a reality. You also need to gather the appropriate tools. For example, if you want to become a singer, you need to create a musical environment that is conducive to singing; probably buy, rent, or borrow a musical instrument to accompany yourself; learn how to read music; and practice singing every day. If you want to become an author, you need to create an environment that encourages you to write; buy, rent, or purchase a computer; read everything you can get your hands on; and learn the basics of grammar and sentence structure.

You are on the path to realizing your full potential when you lay the groundwork for attaining your empowerment goals by creating a conducive environment and gathering the appropriate tools. You become unstoppable. When you believe in yourself and value your goals, anything and everything becomes possible. It's all a matter of perception, preparation, and implementation.

Your Power Tools

Tim surveyed the mess he had gotten himself into. He had agreed to clean up two and a half country acres that had been thoroughly decimated by the former residents. This included a house that was partially burned down, 22 junk cars, a caved-in chicken coop, and an assortment of broken appliances, car parts, tires, broken glass, and trash that was spread over most of the property. In his mind, Tim could see the whole place clean and beautiful once again, but it seemed the more he cleaned, the more there was to do. The task seemed hopeless, particularly after he tried to pull down what remained of the house and only succeeded in breaking the heavy rope in pieces. Tim videotaped the whole process. He now laughs when he watches the tape, but at the time, it was horribly frustrating for him.

Just about the time he was thinking of giving up, Tim happened to mention his problem to a friend who owned a construction company that specialized in backhoe and excavation work. After reaching a financial agreement that worked for Tim, which included making several payments throughout the next year, his friend brought in his equipment, and within a week the house was knocked down and loaded into four large dumpsters. The junk cars were hauled off, and the appliances, tires, and junk were taken to the dump. Tim spent the next few weeks picking up the remaining glass and trash by hand and putting it into garbage bags.

When the project was finished and the property completely cleared of debris, Tim stared in amazement at how quickly his dream had become a reality. The land was beautiful once again. More than anything, this experience helped Tim understand the value of the right tools and how they influence the success of goals.

Tools help make life better by aiding you in your quests. In terms of your empowerment process, after setting your goals and formulating your plans, you must then survey the tools that are available to help you empower your life.

Tools come in many forms and perform many tasks. Depending on the context of your goal and plan, you must determine the tools that will help you do what you need to do. This is where knowledge and information relating to your goal can be very handy. Make every effort to learn from other people's successes as well as their mistakes. Be prepared to ask for advice when you need it, but always evaluate every bit of advice you receive as to whether it works for your situation. Keep in mind that everyone and every situation is unique.

Tools that help you become more organized are usually practical tools. Making lists and using planners, including those on your computer, can be valuable tools. When used regularly, these tools are great for helping you keep your focus on your empowerment goals and plans.

Meditations, rituals, prayers, and affirmations are also tools that can help you maintain your focus. No matter how well you plan, there are those challenging times when everything seems to fall apart, and you don't know how you're going to make it through the experience. This is when meditations, rituals, prayers, and affirmations become invaluable tools for inspiring you and keeping your spirits up. Energy flows in cycles, and your life reflects this as it is continually moving from the positive to the negative and back to the positive. The positive times energize you, while the negative times test your faith. Having useful tools can help you cultivate more positive times.

Preparation and Tools in Wicca

Within the practice of Wicca, preparation and magical tools are essential components. Every ritual, magical work, prayer, and affirmation has the underlying current of intention and expectation, desire, and merging. The power of thought is your most useful tool in magic. What you turn your mind to determines what you experience.

For several years, I had the rare opportunity to work with IBM Senior Scientist Marcel Vogel at his laboratory in San Jose, California. Marcel felt that everything was interconnected. He also believed in the power of thought. He said that thought equaled energy. If you have a strong enough field of thought energy, you can manifest your thoughts into reality. I participated in several experiments to demonstrate that reality definitely responds to what you think, feel, say, and do.

One experiment with the De La Warr Radionics Camera (thought-photography camera) clearly showed the power of thought. Together Marcel and I imagined the image of a five-pointed star for a few minutes, and when we checked the photographic plate, sure enough, there was the clear image of a five-pointed star. We thought of a circle, and the image of a circle appeared on the photographic plate. This experience permanently changed the way I view reality, and it showed me that what I turn my mind to greatly influences the quality of my life.

Your thought processes determine what you do, how you feel, your level of empowerment, and whether you are successful in becoming the person you want to be. It is important to steer your thoughts in a positive direction so that you can attain your goals. It's also helpful to listen to what other people have to say and how they can teach you. At the same time, avoid basing your decisions on what others do or tell you. To be truly empowered and satisfied with your life, you need to make your own decisions based on who you are, how you feel, and the direction you want your life to take.

When performing Wiccan rituals, you set up your altar, draw a magic circle, call in the elements, and follow traditions that span generations. A lot of what you do in ritual is more a matter of remembering rather than learning new information. Knowledge and genetic information are transferred as each wave of children is brought into the world. Ritual is something that people do on an almost instinctual level, much like salmon returning to their birthplace in order to spawn, die, and be reborn in their descendants.

Rituals can be powerful tools in and of themselves, whether traditional or innovative ones you formulate yourself. In Wicca, rituals create magical spaces where the bounds of reality are expanded in ways that defy what is usually thought possible. Fortunately, the realm of possibility keeps expanding, and magic making speeds up that expansion on a personal level. Once you experience divine rapport in ritual, your life permanently changes. There is forever a connection that continues to grow and empower you as you continue on your spiritual path.

When you make magic, you prepare your space. Your altar is the gathering place for all the items you need to manifest successful results. First, your tools are consecrated and empowered with energies of the Goddess and God, which makes them a conduit for divine energy. In essence, you empower your tools, and they in turn empower you.

Once your ritual tools are charged with divine energy, they are set on your altar. The altar, as the Lady's Table, is sacred. Your sacred space, which generally includes your altar, is a tool for focusing your thoughts, for doing magic, prayer, affirmation, and mediation. It is a place filled with divine energy that provides you with peace of mind.

Making an Empowerment Stone

Many tools are available to help you prepare and implement your empowerment goals; tools are meant to make the process easier. The ultimate metaphysical tool, the "philosopher's stone," has been written about and sought after since Zosimos the Theban first described it in the third century C.E. Through the ages, it has been known by several names, including "materia prima," "magnum opus," "soul of the world," and "spirit of truth."

The philosopher's stone reportedly is made from the seed of gold and can only be used with the help of the divine. Its uses include bringing about a permanent transmutation of base metals into gold and restoring life by cleansing the body of impurities. It doesn't prevent death, but instead prolongs life, and as such is also called the "elixir of life" when made into a tincture.

On an energetic level, the philosopher's stone represents creation and the forward thrust that motivates us to strive to improve our lives. It is a link from the human to the divine, or in other words, from the individual self to the higher spiritual self that unites us all together into Oneness. Historically, the stone was a tool that allowed people to transform into who they wanted to be by acting as an energetic mirror and reflecting the "golden" properties of their higher spiritual self. Golden in this case being "something of immense value," no matter what form it takes: love, health, or prosperity.

Along this same vein, by following basic metaphysical steps, you can make your own philosopher's stone. It can be used to bring out your "golden" qualities and empower you. By making an empowerment stone, you are making a magical tool that you can use to tap into your higher spiritual self. As with the philosopher's stone, it is a link between you and Oneness. The more you work in partnership with the Goddess and God with regard to your empowerment process, the greater the power for manifesting your empowerment goals.

To make an empowerment stone, you need to first find a stone in nature, a quartz crystal, or gemstone that you want to use. Prepare the stage by setting up your altar and drawing a magic circle. Next, clear the stone by placing it between your hands as if praying. Now take a deep breath in and hold it. In your mind's eye, imagine a clear mountain stream. Then exhale by pulsing your breath outward through your nose. As you do this, actually imagine sending your thought energy of the clear mountain stream into the stone itself. Your pulsed breath acts as a carrier wave for your field of thought energy. This is called the pulse-breath technique and is one of the easiest and most convenient ways to clear crystals and other objects of unwanted energies. Repeat this process three times to completely clear the stone of any residual energies. Your stone is now ready to be empowered.

Next, put the stone on your altar in front of your representation of the Goddess. Take your magic wand and draw an energetic thread of bright white light between the Goddess and your stone. Now, place the stone in front of your representation of the God, and again imagine a bright thread of white light moving back and forth between the two. Lastly, place the stone halfway between the Goddess and God and imagine the magical triad—the Goddess, God, and divine Oneness—filling the stone.

Once again, put the stone between your hands. Now imagine being empowered. See and sense all of your empowerment goals being attained in good time. Feel the joy, happiness, and satisfaction of manifesting your empowerment goals. Take a deep breath and hold it. In your mind's eye, be there in the future enjoying the attainment of your goals. Now pulse your breath out through your nose, and as you do, imagine planting this image into the stone. Take another deep breath in, and once again focus on the pleasure you experience attaining your goals. Make your picture of success bright, colorful, and clear in your mind's eye. Then pull this image into the stone as you pulse your breath out through your nose. Once more, take another deep breath inward and imagine attaining your goals. You feel empowered and uplifted. Once again pulse your breath out your nose, and plant this affirming image into the stone. You may feel the stone sweat, tingle, or pulsate in your hands as you work with it. When you are done pulsing your breath and planting the image into the stone, carry the stone with you in your pocket, wallet, or purse to empower you each and every day.

Like the young Harry Potter in J. K. Rowling's book (and consequent movie) *Harry Potter and the Sorcerer's Stone*, empowerment can move you out of the closet under the stairs to a divine place where you are appreciated because of your heritage and personal powers. It's vital that you realize who and what you are and who and what you can be. Your empowerment stone is a connecting path between the two. Whenever you doubt your mission in life, hold onto and consult your empowerment stone, and it will be a tool that helps you stay on course. In this way, you will be better able to stay on your chosen path.

Empowerment is about setting your sights high enough within the given environment so that when your goals happen, you find yourself where you want to be while feeling that all of the aspects of your life are being energized. It's as if a beautiful white light shines on you from all directions, and you become one with all of creation.

Love

When I was beginning my training in Wicca, a young woman named Tonya came to the Beltane circle with one of the members of the group, Eric. From the beginning, it was apparent to the members of the circle that the relationship was one-sided in the sense that Tonya seemed to be always doing the chasing, and Eric always seemed to be running the other way. To make things worse, Tonya told members of the group that the only reason she was thinking about joining the group was because it was important to Eric. But unfortunately, the harder she chased, the more he seemed to want to get away. From her perspective, the situation seemed hopeless.

One night, I pulled Tonya aside and began talking to her. I explained that she needed to step back from the situation and begin accentuating her attributes and becoming more desirable. As a final note, I told her that she should only go through the initiation if she really wanted to practice Wicca because otherwise she was doing it for all the wrong reasons, which would ultimately backfire. In terms of spirituality, you must seek and find the path with a heart. You sometimes walk this path with others, and sometimes you walk it alone. At some point, as the traditional song goes, "You must walk that lonesome valley by yourself."

Tonya finally began taking control of the situation. As if on cue, once Tonya quit chasing Eric, he began taking more of an interest in her. The more she became more Goddess-like—gaining self-confidence and poise—and the more she pursued her own interests and goals, the more Eric seemed to suddenly find Tonya appealing. He began pursuing her. By the time she became initiated—a decision she alone made—their relationship had progressed to the point where he asked her to marry him.

Because Tonya learned to use her innate, Goddess-given feminine tools, she gained a stronger rapport with the divine and crafted the situation so it worked for her rather than against her. This is often the key to empowerment.

Most of the time, your biggest opponent is yourself. When you don't truly believe in your own success and you don't think you deserve it, it creates a negative pattern that can only end in failure. Every time you embark on the adventure of attaining an empowerment goal, you must believe in its successful completion. It is your successes that keep you striving for more, not your failures. Empowerment comes from your successes rather than your failures, although your failures often have much to do with successes, because energy is a dynamic force that moves back and forth.

Negative people can disempower you faster than anything, and as such, you need to distance yourself from them. Usually this can be done with grace and kindness, but sometimes you just have to cut that toxic friend or family member out of your life, quickly and permanently. Surrounding yourself with people who encourage you and help you is an important part of empowering your life with Wicca. This is also true in terms of the divine.

Work with Goddesses and Gods who are beneficial and help you manifest your goals (check Appendix A for a list of empowering Gods and Goddesses). If your goal is to bring more love into your life by strengthening your relationship with your partner, it would be wise to ask for the blessings of a love Goddess such as Aphrodite, Venus, or Freya, or love God such as Pan, Angus Og, or Adonis. Also remember to focus on the bright, positive aspects of a deity rather than the negative aspects when doing the goal empowerment techniques. I guarantee the process and end result will be much more to your liking.

The Third Empowering Step: Love Meditation

Make sure you won't be disturbed by others while meditating. Turn on the answering machine, turn off the ringer, or unplug the phone completely. Put your pets and cell phone in another room. Turn on some soft meditative music and sit or recline in a comfortable spot. Take a slow, deep breath in until your lungs are filled with air, and then exhale, letting go of all the tensions in your neck and shoulders. Repeat this three times, allowing yourself to get more relaxed and comfortable with each breath you take.

Now close your eyes and imagine yourself walking down a white stone staircase. The sides of the stairway are covered with lacy green ferns. As you walk farther down, step-by-step, you begin to feel and smell a dampness in the air. You take a deep breath in, and take another step down. As you take another deep and complete breath, and take another step down, you hear the splashing sound of water. As you near the end of the stone staircase, you see a pool of water that looks like a natural spring. As your feet touch the last stair, you notice that the bubbling spring is surrounded by an array of small, colorful, and shiny stones and lush vegetation.

The ground around the spring is soft and the short, thick grass cushions your feet. You marvel at the intensity of color from the deep greens of the foliage and the reds, blues, and yellows of the stones to the deep blue-green florescence of the spring water itself. Moving closer to the water, you gaze into its depths. Instinctively you pick up a bright green stone, charge it with your energy, and gently toss it into the water as an offering to the Goddess. Then you pick up a bright red stone and gently throw it into the water as well, as an offering to the God. As the small stones hit the water, you watch the ripples as they move out toward the shore. Watching the rippling water, you say a silent prayer: "Dear Goddess and God, please show me my lover."

Once the ripples from the stones fade and wash into the edge of the pool, you look down into the watery depths again. As you take a deep breath in, you begin to see the image of a face within the watery abyss. You focus all your attention on the image, but it remains vague and without definition. Looking around on the ground, you spy a two-foot stick that is about one inch in diameter. As you pick it up, you see that the stick has several distinguishing knots in it that give it character and make it unique. Picking up a small white stone from the ground, you instinctively insert it into one of the knots, where it fits perfectly. You then dedicate the stick to Goddess and God and empower it, making it into a magical wand.

Moving back to the edge of the pool with your wand in your right hand, you point it toward the image of the face in the water and begin drawing small clockwise circles around the image, over and over. Each time you draw a circle, the image becomes more defined, until at last you can see your beloved's face clearly in the depths of the water.

Staring deeply into your lover's eyes, you feel yourself merge and become one with your beloved. Take a deep breath, and imagine effortlessly diving into the pool of water. Become one with the water and your beloved. Imagine taking your lover's hand in yours and swimming together upward to the surface of the pool. As you reach the surface, you both float to the edge of the pool. You jump out of the water and sit on the grassy edge for a few minutes, just enjoying each other's company and absorbing the beauty of the natural setting. After a while, you walk hand-in-hand to the white stone staircase edged with ferns. Together, you begin ascending the stone staircase, one step at a time in a merged state of everlasting love. Each step you take, you feel more refreshed and revitalized, filled with energy and light.

Now take a deep breath in through your mouth, still your breathing for three heartbeats, and slowly exhale through your nose. Repeat this three times. Now take another deep and complete breath and begin moving your hands and feet. Open your eyes and become aware of where you are, in the present time and place. Take a few moments to stretch and get your body moving again.

When you are done and while the thoughts are still fresh in your mind, write your impressions with regards to the meditation in your empowerment journal. Remember what it was like to use the wand as a tool to bring your lover's face into focus. What was it like merging together as one? Carry the feeling of everlasting love with you as you move through your daily life. It is certain to empower you!

Love Affirmation and Prayer

Tools are only effective if you remember to use them, otherwise they sit on a shelf and collect dust. Affirmations are ways to help you get into the routine of using your empowerment tools in ways that will ultimately make your life easier and more fulfilling. Examples of affirmations that reinforce the idea of using your tools are:

      "Every day I use my empowerment tools to help me in my plans to make my love goals become a real part of my daily life."

● "Today and every day, I discover and use my love empowerment tools to the best of my ability."

When you say a prayer, you establish a communication link between yourself and the divine. Because of this divine connection, prayers are great opportunities to communicate what you want from the divine by asking for it in the prayer.

In terms of empowerment tools, the more divine energy you run through them, the stronger your connection will be to the divine when you use the tool. Bringing divine energy into your empowerment process as much as possible sets the stage for miracles to happen on a daily basis.

"Miracluleux," the Latin root for the word "miracle," means a wonder or marvel, and Webster's Dictionary defines it as "an extremely outstanding or unusual event, thing, or accomplishment." Miracles are often associated with divine intervention and help. The idea behind empowering your life with Wicca is to enable you to accomplish outstanding things in your life every day until they become usual rather than unusual. Bless your love empowerment tools by saying:

Great Goddess and God, I pray you
Bless my love empowerment tools,
So that they resonate with your divine energy,
And the infinite power of Oneness.
In the Lady and Lord's name, blessed be!

Sacred Love Space

Creating an uplifting and inspiring sacred space and environment helps you in your empowerment quest. To do so, add plenty of pictures of you and your loved ones to your sacred love space. Also add a piece of rose quartz, rose scented oil, and two clean pink candles. Next, place your chalice on your altar. Before setting these items on your altar, rub them with a thin film of scented oil. Then hold them in your hands, one at a time, and empower them by saying:

I dedicate this empowerment tool to the love Goddess and God. May
they bless and fill this tool with divine love.

Now fill the chalice with water and allow it to sit on your altar for 24 hours. After that time, pour the water onto the ground outside, under a healthy potted plant in your home, on a flower bush, or on a tree. As you do, say:

Today, may love and joy flow into my life.

Continue to fill the chalice every day and pour it onto the ground the next day for 28 days (a moon cycle). Each time you do, repeat:

Today, may love and joy flow into my life.

Love Ritual

Use this ritual to make a love empowerment talisman to reaffirm the love you share with your partner or to help you find someone to love and be your partner.

You will need paper and a pen, plus the piece of rose quartz and the two pink candles from your sacred love space. Begin by drawing a magic circle around your sacred love space and empowering the elements. Now, use the pen and paper to write what attributes you would like to impart into your love empowerment talisman, whether it be a feeling of love, better communication, a stronger spiritual bond, or more passion in your relationship. Be specific. Next, decide and write down the talisman's area of influence, for example, an area 3 feet, 5 feet, or 10 feet. As with most things in magic, it is best to start small and work up from there. You will have an easier time programming your stone for a small rather than a large area of influence. After you are done, set the paper on your love altar where you can easily see it.

Light the first candle and dedicate it to your favorite love Goddess. Set it in its holder on your altar and light the second candle, dedicating it to your favorite love God. Set it in its holder on your altar to the right and about nine inches apart from the first candle. Now clear the piece of rose quartz by holding it in your power hand and imagining a pure, clear mountain stream. With the image fixed in your mind, take a deep breath and pulse your breath hard out your nose while visualizing the stream clearing the crystal of any unwanted energies. Actually imagine planting the stream into the stone itself. Repeat the pulse-breath technique three times.

Place the stone on your love altar between the two candles. Take a few minutes to review the paper with the attributes and area of influence written on it. Read out loud what you have written. Now take a deep breath, hold it, and in your mind's eye, imagine the talisman attributes you wrote down. As you sharply pulse your breath out through your nose, imagine planting those attributes into the stone itself. Repeat the pulse-breath technique three times, each time imagining you are planting the desired love attributes into the talisman stone.

Now set the stone between the candles on the altar so that it is illuminated in the flames. Gaze at the stone and become one with it. Take a deep breath and merge with the stone. Imagine entering the stone and walking around inside of it. Spend at least 30 minutes merging with the stone. Keep in mind that your intention, expectation, desire, and the depth of your merge determine the power of your talisman. The stronger they are, the more powerful your talisman stone. During the time you are merging with the stone, pick it up and hold it in your hands. Actually see and sense the atomic structure of the stone changing as you charge and transform it into your love empowerment talisman, a magical tool to help you create more love in your life. If you like, you can imagine a laser beam of light flowing out of your third eye or from your hands into the talisman, charging it with your thought energy. If your mind wanders, just bring your focus back to the stone, take a deep and complete breath, and merge more deeply with it. When you feel you have amply loaded the talisman with the love attributes and area of influence that you desire, activate it by holding it in your power hand and saying:

Divine talisman of love,
Filled with [state your attributes],
By the loving power of the Goddess and God,
So be it! Blessed be!

Now clap your hands loudly three times, setting the pattern of energy in your talisman into place. Thank the Goddess and God, bid farewell to the elements, and pull up your magic circle. Allow the candles to safely burn down. Put your love talisman on a bedside table or carry it on your person to improve and strengthen your relationship with your beloved or to help you in your quest to find a loving primary partner.

Oracle of Love

Augury, the art of divining bird messages and feathers, has been practiced for more than 30,000 years. Cave paintings in France depict the use of augury by ancient shamans. Just like the ancient shamans, each of us has the innate ability to commune with birds and other animals. New Age Wicca encourages practices such as bird augury and shapeshifting to better understand divine intervention and messages and to get in touch with and heal the earth. The best way to acquaint yourself with bird augury is by paying attention to birdsong, bird movements, and feather signs.

Begin by thinking of one question about your love empowerment goals. Write the question down in your empowerment journal and note the date. Then go outside and take a walk. As you walk, ponder your question, and at the same time, look around on the ground for a feather. Continue walking until you find one. When you do, make a note in your journal as to the color of the feather, the direction the feather was pointing when you found it, the time of day you found it, and whether the bird was present when you found it. If the bird was present, determine whether or not it sang out when you discovered the feather. Next, refer to the following list for the oracular meaning of the feather color:

- White: Birth, initiation, love, joy, purity
- Blue: A gift, love, happiness
- Green: Magic, adventure, dreams, prosperity, new ventures
- Rose: Romance, love, spiritual union
- Red: Magic, good luck, love, passion, fortune
- Yellow: Friendship, fellowship, companionship
- Yellow and Green: Prosperity and healing to come
- Orange: Happiness to come in the future
- Brown: Good health, happy home, good fortune
- Gray: Peace of mind, tranquility, harmony, wisdom
- Blue and White: A new love, a love affair
- Brown and White: Joy, good health, and much happiness
- Gray and White: A new and happy event or situation
- Black and White: Beware of problems and danger
- Black: Misfortune, bad luck, death

Make a note of the oracular meaning in your journal, as well as any other insights you derived from the experience.

Health

I stood staring intently at the vibrant-looking woman in front of me at the check-out stand of the local health food store. She seemed familiar, but I couldn't place her no matter how hard I tried. Something about her was different, making my mind work even harder to identify her.

"Stephanie," I spontaneously cried out in surprise, causing the woman to turn around, at which point she, too, recognized me. What surprised me was that I had worked with Stephanie a couple of years ago, and she had been in ill health and very depressed and negative about everything and everyone. She was a bookkeeper for a computer software company that was always one step ahead of its large list of creditors. She was forever trying to collect from an equally large assortment of people that owed the company money. The job was disempowering and caused ulcers in its employees. Stephanie was fired from the job, and at the same time, her dysfunctional marriage was breaking up because her husband was running off with her best friend. The last time I saw Stephanie, things were especially bleak in her life.

After our chance meeting, Stephanie and I began talking, and she told me how after she was unemployed and her husband had left, she began using affirmations and prayers as a way to uplift her spirits and keep her faith. She said staying positive and believing in herself was the main thing that kept her going.

She recounted how one day a media company called her for an interview, and she eventually took the job as their receptionist. At one time, media had been her passion; she had majored in it in college. As events kept rolling into place, she felt her life come together. She quickly rose up to the level of production supervisor.

What amazed me most was how much Stephanie's attitude and change of environment had improved her appearance and overall health. She went from being a dour, negative person to someone who exuded confidence, was positive, and had a beauty that energized herself and everyone around her. By changing her mind through affirmation and prayer, and by changing her environment to one that was energizing rather than depleting, she empowered her health and lifestyle.

The people who live on the Kalahari desert and who are the subject of the movie *The Gods Must Be Crazy* live in an environment that is as harsh as any that you could imagine. Yet they maintain a positive attitude that helps them survive and even flourish in an environment that would be most people's worst nightmare. What this again shows is that both your environment and your attitude toward your environment influence your health.

Sometimes it's easier to change your attitude toward things than it is to change everything around you. This doesn't mean that you should accept everything for what it is and not try to change it. What it does mean is that change needs to be consistent with the patterns of yourself, nature, divinity, and Oneness. When you achieve this unity, you feel a peace that will unify you with the "great beyond," a place where all things are united together as one.

The openness and objectivity required in assimilating new ideas are usually only reserved for the young, but if continually cultivated, new ideas can flourish in everyone, no matter what their age. Use the following meditation to empower your attitudes and environment to help you attain your health goals.

The Third Empowering Step: Healing Meditation

Imagine that you have received a special invitation to attend an exposition entitled "Health Empowerment Tools Expo," presented by the Goddess and God in a castle in the clouds. Begin by sitting or reclining in a comfortable spot. Close your eyes and take three deep, complete breaths. As you breathe in, imagine your lungs being filled with a healing white light. As you exhale, see and sense the light moving throughout your body, making you feel relaxed and healthy. After the third breath, feel yourself become lighter than air and begin floating around the room. Imagine moving through the doorway of the room and floating through your home and out your front door. You gradually float above the trees and eventually up to a collection of white, pillowy clouds that resemble a castle in the sky.

Moving through the doorway into the castle in the clouds, you find yourself in a giant hall filled with booths occupied by supernatural beings demonstrating all types of different tools for health. As your feet set down on the shiny blue-tiled floor of the cloud castle, you are greeted by a woman and a man, whose appearance seems ageless. The woman, who has long auburn hair, takes your left hand, and the man, whose blue eyes remind you of the summer sky, takes your right hand. They begin escorting you around the hall.

Soft music is playing in the background as the Goddess and God guide you down an aisle to a booth with a long table, displaying a variety of foods, herbs, and vitamins. Behind the table is an uncommonly tall, white-haired man with four eyes that all blink at different times and act independent of one another. In his long, narrow fingers, he holds out a glass of orange liquid that he says is a potion for healing pain. The Goddess and God let go of your hands, you take the glass from the four-eyed man, and you begin slowly drinking it. It tastes fruity and feels cool and soothing on your throat as you swallow. You can feel the potion flowing into your body, and almost immediately you experience a tingling sensation that fills you from head to toe. The tingling gives way to an energizing feeling that gradually neutralizes any pain you may be feeling. You thank the four-eyed man for the potion. Then the Goddess and God once again take you by the hands and guide you to another booth.

You see what looks like a massage table in the booth and a thin, agile woman with green-tinted skin, golden hair and eyes, and elfin-like features. The Goddess and God let go of your hands, and the woman motions for you to lay on the table. You lay on your back, watching as she picks up a small, round tool that starts emanating a bluish-white light the moment she touches it. The woman begins passing the tool over your body, starting with your head and working down to your feet. The light feels warm and soothing as it starts working its way into your body. Soon, you feel its healing effects cleanse you of all pain and discomfort, leaving you energized and revitalized. Getting up from the table, you marvel at how light your body feels.

Once again taking you by each hand, the Goddess and God escort you back to the doorway of the castle of clouds. Together they touch you on the forehead and bid you goodbye, telling you that they are always available whenever you need their help. All you have to do is ask. Moving through the doorway, you find yourself outside the sky castle of clouds, only this time you are floating downward like a feather, slowly and lightly descending to earth. You float back into your home and into the room where you are comfortably meditating.

Now take three deep breaths by inhaling through your mouth and exhaling through your nose. Each time you breathe in and out, you feel more and more calm and relaxed, yet completely aware. Now slowly open your eyes and come back to the present time and place. Stretch your muscles like a cat, feeling the healing effects of the meditation on your body.

While the meditation is still fresh in your mind, write in your empowerment journal your impressions and experiences during the meditation. Include the date and what you liked most about the meditation. Next, write down how you felt when the light tool cleansed and energized you, helping you to feel well and whole again.

Healing Affirmation and Prayer

As you've seen, a positive and empowering environment is vital to good health. In terms of tools, knowledge can be one of the most powerful tools in your health empowerment process. The following affirmations address these two concepts:

- "Every day, I empower my health and realize my full potential by learning all I can about wellness and applying it to my life."
- "Today and every day, I create a healthy and happy environment at home and work."

When you ask for divine help, the request is often in the form of a prayer. Like the sleeping kings and queens of Celtic mythology, the Goddess and God are always waiting for you to call them into action. After all, they have a vested interest because they are part of you and you are part of them. By virtue, prayers are important tools for making extraordinary things happen in your life:

Goddess and God, please bless my life with good health by helping me create a healing environment to live and work in, and by helping me discover and use the best possible health empowerment tools. Please guide and protect me in my quest for good health and happiness. May you shower me with healing power. So be it! Blessed be!

Sacred Healing Space

Add a clear quartz crystal (a necklace with a quartz crystal stone will also work well in this application) and two, clean green candles to your sacred healing space. Also add a vial of lavender scented oil, some self-help healing tapes, a cookbook with healthy recipes, and your ritual bowl. Rub a few drops of lavender oil on the crystal, candles, and bowl. Then hold them in your hands, one at a time, and charge them with divine energy by saying:

I empower this tool with the healing energy of the Goddess and God. Blessed be!

Next, fill the bowl with clean earth and place it on your altar for 24 hours. After that time, return the soil to the earth. As you do this, say:

*Today, I feel the divine healing energy of the sacred land and the
Goddess and God, filling and completely revitalizing me.*

Continue to refill the bowl every day and return the soil to the earth
the next day for 28 days (a moon cycle). Each time you do, repeat:

*Today, I feel the divine healing energy of the sacred land and the
Goddess and God, filling and completely revitalizing me.*

Healing Ritual

In this ritual you make a health empowerment talisman that can be
programmed for specific medical problems you may have or for the
improvement of your overall health. (If you have a serious medical
problem, you should see your doctor. A talisman is not a substitute for
getting medical advice.) Consult your health empowerment goals and
choose one(s) that you want to work on with your talisman.

You will need paper and a pen, plus the clear quartz crystal and two
green candles from your sacred healing space. Begin by using the pen
and paper to write down the attributes that you want to program into
your health talisman, such as sending a steady stream of healing energy
to your stomach, back, and heart, or neutralizing your anger, worries,
and stress. After deciding the healing attributes you want to put into
your talisman, determine the talisman's area of influence. If you are
going to wear your talisman and you want it to protect you from disease, then you might want to make sure the area of influence covers
your entire body and radiates about 10 feet in all directions. After you
are done, set the paper on your healing altar so that you can easily refer
to it.

Next, draw a magic circle, empower the elements, and light one of the
green candles, dedicating it to the Goddess of health whose energy you
want to invoke into your ritual. Now set it in its holder on your altar.
Then light the second green candle, dedicating it to the God of health
whose energy you want to invite into your circle. Place the second green
candle at the right and about nine inches away from the first one. After
you light the candles, take a few minutes to review your list of healing
talisman attributes and its area of influence so that you have a clear
image in your mind of exactly what you want.

Now grasp the clear quartz crystal in your power hand and imagine a single point of white light on a black background in your mind's eye. Take a deep breath inward and hold it. As you hold your breath, focus your mind on the single point of light, and then pulse your breath firmly out through your nose while planting the image of the point of light into the crystal, cleansing it of any unwanted energy that might be lingering in it. Repeat the pulse-breath technique a total of three times.

Next, put the crystal between the two candles so the flames illuminate the stone. Begin gazing at the crystal and merging with its essence. Imagine the healing attributes you listed and area of influence entering the stone. Imagine your thought energy actually shifting and rearranging its molecules until the crystal radiates with healing energy. Hold the crystal in your hands, take a deep breath in, and pulse your breath sharply out your nose as you imagine planting your healing thought energy into the talisman. Repeat the pulse-breath technique a total of three times. Continue to hold and gaze at the healing talisman for at least 30 minutes until it's fully charged and ready to be used as a health empowerment tool. Activate your talisman by saying:

Dear Goddess and God of health,
Please activate this healing talisman
With your divine blessing and power
So be it! Blessed be!

Now set the pattern in place by clapping your hands firmly together three times. When you are done, thank the Goddess and God, bid farewell to the elements, and close the circle. Allow the candles to safely burn down. Carry the talisman on your person for best results.

Oracle of Health

While vacationing in Hawaii, I fell asleep under a tree on the beach in Waikiki. Suddenly, I woke up to loud birdsong and felt something wet on my arm. I was none to pleased to discover I had bird dung on my arm. On the way to the restroom to wash my arm, I found a black and white bird feather. I realized at that point the birds were trying to tell me something. I immediately went looking for my husband, who was swimming in the ocean. He got out of the water, and I told him about the bird dung and feather. I also asked for the car key, so I could get my bathing suit. He looked in his bathing suit pocket for the key only to find that it was gone. We had no other way into the rental car, and no money because my purse and his wallet were locked in the car. I borrowed a dollar from a kind-faced young man and called the rental agency. A man came out and unlocked the car for us and gave us another key. Needless to say, I now pay close attention to any bird feathers I find, birdsong I hear, and the movement of the birds around me.

Begin this oracle of health by thinking of one question about your health empowerment goals. Write the question down in your empowerment journal and note the date. Then go outside and take a walk. As you walk, ponder your question, and at the same time, look around on the ground for a feather. Continue walking until you find one. When you do, make a note in your journal as to the color of the feather. Also note the direction the feather was pointing when you found it, the time of day you found it, and whether the bird was present when you found it. If the bird was present, determine whether or not the bird sang out when you discovered the feather. Refer to the feather color list earlier in this chapter for the oracular meaning.

Make a note of the oracular meaning in your journal, as well as any other thoughts or experiences you had while on your feather augury walk.

Prosperity

A company in the student loan business was suffering because loans were being bogged down in the processing department and taking sometimes more than three months to process. Students were constantly calling wondering about the status of their school loans that paid for tuition, books, and housing. The paperwork had become overwhelming, and schools and students were starting to take their business elsewhere. It was a problem that was getting worse rather than better—not a good sign for the future.

When the situation seemed hopeless, Karen and Nick, two programmers in the systems department, came up with a program that tracked the loan applications within processing. At the same time, they devised an electronic system where loans could be approved in 48 hours. After a brief period of implementation, where all the tools, in this case computers and software, were put into place, the processing of loans became streamlined and extremely fast compared to the previous system. Students now called to say thank you for being so quick, and as a result, more schools continued to sign up for electronic processing, something that went on to become the standard not only for student loans, but for all lending institutions.

What happened in student lending is indicative of the changes that occurred in business offices everywhere. Typewriters, once the workhorse of offices everywhere, were replaced by computers and word processors. Technology in general has created tools that are much more efficient, and businesses benefit from these tools. You can use fax machines to send documents instantly from one location to another, and e-mail to instantly communicate with anyone in "real time," rather than the delay experienced with "snail mail," a term now associated with the standard postal service. (And to think that a hundred years ago, people thought the pony express was fast!) Times definitely change, as do the nature of tools. You can use these changes to empower your prosperity goals.

In many ways, the only constant in life is that it continually changes. Tools and technology are where the most dramatic changes seem to happen. This is why they are essential in manifesting your goals. Make every effort to stay current and learn about new innovations. Always be willing to intelligently try new things. The balance between the "new" and the "old" is something that you are continually trying to maintain in your life. This is the essence of empowering your life with Wicca.

Sometimes it seems too hard to keep going and is easy to give up, but the people who regularly attain their goals are those who keep going. Whether through intention, expectation, desire, or determination, the idea is to overcome the odds against you, work with those things that empower you, and become who you want to be. Tools help you to achieve this result. Make every effort to hang in there even when the going gets tough, and you will discover new ways of manifesting your goals.

It is not only a matter of using the best tools for the empowerment job, it's also a matter of faith, which is an overriding factor in all of life, whether you believe or not. Science hasn't established that it can predict

"A" to "B" to "C." There is much that exists outside the arena of traditional science, including anything having to do with faith. Yet people who exhibit tremendous amounts of faith continue to do things that are scientifically impossible. This means there is something more to faith than science has determined—faith can be a very powerful tool when empowering your life and your magic making.

The Third Empowering Step: Prosperity Meditation

Begin by sitting or reclining in a comfortable, undisturbed spot. Close your eyes and take three deep breaths. As you breathe in, visualize a golden light filling your lungs, and as you breathe out, imagine the light surrounding your being, giving you an aura of good luck. After the third breath, you feel relaxed and ready for anything that might come your way.

Now imagine yourself on a space ship that sails around the galaxy, looking for evidence of lost civilizations. After touching down on an unknown world, you gather your tools, which include a techno-trowel, a sifting screen, and a brush. Suiting up, you step out of the ship and survey the landscape, which has a red-tint to it. The area has a few oddly shaped trees and bushes here and there. Mounting your all-terrain vehicle, you point it north and begin making your way to a site that has evidence of a civilization that predates any prior discoveries. Your excitement heightens as you drive closer to the archeological dig.

As you approach the dig, you shut off your vehicle. You step down from your vehicle with your tool pouch securely mounted around your waist. Instinctively, as if pulled by an unknown force, you gravitate to a particular area where you pull out your trowel and start digging in the ground.

Scooping up a shovel full of reddish dirt, you take out your sifting screen and begin moving the dirt through it. You hear a slight clinking sound as you look down into the screen and see an odd-looking medallion resting at the bottom of the screen. It is golden-colored with emeralds, rubies, and diamonds embedded in a design that resembles a triple DNA helix. Using your brush, you clean the rest of the dirt from the medallion and reveal an inscription that spans its middle section. The inscription reads, "This tool of tools will bring unlimited riches to the one who can command its power."

When your hand touches the medallion, it begins to light up and get warm to the touch. As you place the medallion next to your trowel, the trowel turns to gold. You place the medallion next to your screen and brush, and they turn to gold. You place four reddish rocks next to the medallion, and they also turn to gold. It seems to turn all inanimate things into gold. You resist turning everything into gold, knowing that if you did, gold would become worthless and no longer a sign of prosperity. This knowledge is as powerful a tool as the medallion itself. The realization has an empowering effect on your entire being, like understanding that money can't buy everything you want in life because no matter how much you wish it otherwise, some things take time and effort. These in many ways are the things that really count when it comes to life, otherwise you feel an emptiness inside. Prosperity is something that you engender each and every day of your life. Even if you're not doing what you want to be doing, you can make prosperity plans and goals for the future and attain them.

Now take three deep breaths by inhaling through your mouth and exhaling through your nose. Imagine taking the medallion with you and getting back on your all-terrain vehicle. Drive back to your space ship and remove your space suit. Hold the medallion in your hands and take a deep, complete breath. Think about the riches and abundance you want to manifest in your life. Now take another deep breath and slowly begin moving your toes and fingers. Then slowly open your eyes and stretch your body to bring you back to the present time and place.

Write your impressions and experiences, particularly with respect to the medallion and the knowledge that it brought with it, in your journal.

Prosperity Affirmation and Prayer

Empowerment comes when you are doing what you want to do, feeling what you want to feel, and moving in the direction you truly desire. Use these affirmations to effectively use your prosperity tools to manifest your prosperity goals:

- "Today and every day, I discover and learn effective new ways to use my wealth empowering tools."

- "Each and every day I use my prosperity tools to empower myself and manifest my riches into my life."

Use the following prayer to help you use your tools to manifest your prosperity empowerment goals:

Dear Goddess and God,
Bless my prosperity tools
So that they may empower my life
And make each day extraordinary.
Ayea! So shall it be!

Sacred Riches Space

Your prosperity tools can help you more readily manifest your goals. Add your magic wand, a vial of patchouli-scented oil, two clean golden candles, and a golden-colored medallion to your sacred riches space. Rub a bit of the patchouli oil on your wand, candles, and medallion. (Not too much—a little patchouli oil goes a long way!) Then hold your prosperity tools between your hands and empower them with divine energy, one at a time. Say:

May the divine abundance and powers of prosperity of the Goddess and God fill this tool, now and forevermore. Blessed be!

To further empower your prosperity goals, add self-help tapes, books about making and investing money, as well as your bank book, checkbook, and eight dollar bills to your sacred riches space. Over the next month, listen to the tapes regularly, spend the eight dollars on a basic prosperity tool (have fun and use your imagination), and read through a few of the books to help you more easily attain your goals.

Prosperity Ritual

In this ritual, you make a prosperity empowerment talisman that can help you in your quest to achieve your prosperity goals. The most productive thing to do is to select one of your prosperity goals, such as finding a new job, and use it as the focal point of your talisman. After making the first one, you can then make talismans for some or all of your empowerment goals. Remember, it's often easier and more advantageous to work on one goal at a time.

You will need a sage smudge stick, pen, paper, two gold candles, and the gold medallion from your sacred riches space. The first thing you need to do is write down the prosperity goal you are working on. Then write down the kind of energy you want to load into the talisman to help you manifest your goal. This means determining what you need most to make it all happen and bring more riches and abundance into your life. If your goal is finding a new job, then you need to load the talisman with the attributes that will help you in that endeavor, such as networking with helpful people, excelling at interviewing, and discovering the best job possibilities.

Begin the ritual by drawing a magic circle and empowering the elements. Then light the first gold candle, dedicating it to your favorite Goddess of prosperity and abundance. Put the candle in its holder on your prosperity altar. Now light the second candle, dedicating it to your favorite God of prosperity and wealth. Put the second candle to the right and about nine inches apart from the first candle. Light the smudge from the Goddess candle flame and thoroughly smudge the medallion in the purifying smoke for a few minutes. Also smudge yourself in the smoke and then extinguish the smudge stick.

Put the medallion between the two candles on your altar. Take a few minutes to review the list of prosperity attributes you want to load into your talisman. Read the list out loud three times. Then take a deep and complete breath and enter a merged state with the Goddess and God. Begin gazing intently at the medallion until you become one with it. Imagine you have supernatural powers, and you can actually energetically enter the medallion itself and alter its interior structure to help you manifest your goals. Hold the medallion in your hands and continue to gaze at it for at least 30 minutes. During this period of time, plant the desired prosperity attributes and the talisman's area of influence (I suggest 20 feet) into the medallion itself, using the pulse-breath technique discussed in other rituals earlier in this chapter. Imagine breathing in bright golden light, and then as you pulse your breath out through your nose, imagine the prosperity attributes on your list, the talisman's area of influence, and the bright golden light being planted into the medallion with your thought energy. Repeat the pulse-breath technique a total of three times. Once you are finished loading the prosperity attributes, influence, and golden light into your medallion talisman, ask for the blessings of the Goddess and God. Hold the medallion in your power hand and say:

Great Mother Goddess and All Father God,
Please bless this talisman with [say what properties]
Empower it with your abundant light
May it bring prosperity and riches to me
So be it! Blessed be!

Set the prosperity pattern in place by clapping loudly three times. When you are finished, thank the Goddess and God, bid farewell to the elements, and pull up the circle. Allow the candles to safely burn down. Wear your medallion to draw more riches into your life each and every day and to manifest your prosperity empowerment goals, one at a time.

Oracle of Wealth

Begin by thinking of one question about your prosperity empowerment goals. Write down the date and question in your journal. Now go outside and take a walk. Think about the question as you walk. Also, look around the ground, in the bushes, and so forth, for a feather. When you find a feather, write the color down in your journal, as well as the direction the feather was pointing when you found it, the time of day you found it, and whether the bird was present when you found it. If the bird was present, record whether or not you heard the birdsong when you found the feather. Then refer to the feather color list earlier in this chapter for the oracular meaning.

Make a note of the oracular meaning in your journal. You can repeat augury as often as you like as a means to clarify the answer to your prosperity empowerment question.

Chapter Four

The Fourth Empowering Step: Becoming One with Your Empowerment Goals

If you've ever played music or sports, you probably have experienced moments when everything seemed to come together, and you felt you could do no wrong. This aura of super empowerment can be catching, especially when it spreads to all aspects of your life and to the people who you interact with on a regular basis.

In my twenties, I was the singer in a rock band. One Saturday, we were asked to play a benefit for the Smith River, which at the time was the only California river that was not dammed. Having played a wedding earlier in the day, our band hurried to a place that was a re-creation of an Irish Pub, complete with Guinness on tap. The minute we walked in and started setting up our instruments, the place seemed to have a magical feel to it that was hard to describe with words. When we started playing, our music seemed to reverberate from every part of the building, and the sound was incredible.

As a band, we had never played so well as that night, which was evidenced by the many compliments we received from the people at the benefit. The feeling I had that night was one of the most magical and empowering experiences I have ever had in my life. When we finished playing music that night, I felt that anything was possible.

In 1975, the Golden State Warriors entered the national basketball championships against the Washington Bullets as the decided underdogs, who by the experts were given little chance for victory. Led by a supposedly washed-up Rick Berry, the Golden State Warriors became unbeatable and won the championship in four straight games. By the fourth game, the energy was so intense for Golden State that the once all-powerful Washington Bullets looked beaten before the game even began. There was an energy that seemed to have pattern, and this pattern influenced the overall flow of the game.

These are two great examples of what a feeling of empowerment can do when planted in a positive and supportive environment. It is a feeling and energy that escalates and snowballs, gaining momentum to a point where it is unstoppable. Energy is volatile and can sometimes switch directions in an instant much like a wildfire, but in the end it follows patterns just like everything else. Understanding and influencing these energy patterns are keys to empowerment.

Being at One with Yourself and Your Goals

The more you become your empowerment goals and make them part of your life, the more unstoppable you become. When you and your goals become one, things start to happen, and you begin to realize your plans and patterns. You no longer just believe you can change your life for the better, you know you can do it!

One of the best ways for being at one with yourself and your goals is to set a certain amount of time aside for reflection and thought. Use this time for getting to know yourself—your likes, dislikes, strengths, weaknesses, attitudes, fears, wants, and needs.

A saying in Wicca is "To know yourself is to know deity, and to know deity is to know yourself." This saying implies that you are an integral part of the divine. You are one with the divine. As planets reflect the rays of the sun, you reflect the rays of divine light in everything you do. As an individual, you are like the light of a candle, but when you put your light together with everything else that is Oneness, you create a light whose intensity eclipses that of the sun.

At this point in your process, it's important to keep your empowerment journal with you at all times. Go over your lists of empowerment goals at regular intervals, such as reviewing short-term goals every day, and mid- and long-term goals at least once a week. Spend time getting comfortable with your various empowerment goals.

Tweak or change your goals over time to better suit you. Your goals and view of the future must be in sync with who you are or your empowerment will be diminished. Have the courage to discover your full potential. A seed lies inside you waiting to be planted, nurtured, and cultivated, bringing you love, health, and prosperity.

Meditations, affirmations, and prayers are some of the tools you can use for becoming one with yourself and your empowerment goals. Post these affirmations and prayers in places such as the refrigerator, the bathroom mirror, or on your desk, so you see them often. In this way, they impact your psyche and the many aspects of your being. Collecting all of your empowerment meditations, affirmations, and prayers in a notebook or 3-hole binder can help you become one with yourself and your goals.

Performing rituals, exploring oracles, and working with your sacred space can bring more energy into your pattern, helping you become one with your goals. The more energy you generate, the more power you have to manifest your goal into reality.

The perception of the past and the molding of the future are done within a moment, termed "the eternal now." This moment constantly fluctuates like a strobe continually in motion. Each image, which is a micro view of life, is captured for an instant and then let go. In a macro view, your life is like a movie played out frame by frame, which when put together creates the whole cinema of your life. Rather than individual sequences, the strobe creates a sense of movement as you move through the various stages of your life.

The macro view is also called a holistic view or "the big picture." This larger picture is what connects all the particulars so they all work harmoniously together. In a spiritual sense, it is the wonders of divine creation and how everything intricately works together so well in terms of the natural cycles of life.

Building Your Feeling of Empowerment

Every morning you need to wake up with the enthusiasm and the desire to live life, to move forward. Those hours and minutes when you first wake up are platforms and stepping stones for the rest of your day. It's important that this time be positive and re-enforce your feelings of empowerment and happiness. Just as it's important to get up and eat a healthy breakfast, it's also important to feed your mind and spirit with something that is also healthy, and in this case inspirational.

Personally, I like to place books that I want to wake up to either next to my bed on my nightstand or in the bathroom. Three books I would recommend that have inspiring biographical stories are *A Cup of Chicken Soup for the Soul* by Jack Canfield, Mark Victor Hansen, and Barry Spilchuk; *It's a Miracle*, stories from the television series selected by Richard Thomas; and my book, entitled *A Witch Like Me*. (See the Bibliography at the end of this book for details.) The first book is great because of its short inspiring stories, the second because it gives hope that anything is possible, and the third because it shows that you are not alone in your quest for something that "works" in your life and in turn gives you a feeling of empowerment and worth.

Recent Gallup Polls have established a correlation between happiness and your level of empowerment or confidence. If your mother calls you every morning to tell you everything that's wrong with you, then it's time to unplug the phone or at least let the answering machine take the call because you don't need that in your life. These experiences break down your level of empowerment and are not helpful. You need to wake up to experiences that help you feel like you can achieve your goals and become whoever you want to be. This is why it's important to create an atmosphere with uplifting music, pleasing pictures, and welcoming decor that reflects what you are doing and where you are going in your life.

One simple way to begin is by collecting pictures and photographs that reflect positive images of the future to you. Pictures of your ancestors can also be empowering in the respect that these people often came over to this country in search of a new life, brought to foreign and often unfriendly shores by an image in their dreams. You are a product of this determination and will to create something better.

It is your destiny to seek higher realms of being. You are encoded with a genetic map that compels you to do things other than swim back and forth in a pool of water. This power moves you forward whether you like it or not, alluding to the existence of a divine force that over-rides all other energies. Much like springtime love, there is no way to stop it, so you might as well flow with it and enjoy the divine ride!

Getting Excited About Your Future

In the classic movie *It's a Wonderful Life*, the main character, George Bailey, is visited by an angel and given the unique opportunity to see what life would have been like if he had never existed. What the experience showed him was that his life touched many other lives in an intricate number of ways. Before the experience, George was feeling he had no future and that he would like to end his life. After the experience, he was once again excited about life, and his future was suddenly filled with options and hope.

Take time to imagine what your future could be when your plans start coming to fruition and your goals become a real part of your life. Dare to imagine life as you would like it to be in the future. As you define this image in your mind, remember to include your relationships with others. Think about the whole of what you are imagining as well as each individual part. Positive interaction with others can be helpful, while negative interaction can undermine your overall empowerment.

It's pretty much impossible to avoid negative people, particularly when they are family members or co-workers. At the same time, you can minimize their overall impact on you. If your in-laws tell you that they don't approve of your lifestyle or career, it's probably time to distance yourself from them while working on empowerment and attaining your goals. Don't let them sabotage your efforts. After all, the less negative people influence you on a daily basis, the better your empowerment results.

There is a scene in the popular movie *Fun with Dick and Jane*, in which the character played by Jane Fonda asks her affluent parents for financial help because her husband has lost his job. Her father declines to help and throws salt into the wound by telling her that he envies her hardship because it's such a grand opportunity for her to grow in the puritan sense. He echoes the middle-class puritan ethic that life must be a struggle, and through this struggle, we grow as human beings, impervious to the misery around us. Personally, I think this buggy-whip point of view is outdated and life has more to offer than struggle and hardship.

When you turn your mind toward empowerment, life ceases to be a struggle. When you apply yourself, you manifest your goals. Most struggles are within yourself. Once you create a positive focus, they lessen and eventually cease. It's bad enough that the world can sometimes work against you, but it's even worse if you work against yourself. This is why it is important to start at home and work outward. Get your immediate environment together first.

Even in the darkest of times, never give up hope that your goals will become reality. Belief and determination are often the tools that help you through the hard times and eventually move you into the future that you envision. Set aside at least 30 minutes a day to imagine what your future could be. Imagine your love life the way you want it to be. Imagine your health as you ideally want it to be, and imagine yourself living where you would like to and doing what you want in life. If they are truly the things you desire in life, then you should start getting excited at the prospect of them becoming part of your life.

The more excited and determined you get about your image of the future, the more positive energy and effort you put into making it happen. Other people can help you, but you are the one that ultimately makes it happen for yourself. To do this, you must have confidence in your abilities to make your future happen. That is what the Fourth Empowering Step is all about.

Establishing a Rapport with Helpful Energies

As you do more rituals, you will begin establishing patterns as to which Goddesses and Gods help you for specific purposes. Begin by establishing a rapport with divine energies that can help you with your future patterns.

Different aspects of the divine work with you, depending on the goal you aspire to accomplish. This is why it's important to choose accordingly. If you want to be a artist, you might choose Gwydion; if you choose to work with the earth, you might require the help of Anu, Celtic Goddess of the earth, who in earlier times was called "Danu," Mother

Goddess of the many tribes that migrated out of the Danube Valley. (See Appendix A for a complete list of empowering Gods and Goddesses.) Ultimately, these tribes influenced the way we speak, write, and think. No matter how far we think we have traveled, we are still just a step away from the source, the Oneness that ultimately binds all of us together.

In Wicca, you usually gain rapport with a particular pantheon of Goddesses and Gods such as Celtic, Roman, or Greek. As you interact with these divine energies more and more, they help to empower your patterns and can be of great value to you and your overall success.

Sometimes you may find as you progress in life that the divine energies that you connect and interact with change through time. Instead of working with a particular pantheon of Goddesses and Gods, you may find yourself working with different energies than the ones you began using. This is part of your evolving process. At some point, you'll see the universal quality of energy.

The reason for this progression is that when you begin, it's easier to imagine things in terms of particulars and later extend them to the universal whole. The more you work with divine energy, the more you will naturally visualize this energy in terms of its universal whole. When this happens, it doesn't matter what name you call it; it is all the same energy. It is Oneness.

Love

In the movie *African Queen*, the two main characters, played by Katharine Hepburn and Humphrey Bogart, are not immediately attracted to one another, and their initial interaction is not empowering. As situations and conditions change, they become more reliant on one another, and as a result begin to empower each other. She has the determination to do what has never been done, and he has the expertise to win what has never been won. Together they empower each other and achieve what they set out to do—blow up a German ship. These are the events that make life memorable; everything else is left to the archives.

To make things happen, you must first believe that they will happen. Your expectation is what sets the stage. In terms of love, you need first to love yourself and believe in your ability to love and give of yourself before you can expect anyone else to love you and give of themselves.

Love is a powerful source of empowerment because of its intimacy. Love helps you to let down your walls. You open yourself to an experience that is the most intense and enjoyable you will ever have in your life. As with most things, there is a polarity. When you leave yourself that open, you are also risking being intensely hurt.

Many of us have been hurt by love, and we allow these past hurts to close our hearts off to love. Instead of getting hurt again, we figure it's easier not to love at all. But what happens when you refuse to take the risk is you also close your energy down and cease to move forward in love, making empowerment more difficult.

It's necessary to confront your fears, or at least acknowledge them, in order to fill your heart with love for yourself and others. This is the place where you become one with everything around you. The more you struggle, the harder the process becomes. You must learn to flow with the energy that circles you. It's a matter of converting struggle into flow so that you don't fight yourself. The idea is to flow with the energy of Oneness, to focus on your natural proclivities and abilities and start actualizing your full potential as a living, breathing, loving person.

The Fourth Empowering Step: Love Meditation

To enhance this meditation, you can put on soft music that has a springtime feel to it, fill the room with the scent of fresh flowers, and do anything else that reminds you of spring. Begin by sitting back or reclining comfortably. Loosen any tight clothing, belts, or shoes. Uncross your hands and feet, take a deep breath, and let go of any tension you may be feeling as you exhale. Do this several times, feeling more and more relaxed with each breath you take.

Now breathe in again, and this time imagine breathing in a royal blue light that spreads throughout your body, breaking up any negative feelings you may be harboring. As you exhale, imagine your body, mind, and spirit letting go of any feelings of hate, anger, frustration, and fear that you have inside. Repeat this process twice more, breathing in blue light and exhaling and releasing all of those negative feelings that hold you back from being who you truly want to be.

Now breathe in again, and as you exhale, in your mind's eye, imagine walking on an earthen path that weaves its way through the trees, bushes, and vines that grow on both sides. The time of year is early spring when the trees begin getting their new leaves, and the bright colors of the flowers begin adorning the landscape in divine ways. Breathing in deeply, you smell the sweet fragrance of the pink, white, and grape hyacinths that dot the parameter of your path.

The sun is shining and the chill of winter is being replaced by the warmth and vitality of spring. You can feel it all around you. Embrace this overall feeling of "aliveness" and allow it to become part of you. Breathe in the vital energy of spring. As with the trees and flowers around you, you feel yourself awakening after a period of dormancy and flowering in new and exciting ways.

You follow the path to a giant oak tree that looks to be the mother of all oak trees. Underneath the oak is a circle of violets. As you approach the circle, a bluish-green fairy appears. In her hands she holds a crystal ball. She holds the crystal for you to gaze into, and you can see a future where all of your love empowerment goals come true. As you gaze at the crystal, you are filled with excitement because everything you ever wanted has suddenly become reality. You can see yourself stepping through a time portal that links the present to the future with one degree of separation, which in this case is your perception and the will to make it happen.

Take another deep, complete breath and imagine stepping further into the latticework of the crystal, into the reality you desire. See yourself following a path of light that leads to the center of the crystal. The closer you get, the more energized you feel. Finally, you enter a core of the crystal, where there exists an ocean of white light. As you effortlessly swim in the soft white light, you are immersed in a feeling of love that begins to fill every cell of your body.

Continue bathing in the white light until you are filled to the brim with love. In this state of being, you realize that love comes from within and excludes nothing. It is unconditional. Love is infinite and as such has no boundaries you can attach to it. Swimming in this crystal of white light, you sense love everywhere around you. There is a constant influx of feelings of love that keep moving into your sphere of being. The more you float in the white light, the more you become one with that divine feeling of love that permeates all things. You, too, feel like a flower that is opening slowly and just beginning to come into its moment of florescence.

Now breathe in this feeling of love and breathe out this feeling of love. Breathe in the white light and breathe out the white light. Each time you do this, imagine the white light flowing farther out around you. Breathe in the white light, and breathe it out into the room around you. Breathe in the white light, and breathe it out into your home and the area around it. Breathe in soft, loving white light, and breathe the light out into the community you live in, into the country, the continent, the planet, and the universe you live in.

Now take another deep and complete breath, feeling relaxed and refreshed. In your mind's eye, imagine becoming one with the white light, within and without. Continue breathing the loving light, allowing it to revitalize and soothe you.

Begin to move your awareness back to the present time and place by taking another deep breath. As you exhale, move your toes, fingers, hands, and feet. Take another deep breath in, and as you exhale, slowly open your eyes.

While the mediation is still fresh in your mind, make a few notes in your empowerment journal about how you felt before, during, and after the meditation. Also make a note of any insights you may have gleaned from the experience.

Love Affirmation and Prayer

An important part of the empowerment process is to remind yourself that you love who you are each and every day. If you aren't the kind of person you can love, then your first goal is becoming a person you can love. Only by learning to love yourself and being comfortable with who you are can you learn to love others.

An affirmation you can use to empower your sense of self love is:

Every day in every way, I love who I am and who I am becoming.

Empowerment is so much easier when you become aware and acknowledge that you are part of divine creation. When you are at one with the divine, you make a connection that is as old as life itself. Use this prayer each morning and night to help you become one with the divine:

Oh bright and shining ones,
Mother and Father of all creation,
May I know divine love and joy
May I become one with your loving light
I ask this in the Lady's and Lord's name, blessed be.

Sacred Love Space

Add a picture or symbol that you associate with your love empowerment goals to your sacred love space. The picture can be of a loved one or of something that represents love to you. In terms of symbols, it might be a tarot card, rune, crystal, flower, or a design you create yourself.

Before placing the picture or symbol on your altar, hold it in your hands and bless it by saying:

Goddess and God, please bless this symbol
So be it! Blessed be!

Also put a rose-colored candle, a white candle, and a green candle on your altar. Bless each of them by holding each in your hands and saying:

Goddess and God, please bless this candle
So be it! Blessed be!

Also, add either rose petals or rose oil to your sacred love space. In mythology, roses were said to have been a gift of the divine, given to mortals when Venus, Goddess of love, arose from the sea.

Love Ritual

This ritual is best done during a full moon. Use it to gather and direct a considerable amount of focused energy toward making your love life what you would like it to be. You will need the rose-colored, white, and green candles from your sacred love space, a pen, and rose oil.

Begin by drawing a magic circle of light around your love space and empowering the elements. Next, you need to choose three different Goddesses, Gods, or divine energies that you associate with love. Use the pen to inscribe one of their names upon each of the candles. Next, rub the candle with a thin film of rose oil. As you rub the oil on the candle, imagine the candle being empowered by the divine energy whose name is inscribed on it.

Now, put each candle in its holder on your love altar in the order of rose, green, and white. Wipe any remaining oil from your hands. Light the rose-colored candle. As you do, dedicate it to the divine energy you have inscribed on it. Next, light the white candle, dedicating it to the divine energy inscribed on it. Then light the green candle, dedicating it to the divine being you inscribed on it. Now, staring into the flame of the first candle, recite the name of the divine energy inscribed on it nine times, in three series of three. Next, stare into the green candle and recite the name written on it nine times. Do the same with the white candle. Afterward, start at the rose-colored candle and repeat the process two more times.

The idea is to build energy each time you move through the candles, until the very end, when you release the energy toward your expectation for love by shouting out in a jubilant voice "Ayea" nine times. As you do, extend your arms upward and reach for the sky, sending the energy from the ritual outward to help manifest your expectations and love empowerment goals.

When you are done, allow the candles to safely burn down. Thank the divine energies you inscribed on the candles, bid farewell to the elements, and pull up the circle.

Oracle of Love

Crystal gazing is a technique that has been used through the ages to glimpse into the future. You will need a clear quartz crystal (not necessarily a crystal ball), a candle, and a specific question regarding your love goals that you want to have answered.

First, clear the crystal by holding it in your power hand and taking a deep breath in. As you still your breath, imagine a pure, clean mountain stream moving out from the source of creation into the crystal. Then pulse this image into the crystal by breathing sharply out through your nose and imagining planting the image into the stone itself. Repeat this pulse-breath technique three times.

Once the crystal is cleared, place it in front of a lit candle so that the light shines through the crystal. Focus on your question as you move your mind and being into the latticework of the crystal. Now ask for divine assistance by saying:

Great Goddess and God of healing,
Empower this crystal as a true oracle
Please show me my future as it will come to me.

Continue to gaze at the crystal and watch the light as it dances within the stone, creating images of your future. Looking more closely, these images become clearer to you. Within the images in the crystal, you see the answer to your question. Do this for at least 20 minutes.

When you are done, snuff out the candle and note the day, the question, and the images you saw in the crystal in your empowerment journal.

Health

One of the most warm and caring people I have ever had the pleasure to know was Dr. Marcel Vogel, head of the Psychic Research Institute in San Jose, California, during the 1980s. An incredible scientist with hundreds of patents to his credit, he retired from IBM and set up a lab in San Jose that researched the idea that disease often begins energetically and then appears physically. He researched and specifically cut New Age healing crystals that can be used to influence the energetic body in order to produce healing effects on the physical body. He was the person who taught me most of what I know about healing crystals, including the pulse-breath technique.

I was privileged to see Marcel do many healings. He had an intensely magnetic personality and used that magnetism to attract energy, which through focus, he was able to produce amazing scientific results. Like the human body, crystals vibrate at the frequency of water, and as such are used as natural energy conductors and amplifiers. Using measurements that he ascertained from the Cabala, Marcel created particularly effective healing crystals, whose powers are still being revealed.

Just as disease often begins in the spiritual and mental and moves into the physical, healing patterns can also start in the spiritual and mental, and in turn affect the physical body. By being aware of your divine connection, you can empower your life. You can become like a vibrant plant that is less likely to be susceptible to a disease than one that is sickly and on the edge. This is why it is important to keep your energy level up and make an effort to remain positive at all times. One sure way to do this is through empowerment.

The Fourth Empowering Step: Healing Meditation

You will need a quartz crystal that has been cleared of unwanted energies either through smudging, the pulse-breath technique, or by rinsing it in cool water for at least one minute. You will also need soft and healing music and a comfortable spot in which to meditate. Turn on the music and sit back or recline comfortably. Take three deep breaths, feeling yourself becoming more relaxed with each.

Now in your mind's eye, imagine the music is like a river and your light-filled being is floating on the notes that take you downstream. Farther you flow, letting the music guide you as you glide smoothly down the river. Feel your senses become more fluid and harmonious with everything that is around you until a current of peace and tranquility envelopes your entire being. You feel at one with the music.

Now in your mind's eye, allow the music to take you to an island in the middle of the river of light. The island shines so brilliantly that it seems like it must be part of the sun. As you reach the island's shore, your feet touch the soft ground. Allow the music to take you inland to a verdant meadow where wildflowers abound in color and fragrance. Also in the meadow are a group of magical beings dancing in a clockwise circle. Instinctually, you join hands with two beings who extend their hands to you, and you become part of the healing circle.

Now imagine the music transforming into a radiant flame that shines through every cell of your body with an effect that is both healing and invigorating. All disease seems to melt away as the light shines through you. Imagine the healing flame becoming so hot that it wipes out any unwanted bacteria or disease in your body. With each note, you feel the musical flame cleansing you more and more. As you do this, imagine yourself becoming healthier and healthier.

Now fine-tune the light so that it kills all the unwanted, harmful energies in your body. Respectfully ask for the help and blessings of the Goddess and God as you visualize a lavender-colored light enveloping your being. Now breathe in deeply and pulse any unwanted energies out of your body through your exhaled breath. Do this several times until you feel free and lighter.

Once again, bring your awareness back to the music and envision it transporting you back on the river of light. Now breathe in deeply and slowly come back to the present time and place. Breathe in and move your toes and fingers, hands, and feet. Open your eyes slowly.

Take your time coming back to the present time and place. Remember the image of the healing light and realize that you can enlist this light to help protect you from unwanted and unhealthy energies that may attack your health and disempower you. By allying yourself with positive energies that can help your health, you increase your chances for living a long, healthy life.

Healing Affirmation and Prayer

As with many things, good health is a matter of adapting some of your attitudes toward your body and its overall health. Being good one day and bingeing the next are not necessarily good ideas. A better approach would be to moderate the things you do rather than ping-ponging from complete abstinence to total indulgence.

Every day it's important to remind yourself that you want to be in good health and that you are doing things to make that happen in your life. Use this affirmation:

Every minute of every day I am moving toward my optimum health, and I practice those things that help make me healthy.

When praying for good health, ask for the help of your favorite healing deity. For example:

Great Goddess Bridget, I pray you
Please bless me with good health,
And show me the way to better health
Grant me your divine wisdom every day.
Blessed be Bridget, Great Lady!

Sacred Healing Space

Select a picture or symbol that represents your ideal health and add it to your sacred space. The picture can be of someone you aspire to be like health-wise, or a symbol that to you implies optimum health. Before placing the picture or symbol on your healing altar, empower it by holding it in your hands and saying:

Great Goddess and God, give this your blessings,
So that it may help me manifest good health.

Place it on the altar along with a blue candle, a green candle, a gold candle, and either sage leaves or oil, which you have also empowered. When doing healings, blue breaks up the old negative pattern, green plants the seeds for new healthy patterns, and gold gives it the light to grow and come to fruition, which is in this case optimum health.

Healing Ritual

Perform this ritual to bring healing energy into your being or to direct it to someone in need of healing. Full moons and Sabbats are excellent times for doing this ritual, but it can be done anytime during a waxing moon phase. You will need a pen in addition to the blue candle, green candle, gold candle, and sage oil you've already gathered and empowered.

Begin by drawing a magical circle of light and empowering the elements. Next, choose three Goddesses, Gods, or divine energies that best represent healing and good health to you. Use the pen to write one name

111

on each candle and then rub each candle with sage oil before setting the candles in their holders. Wipe any remaining oil from your hands. Now, one by one, light the candles while dedicating them to the Goddess, God, or divine energy inscribed on the candles.

Standing before your altar, take a few minutes to focus your awareness on the health problem or illness that you wish to direct the healing energy toward in this ritual. Next, gaze at the blue candle and begin chanting each of the three names on the candles, nine times, in three series of three. As you do this, imagine directing bright cobalt blue light toward the area needing healing. For example, if you selected Celtic deities, visualize blue light flowing to the area needing healing, and chant:

Anu, Anu, Anu
Anu, Anu, Anu
Anu, Anu, Anu
Math, Math, Math
Math, Math, Math
Math, Math, Math
Kerridwen, Kerridwen, Kerridwen
Kerridwen, Kerridwen, Kerridwen
Kerridwen, Kerridwen, Kerridwen.

Next, gaze at the green candle, visualize green light again flowing into the area needing healing, and chant the three names nine times, in three series of three.

Now gaze at the gold candle, imagine gold light flowing into the area needing healing, and once again, chant the three names nine times, in three series of three.

Build the energy up higher each time you move through the sequence of blue, green, and gold until you finish with a resounding, "Ayea! Ayea! Ayea!" On the last "Ayea," stretch your arms and hands upward, releasing all the energy accumulated in the ritual toward the area needing healing. If you are doing a healing ritual for yourself, if possible put your palms directly on the area where you are having the problems. Imagine all the healing energy moving into the problem area and healing it. Do this for several minutes.

When you are done, allow the candles to safely burn down. Thank the divine energies that you inscribed on the candles, bid farewell to the elements, and pull up the circle.

Oracle of Health

Also called scrying, crystal gazing is a way to tap into that part of yourself that links you to universal health. Use a clear quartz crystal, and cleanse it of any unwanted energies using the pulse-breath technique, smudging, or by rinsing it in cool water for at least a minute. You will also need to focus on a specific health question that you want to have answered.

Place the crystal in front of a lit candle and begin asking yourself the question as you move deeper and deeper into the crystal. Now ask for divine assistance by saying:

Great Goddess and God of healing,
Empower this crystal as a true oracle
Please show me my future as it will come to me.

Begin seeing images of your future health and images of how you can empower your present health in the light dancing within the crystal. Do this for about 20 minutes. Sense the answer to your question as you move even deeper within the crystal, making everything in your life regarding your health suddenly very clear to you. You have what you need to move forward.

When you are done, snuff out the candle and write down in your empowerment journal the date, your question, and the images you received during the scrying experience.

Prosperity

The following story from the book *It's a Miracle* is an example of someone becoming empowered, and in doing so, making magical things happen. Lisa was a type "A" personality, always on the go and spending most of her time working as a professional and raising a family. One day driving on the freeway, her sight went blank, and for few moments she couldn't see anything, which of course had a frightening impact. After dozens of doctor visits and an assortment of tests, with her condition steadily worsening, her doctor determined that she had a rare disease that would end in blindness.

Lisa's first inclination was to give up. She mostly stayed in her room where the surroundings were familiar and let her husband tend to her needs. After some time had passed in this manner, she was persuaded by a friend to attend an art class. Despite her reluctance, she went to the class and became empowered by the experience, even though some of the other members of the class thought she was crazy for even trying.

People thought the idea of a blind person painting was ridiculous, but that didn't seem to bother Lisa as she began pursuing her new found love of art. By working with the paint, she discovered she could feel the differences between the various colors, and by conceptualizing the canvas in her imagination, she was able to begin creating paintings that were amazingly realistic. Lisa now paints full time, and one of the largest art galleries in the country has featured her work. She feels that she is very fortunate, that she has an angel on her shoulder, which she says is most likely a leprechaun.

Any time someone tells you can't do something in life, tell them the story of Lisa. Her story proves that you can do anything you want if you set your mind to it. Often, self-doubt is your worst enemy. This is why stories such as Lisa's are an inspiration that can help motivate you toward manifesting your empowerment goals.

Although at times it seems that science has explanations for everything, there are still many events that defy what is believed possible. What this means is that the boundaries of reality are continually being broadened to include things that were never before thought possible. The possibilities are expanding. The idea that a blind person can feel color and become a painter of realism is one of those things that pushes that possibility envelope. That's where miracles, magic, and the postulations of science all come together as one.

Overall, scientific evolution has been a good one because we have been able to coalesce our knowledge and make life easier in a physical sense. What science doesn't explain is why the spiritual and energetic work the way they do. Obviously, there is more going on than we can account for in a traditional scientific approach.

We constantly design devices that can measure subtler and subtler forms of energy, and as such we are bound to come to revelations that we never before thought possible. This is what the future is all about— your only choice is to evolve, to propel yourself forward. Trying to remain the same is futile because change is the only constant in life. This is the irony of people who dedicate themselves to an idea or way of life that is bound to change as people continue to move into the future.

Technologically we've created wonders, but as people, we are still grappling with the same basic questions: Who are we? What is the purpose of life? Where did we come from? Where are we going? This is the nature of spirituality and its connection to our prosperity. We continue to create because we are creation. We make choices, but at the same time much of life seems to be guided by circumstances beyond our control and awareness. Sometimes it feels like walking around a room in the dark, bumping into everything. Through experience, our awareness becomes more finely tuned to what's going on around us, and we stop bumping into so many things and begin to see a path of light in the darkness.

The Fourth Empowering Step: Prosperity Meditation

Begin by sitting back in your comfortable spot and take a few deep breaths in and out. Each breath sends you deeper into a relaxed state of being. With each breath, imagine yourself descending the steps of a staircase. You inhale and step down; exhale and step down the stairway. Take several slow and complete breaths, and with each breath, step down further and further, descending the staircase that leads to your prosperity empowerment.

At the bottom of the staircase, you find yourself in a room. In the middle of the room is a strange-looking contraption that looks a little like a sled with a seat mounted on it. Venturing closer, you see that in front of the seat are a series of lights, dials, and buttons. You touch the machine, and it completely lights up and begins making a soft whirring sound. You sit down in the seat, and the whirring sound becomes a little louder. Flipping a dial that says one year, you then press the green start button, and the machine begins moving through the time-space continuum. Lights flicker around you as you are transported one year into the future.

The flicker of the lights stops, and the whirling sound of the machine has again returned softly to the background. Slowly you slide off the seat and begin exploring everything around you. Your life is very much the way you have patterned it in your prosperity goals with a few minor updates. You are living where you want to be living, doing what you want to be doing, sharing times with those you care about, and living the lifestyle you envisioned for yourself.

You feel in harmony with the images that are unfolding before you. In the context of the future, you suddenly understand the subtle nuances of the present. You take out your imagination notebook and write down these nuances for future reference. You realize that looking at the future is both informational and therapeutic. On one hand, you better understand the present path you are following and where it will eventually lead you in a year. On the other hand, you can take refuge in the idea that you are going to be successful, and all the people who told you that you couldn't do it were foolishly wasting their energy. Above all, you fulfilled a commitment to yourself when you made your empowerment goals happen. You sense an electrical charge that explodes throughout your body, giving you a sense of euphoria as you bathe in the prosperous light of the future.

Now, moving back to the machine, you once again slide into the seat, turn the dial to "present," and push the green start button. Images flicker by and you sense yourself being returned to the present moment. Once you return, you sit in the seat and ponder all that you have encountered. You then slide out of the seat and return to the stairway. Take a deep breath as you take a step upward. Take another deep breath and move up another step, feeling completely refreshed and renewed with a sense of success and joy. Continue to breathe deeply and ascend the staircase, coming back to the here and now.

Now take several deep breaths, stretch your body, and come back to the present time and place. Slowly open your eyes and begin looking around the room. Before doing anything else, write your observations from the mediation down in your empowerment journal, particularly the subtle nuances that you wrote down in your imagination notebook during the meditation.

Prosperity Affirmation and Prayer

Every day remind yourself that you are good enough to realize your potential and succeed at the tasks you do, and never let anybody convince you otherwise. If someone starts to put you down, run, don't walk, the other way! We can all be tough when we need to be, but at the same time, we can be fragile and need tender care. Sometimes your psyche needs to take a time out from the constant bombardment of life. Use this affirmation to remind yourself you are good enough:

Every day and every night I am filled with shining divine light, and I know I am good enough for the Goddess and God love me, always.

For your prayer, add the blessings of a particular deity, for example, the Celtic Goddess Kerridwen:

Kerridwen the Bright, please fill me with your blessings,
I pray you, Great Lady, guide and protect me
So that my path will always be illuminated,
No matter how light or dark the outside world becomes.

Sacred Riches Space

Find a picture or symbol that represents your success as you envision it. It can be a person, a place, or something of your own creation. Before placing the picture or symbol on your space, empower it by placing it in your hands and saying:

Great Goddess and God,
Please consecrate this object
With your blessings and divine power
So be it! Blessed be!

Also add and empower a green candle, a gold candle, a lavender candle, and some bay oil. Green is the color of fertility and the earth. Gold is the color of prosperity and the Sun, and lavender is the color of the higher, spiritual self, relating back to the divine energy that ties everything together into Oneness.

Prosperity Ritual

This ritual is best done on a high (full) moon or a Sabbat when the elemental energy is at a peak. Your expectation when doing this ritual is to raise and direct a large amount of energy toward the fruition of your prosperity empowerment goals. You will need a green candle, a gold candle, a lavender candle, bay oil, and a ballpoint pen.

Begin by drawing your magical circle of light and empowering the elements. Select three Goddesses, Gods, or divine energies that you want to help you in your prosperity ritual. Using the pen, write the name of one deity on each candle, and then rub each candle with bay oil. Wipe any remaining oil from your hands. Associated with the Sun and sacred to the God Apollo, a garland or crown of bay leaves was the reward for victory or excellence, which makes it an ideal herb to use for prosperity magic.

Now light each candle, one at a time, dedicating each candle to the deity whose name you wrote on it. Now focus your awareness on your expectation, which in this case is your prosperity goals becoming reality. When the image of a prosperous future becomes clear in your mind, begin chanting the names of your prosperity deities, nine times each, in three series of three. With each name you chant, gaze at the candle the name is inscribed on. For example, using the Celtic deities, you would chant:

Lugh, Lugh, Lugh
Lugh, Lugh, Lugh

Lugh, Lugh, Lugh
Rosemerta, Rosemerta, Rosemerta
Rosemerta, Rosemerta, Rosemerta
Rosemerta, Rosemerta, Rosemerta
Dagda, Dagda, Dagda
Dagda, Dagda, Dagda
Dagda, Dagda, Dagda.

Repeat this process with the other two candles, each time bringing the level of energy up a little higher. When you feel the energy can go no higher, shout out "Ayea!" three times. On the third "Ayea," raise your arms, hands, and fingers upward toward the sky, directing the accumulated energy toward the success of your present and future prosperity goals.

When you are done, allow the candles to safely burn down. Thank the divine energies you inscribed on the candles, bid farewell to the elements, and pull up the circle.

Oracle of Wealth

Select a question regarding your future prosperity and locate a clear quartz crystal that has been energetically cleared either through the pulse-breath technique, smudging, or rinsing in cool water. Place the cleared crystal in front of a lit candle and look deeply into it at the way the light refracts and creates shapes inside. Focus on your question and ask it out loud. Look into the crystal, watching the patterns and the shadowy interplay of light and dark within it. Now, ask for divine assistance by saying:

Great Goddess and God of prosperity,
Empower this crystal as a true oracle
Please show me my future as it will come to me.

Take a deep breath and merge with the crystal. Become one with it, and as you do, it may seem that your question and the answer to it become obvious to you. Suddenly all the shapes within the crystal have meaning to you with regard to your prosperity question. Merge with the crystal for at least 20 minutes.

When you are done, snuff out the candle and thank the Goddess and God for giving you the insight both into yourself and your future. Make a note of the date, your question, and the answer you received in your empowerment journal.

Chapter Five

The Fifth Empowering Step: Enacting Your Empowerment Plan

In a 2001 interview with *Rolling Stone* magazine, Bob Dylan talked about his creative process in making the album *Time Out of Mind.* Having not made an album of original material in more than seven years, he felt a certain apprehension, but because of a recent spiritual experience, he felt a renewed desire to create music. He had written a batch of songs, but he was playing with musicians he had just met. Having trouble trusting musicians he did not know well with his unrecorded songs, Dylan described the process as a little frustrating when trying to get what was in his head onto the recording.

When talking about one of the songs, "Cold Irons Bound," Dylan said, "There's a real drive to it and I am satisfied with what we did, but it isn't even close to the way I had it envisioned ... You can reach your vision if you have the willpower, but instead you have to steer the event where it wants to go." This event, *Time Out of Mind,* received critical acclaim and went on to win a Grammy award.

It becomes possible to enact your empowerment plan by bridging the gap between your plans, conceptualization, and what turns out in reality, actualization. A process takes place where what you envision in your mind takes shape and manifests itself in physical reality. You have a hand in how this happens, depending on your approach and ability to steer events where you want them to go. At the same time, things are constantly changing, and it is often necessary to tweak your plans while remaining focused. Sometimes it becomes necessary to let it all go and start anew.

Building Your Castle

If you are building the castle of your dreams, the first thing you do is get your castle plans together. The plans represent your vision of the final product. From this, you have to decide how you want these plans implemented. When there are problems with a building, both the architect and builder are quick to blame each other, and when things work out with a building, they are both equally as quick to claim credit. This is because of the integral relationship between design and building. To make things truly work, you must have a balance between the two.

Now that you have your plans for manifesting your goals, you need to figure out how to implement these plans so your goals become reality. Some people are very driven and want everything right now, while others are patient and allow plenty of time for things. Both approaches are valid, and as a whole, you are probably a little bit or a lot of both approaches. As with most things in life, polarities exist that influence your overall actions. From the extremes, you discover balance.

In order to change the way you do things, you need modify the overall structure of your life. You need to set new boundaries and direction as to the scope and structure of your life that reflect your future rather your past. You need to turn your mind to the here and now and toward the future.

When making changes to your life, it's always easier to adapt your present patterns and ways of doing things than it is to create new ones, although sometimes that is just what you have to do. It depends on your specific plan and steps for attaining your empowerment goals. If one of your love empowerment goals is finding someone to love and share your life with, but your basic temperament is to want a lot of space, then you have to find an approach that includes a close relationship with lots of space. To fight your basic nature most often only creates a struggle within yourself.

You can adapt the way you are, but it's almost impossible to totally change who you are without going back and undoing all of your socialization and conditioning. Besides, even if you're successful, fighting your basic nature will often leave you unhappy and unfulfilled. This is why it's important to work with your basic nature and your natural abilities and improve upon these personal qualities rather than struggle against them.

Within this framework, you need to begin laying out the foundation for your plans. If one of your health goals is to eat healthier, then you have to start getting recipes, setting up menus, and making grocery lists to make this happen. Approach and basic nature again apply. Some people insist on setting up a diet and strictly sticking to it, whereas other people have a tendency to work better if they moderate their eating habits while incorporating healthier foods into their overall diet. In both cases, you are steering the event, but what is different is the way you steer the event.

Developing a Method That Works for You

When deciding how you want to enact your plan, you need to choose the method of your approach. More than anything, this method stems from the kind of person you are and what works best for you. Some questions to ask yourself are:

- How controlling are you?
- How detail-oriented are you?
- Do you usually see things in terms of the micro (the details) or the macro (the big picture)?
- How creative are you?
- How much do you like routine?
- Are you easily bored with things?
- How directed and focused are you?
- How much willpower and motivation do you have?

- What times are you happiest when working?
- What times are you most productive when working?
- Do you prefer working by yourself or with others?
- Do you work best when there is an immediate reward involved?

One of the underlying questions when implementing a method to your approach is how much control do you want to have over the empowerment process? With enough willpower and determination, you can probably control most events to get exactly what you want, but you have to be willing to put in the time and effort to deal with all the minute details.

A moderated approach involves influencing the general direction of events and the way they turn out in terms of your goals, but not trying to control everything. After all, this is often physically, mentally, and spiritually impossible. Also realize that control can be illusionary, and writers such as James Redfield, author of *The Celestine Prophecy*, have submitted the idea that control is a large part of what has gone wrong with human relationships.

New Age Wicca keys in on the idea of influencing and directing patterns rather than forcing or controlling them. This is akin to the Eastern thought taught in martial arts classes. When someone goes to throw a punch at you, it is easier and wiser to deflect the punch than to meet it head on. If a person was on a railroad track with a train approaching, it would be much easier to push them off the tracks than to pick them up and physically move them off the tracks.

When you influence events in magic making, you nudge them in the direction you want them to go. How much influence you exert relates to how in tune you are with your intention and expectation as well as how in tune you are with the divine and Oneness. You also need to know the best time and how hard you can nudge to steer the chain of events in the course you have charted for your empowerment plans.

Enacting Your Five-Step Empowerment Plans

Many of the people I grew up with had aspirations of becoming rock stars. After all, with the 1960s came the Beatles, the Rolling Stones, and many other talented bands and musicians. Everyone wanted to be a rock star!

Some of my friends would spend hours practicing and learning their craft, but they would never go any further with it. I met several people who had amazing talent but never took it to the next level, mostly because they were afraid of failing. In retrospect, I think it was a fear of failure that stopped many people from even trying. It's the innate fear of rejection whose positive counterpart is the joy of empowerment. This is why, when it comes to empowerment, no matter how large or small, support groups and people whom you love and trust are much more valuable than all the diamonds in South Africa.

The first thing you need to do is apply your method of approach to your plans. Plan time frames that work with how fast you do things. Miraculous things can happen, but you have to be willing to plan for them and then take the steps to make them happen. In terms of New Age Wicca, this is called magic, which often defies the bounds of current knowledge. That's what makes it magical.

Now that you have mapped out your empowerment plans, you are ready to enact them. Begin by taking each of your five-step empowerment plans that you wrote down in your empowerment journal and decide how you want to approach each of them. Your more important goals and plans obviously take priority over lesser ones; thus, your approach can be different. Looking for a new job when you are unemployed or because you dislike the job you are working at now might have an approach that is much more intensely directed than looking for a job because you are bored with your present one.

Circumstances also determine how you approach a goal. This is dictated by need and necessity. A simple example is if your short-term goal is to go grocery shopping and you are hungry, your need to buy food is greater than if you aren't hungry.

By further defining your five-step empowerment plans, you're making the plan more familiar to you as part of your life. This also starts building your confidence that you can do it. Like learning to walk, empowerment comes one step at a time until movement is fluid and natural.

In terms of the garden analogy, plans are the things that you need to make before you plant your seeds. What this usually means is that you prepare your soil and stake out your garden as to what you are going to plant and where you are going to plant it.

Preparing your soil involves creating an environment that encourages your seeds to sprout, grow, and flourish. Preparation and building confidence in your abilities to enact your empowerment plans are big parts of creating that environment.

You must believe in yourself if you hope to be successful. Otherwise, you will have a hard time getting your plans to grow well. The more comfortable you feel about your empowerment plans, the greater your level of confidence that you can move your empowerment goals from conception to actualization.

Staking Out Your Personal Territory

It's important to decide how your goals fit in terms of the context of your life, as well as how you want to enact your empowerment plans so that they have the best chance of coming to fruition. In addition to laying out your foundation, creating a method to your approach, and enacting your five-step plans, this process includes staking out your personal territory.

When you take the fifth empowering step and enact your empowerment plan, you will find yourself changing your personal boundaries because you are realizing your true potential and moving beyond your past limitations. Staking out your personal territory is part of this process because on a physical level you set up boundaries and sacred spaces for yourself. On a mental level you continue to read and learn, and on a spiritual level you become more in harmony with the divine, particularly through the use of prayer.

In addition to the sacred spaces you've already set up, you can create an empowerment area where you can work on your empowerment goals and plans without distractions. Your empowerment area can be the same area where you do your meditations, affirmations, prayers, rituals, and oracles, and where you have your sacred spaces for love, health, and prosperity. Or your empowerment area can be someplace in nature or in your own backyard.

Some of the things you can do to make your empowerment area more effective is to put crystals around the perimeter of the area. You are less likely to be interrupted if you don't have a phone in the area. Also, you may want a private, secure space in which you determine who enters to keep it clear of unwanted energies.

Many techniques exist for clearing your area of unwanted energy. One of the more effective methods is smudging the area with a sage and cedar smudge stick. This is done by lighting the stick and walking around the area. Use a dish or bowl to catch any hot, falling ash from the stick. Allow the smoke to cleanse and purify the area for several minutes. At the same time that you walk clockwise around the area with the smoking stick, you can repeat the following invocation:

All negative and unwanted energies be gone
In the name of the Goddess and God.
So be it! Blessed be!

As with your sacred space, put pictures and objects that help keep you positive and focused on the things you need to do to enact your plans and manifest your goals. Also having a CD player, a computer with a CD player, tape player, or, if you are so inclined, a musical instrument in your space can be helpful. Some of the keyboards today pretty much play themselves, particularly if there is a sequencer in them.

When staking out and expanding your mental territory, read books, watch informational programs, and gather information that can help you enact your plans and attain your goals. Knowledge is one of the ways to build confidence because it gives you a sense of knowing where you are going and what to expect when you get there.

There are many valuable books, videos, and courses that can provide practical information on everything from relationships, diet, and how to be prosperous. They are resources that you should use regularly. (Many of them are listed in the Bibliography in the back of this book.)

In terms of your spiritual territory, meditations, affirmations, prayers, and rituals help you to stake out and expand your personal territory. Continually merging and working with the divine in its infinite aspects are the best ways to grow spiritually. As you become more in tune with this energy, you start becoming aware of the subtle changes that happen, and how you can influence these changes so that they work for you.

Because the flow of energy is from the spiritual to the mental to the physical and back again, influencing these subtle energies impacts your mental and physical condition. In this case, the effect is empowerment, because it helps you steer events so they flow more in accord with your plans and propel you in the direction of attaining your goals.

Love

In one of my favorite movies, *It's a Wonderful Life*, there is a scene that depicts planning and empowering love. One day at the soda fountain when they are children, Mary whispers in George's deaf ear that she is going to marry him. Of course, he doesn't hear her, but nonetheless, she has begun moving her vision into reality. Time shifts, and they are at a high school dance. The floor starts moving out from underneath them, and they fall into the pool, still dancing.

These events are a precursor to George and Mary's life, where they do indeed get married, but there is always something that keeps changing the course of their lives overall. George Bailey's earlier goals of traveling and building things only become half realized because he never travels to exotic places but his building and loan company is instrumental in building decent houses that working-class people can afford.

Mary shares in George's dreams, and in the end they are graced with family and friends who care enough to help in times of need. George realizes his meaning in life. His empowerment stems from the love he receives from his family and friends. The movie comes full circle from the scene that began with Mary and George at the soda fountain.

In terms of your love empowerment goals, you have to stake out your territory like Mary did. Take a few bold steps to enact your love plan even if it means making some mistakes and altering your course now and again.

The Fifth Empowering Step: Love Meditation

Sit back in a comfortable spot. Take a deep breath, slowly inhaling, holding it for a count of 1-2-3, then exhaling. Do this twice more, becoming more and more relaxed with each breath.

Now in your mind's eye, imagine walking down a path that winds its way toward a body of water. As you walk along, imagine at the end of the path a dock with boats tied to it. Closer and closer the image comes as you smell the sea air and hear the sound of water lapping on the shore.

Reaching the end of the path, you walk along the wooden dock looking at the boats. An old man wearing a sailor's cap beckons you over to one of the boats that has your name painted on the side in large letters. He hands you a folded piece of paper and motions for you step onto the boat. As you do, you open up the paper, which looks like a map with a heart drawn on an island. Instinctually, you understand that this is your destination to love.

Now imagine effortlessly sailing your boat on a sea that glistens in the sunlight. Using the map, you chart your course to the island of your love desires. Floating freely, the movement of the water is relaxing and sensuous at the same time. The warm breeze, feeling like a lover's breath, guides you ever closer, arousing your anticipation.

As you approach the island, you see a person standing on the shore waving to you. Sailing into the harbor, that same person, who you intuitively know is your lover, welcomes you, takes you by the hand, and leads you to the sandy shore.

The warm sand caresses the bottoms of your feet and toes as you walk with your lover along the beach. Together you talk about the type of life you would like to create. Feeling your lover's hand in yours, you savor the moment for its intimate serenity.

Happy and pleasantly relaxed now that your voyage is over and you are where you want to be, you sense a feeling of accomplishment as you take another deep breath in and out. Now breathe in once again, still your breathe for three heartbeats, and then exhale completely. As you exhale, begin to move your fingers and toes, coming back to the present time and place. Take two more deep breaths, each time becoming more aware of your body. Stretch your muscles and begin rubbing your palms together to center yourself. Write your impressions of the meditation in your empowerment journal when you are done.

Love Affirmation and Prayer

Affirmations can help build your confidence and level of empowerment. The following affirmation can be used to reinforce your belief in your abilities to be and do anything you set your mind to. Repeat it at least nine times a day for best results:

Every day, in every way, I am more confident in my abilities to enact my love empowerment plans and manifest my goals into reality.

In terms of prayers, ask for the help of the divine in your quest toward empowerment:

Dear Goddess and God,
Please grant me your blessings,
So that I may be confident,
About my talents and abilities,

Help me to enact my empowerment plan,
And attain my empowerment goals.
I ask this in the Lady and Lord's name
So be it! Blessed be!

Sacred Love Space

Place a picture or small model of a boat that symbolizes your voyage toward your love empowerment goals on your sacred love altar. Every time you see it, envision yourself sailing on the boat toward your love empowerment goals.

Also add four clear quartz crystal points to your sacred love space. Cleanse the crystals by rinsing them, crystal points downward, in cool running water for at least one minute. Next, empower them by holding the stones in your power hand, one at time, and saying:

May the Goddess and God
Bless and empower this stone
With helpful divine energies.

Love Ritual

The purpose of this ritual is to set up a quartz crystal grid with a representation of yourself in the middle to bring more love into your life. You will need the four crystal points from your sacred love space. Perform this ritual just before or on a full moon and leave the grid up until the next full moon. Then take it apart.

Begin by drawing a magic circle of light and empowering the elements. Pick up the first crystal point, and if you're not already standing in the north point of your circle, move there. First clear the crystal by cupping the stone between your hands, imagining a clear mountain stream in your mind, and pulsing your breath out through your nose as you envision the clear image moving into and cleansing the stone. Repeat this pulse-breath technique a total of three times. Next, hold the stone up in your right hand and say:

Dear Goddess and God, divine ones
Please empower this stone with the energy of the northward.

Imagine a great ball of green light moving from the north point to the stone, empowering it with the element of earth. Place the stone back on your sacred love space and pick up the next crystal. Moving to the east point of your circle, repeat the process again by first cleansing the crystal and then holding it up toward the east point while saying:

Dear Goddess and God, divine ones
Please empower this stone with the energy of the eastward.

Imagine a great ball of white light moving from the east point to the stone, empowering it with the element of air. Put the stone back on your sacred space, pick up the next crystal, and move to the south point of your circle. First, cleanse the crystal and then hold it up in your right hand and say:

Dear Goddess and God, divine ones
Please empower this stone with the energy of the southward.

Imagine a great ball of golden light moving from the south point to the stone in your hand and filling and empowering the crystal with the element of fire. Returning the stone to your sacred space, pick up the remaining crystal and move to the west point of your circle. Cleanse the stone, and then holding it up in your right hand, say:

Dear Goddess and God, divine ones
Please empower this stone with the energy of the westward.

Imagine a ball of blue light moving from the west point into the crystal, empowering it with the element of water. Return the stone to the altar.

Now sit comfortably and position the crystals' points around you, pointed toward you in their corresponding direction; north stone in the north point, east stone in the east point, south stone in the south point, and the west stone in the west point. As you sit in the center of the crystal grid, in your mind's eye, join the stones together with a white thread of light. Do this several times.

Imagine love flowing into the crystal points and then flowing into you as you sit in the center of the crystal grid. Take a deep breath and imagine breathing in the color rose and breathing out the color rose. Do this several times. In your mind's eye, imagine enacting your love empowerment plan and attaining your goals. For a few minutes, move your awareness into the future and enjoy feeling filled with love and joy.

When you are done, leave the stones on your love altar to use later in the prosperity ritual. Thank the deity, bid farewell to the elements, and pull up the magic circle.

Oracle of Love

This oracle is about perception and allowing for the supposed random element. Some traditions teach that nothing is random and without cause. Any event begins a continuous wave of events that stem from it. Sometimes the effects are temporary and other times they seem to last for an eternity.

For this oracle, use a book or magazine filled with pictures of paintings. Find one with abstract, surrealistic, or impressionistic paintings because they are less defined and leave more to your imagination. Now hold the book between your hands, take a deep breath in and out, and affirm the book as a true oracle. Say three times:

I affirm this book as a true oracle.

Now focus on a specific question about enacting your love empowerment plans, take a deep breath in, close your eyes, and breathe out as you open the book to a painting. Put your power hand on the page. Now open your eyes. What is the page number? What images, colors, and other things do you see in the painting, and how do they relate to the question you asked? Look into the depths and decipher what the patterns in the painting suggest to you about your future in terms of love. Do this two more times, for a total of three times. Make a note of the page numbers, the three paintings, and the artists who painted them in your empowerment journal, as well as any helpful images you noticed. These items often provide valuable clues to the answer of the question at hand.

Health

As I drove home with my beagle Snoopy's head in my lap, all I could think about was the vet's last words, "This dog should be put to sleep. If you take him home, he will have a seizure and die anyway, meaning trauma for you and your family." I thought about this and the effect it would have on my young son as I drove past our front gate. With the help of my husband, we carried Snoopy's limp body into the house and put him on a blanket in the front room.

For two days, I was barely able to get him to eat five bites of dog food, and my attempts to shove liquid vitamins down his throat were comical at best, particularly each time he coughed them back out after I was sure he must have swallowed them. His condition didn't seem to be improving.

Then a friend of mine who worked in a natural foods store gave me the idea of feeding Snoopy fresh garlic. We were baking bread in a bread machine we had received for Christmas, and we noticed the dog was interested in the smell of the baking bread. He began eating bits of the bread, and we began adding small amounts of fresh garlic to the pieces that he consumed. He also started drinking green tea. Within a couple days, Snoopy showed marked improvement, and he began walking around and wanting to go outside.

It's now been more than two years since I first brought Snoopy home from the vet, and though he still has some problems from time to time, he is still very much alive and part of our family. Every morning he waits at the back door, tail wagging, for his fresh baked bread that we still occasionally spike with fresh garlic.

Snoopy's story is about defying the odds, not giving up hope, and sticking with a plan that works. Make an effort to keep your hopes high and continue trying even when things seem hopeless. This is particularly important when it comes to your health or the health of those you love, whether people or animals. You need to be open to new ideas and willing to try different things if that's what it takes to get better.

The Fifth Empowering Step: Healing Meditation

In this meditation, you are going to build a wellness castle with your imagination that you can visit whenever you feel the need. Begin by sitting back, getting comfortable, and taking a deep breath in. As you exhale, feel all the tension and stress flowing from your body with your exhaled breath. Take two more deep breaths, each time letting go of a little more tension, and feeling more and more relaxed.

Now breathe gently in and out, and in your mind's eye, imagine your wellness castle. Picture it. Now imagine drawing up the plans to create your wellness castle. You might add a healing room, solarium, and indoor garden, as well as an exercise room, spa, heated swimming pool, and an empowerment room. Be creative and add a moon room, a crystal room, and a divine empowerment wing to your castle plans. The idea is to create an imaginary palace you can visit in your mind that feels healing and comfortable, a place where you can completely relax, a place that is physically, mentally, and spiritually healing.

After you have drawn up your plans, imagine yourself gathering the materials and laying out the dimensions of your castle. Now, imagine yourself magically building your dream castle so that it exists on an energetic level. In your mind, construct the castle in such a way that each room heals and empowers you in different ways. It is sometimes easier to start by constructing the main healing room of your castle and then adding more detail as you desire. Take your time and enjoy the crafting process. However you envision your wellness castle, you need to build it firmly in your mind's eye, making it unique and memorable to you.

Upon completion of your wellness castle, see yourself inside the castle, exploring its many magical rooms. Feel the healing energy of the rooms as you move your mind in and out of them. Take a deep and complete breath in, breathing in the healing energies of your wellness castle. Do this several times to absorb the healing energies of the castle. With each breath you take, feel your body, mind, and soul becoming more and more healthy, centered, and harmonious.

Now take another deep and complete breath and realize that your wellness castle is a place of healing that you can return to as often as you like. Take another deep breath in, bringing all the healing energy from your castle with you to the present moment and place. Take another breath in and out, begin moving your fingers and your toes, and slowly open your eyes. Stretch your body completely, feeling refreshed and revitalized. Take a few minutes before you continue your day. Also take a few minutes to write down your impressions of the meditation in your empowerment journal. Draw a basic floor plan of your wellness castle in your journal and date it. Through time, you can add rooms, remodel your castle to fit your needs, and even name your castle.

Healing Affirmation and Prayer

Reinforce your health empowerment plan by saying the following affirmation just before working on your plan:

Every day I work toward my health empowerment plan and every step I take, I am more healthy and happy.

The following prayer adds to this idea by asking for the help of the divine in your plan to improve your overall health:

Divine Goddesses and Gods of healing
Please help me with my plan to be healthier
Please bless my health empowerment plans
So that they will become a reality
Forever guided by your healing light.
Blessed be! Blessed be! Blessed be!

Sacred Healing Space

Put a tiny statue of a castle or a picture of a castle that represents your wellness castle in your sacred healing space. You can use an object that represents a castle, such as the rook in a chess set. Any time you want to return to your wellness castle, just turn your mind toward the statue, picture, or other castle object. Then take a deep breath, close your eyes, and in your mind's eye, return to your wellness castle for a few minutes to recharge your batteries and benefit from its healing energies.

In addition, place seven small gemstones of amethyst, hematite, rose quartz, clear quartz, sodalite, carnelian, and bloodstone on your sacred healing altar.

Healing Ritual

This ritual can be used to align and energize your chakras so that you feel healthier and more centered. Wear cotton or silk clothing for this ritual or go sky-clad (naked). Do this ritual during a waxing moon phase.

Begin by drawing a magic circle of light around your sacred healing altar and empowering the elements. Take each of the seven stones that you placed on your altar and clear them of unwanted energies. Do this by rinsing them in cool water for at least a minute, by smudging them, or by using the pulse-breath technique.

After cleansing the stones, program each for healing and wellness. Hold the stone in your power hand in your mind's eye, imagine yourself in a splendid state of health, strong and vital, filled with energy, and then pulse your breath out through your nose and plant that healthy, vital image into the stone itself. Repeat this process a total of three times for each stone. By now, the healthy, vital image of yourself will be firmly planted in the stone and in your mind.

Now holding the stones in your hand, lie on your back within the magic circle of light with your head pointed north and your feet pointed south. You can use a yoga mat, down comforter, pillows, or a lumbar back pillow for support if you like. Next, put the piece of hematite on your first chakra, located at the base of your spine and your pelvis. The first chakra corresponds to your physical body and is associated with your instincts for survival and trust of others. Breathe in the color red, and breathe out the color red. As you do this, feel the stone's natural power as its healing energy flows into your first chakra before the energy expands throughout your body.

Now place the piece of bloodstone on your second chakra, located just below your navel. Breathe in the color orange, and breathe out the color orange. As you do this, feel the natural power of the stone's healing energy moving into your second chakra. Your second chakra relates to your sexuality and creativity.

For your third chakra, located at your solar plexus just below your breastbone, place the piece of carnelian, a great stone for building power and accessing healing energy. Breathe in the color gold, and breathe out the color gold. Feel the stone's natural healing energy as it moves into your third chakra, the energy center related to power, personal energy, and human will.

Move up to your fourth chakra, located at the center of your chest at your heart. Put the piece of rose quartz on this chakra. Breathe in the color rose, and breathe out the color rose. As you do, feel the stone's natural healing energy moving into your heart area before spreading through the rest of your body. Your fourth chakra corresponds with feelings of love, empathy, and compassion.

Use the piece of sodalite for your fifth chakra, located at the bottom and center of your throat. This chakra corresponds to your communication skills and how well you express yourself to the world. Breathe in blue, and breathe out blue. As you do, feel the healing energy of the gemstone permeate your fifth chakra around your throat area and imagine your link with yourself and the world as a whole being strengthened and becoming one.

Position the piece of amethyst on your sixth chakra, located at your third eye in the middle of your forehead just above and between your eyebrows. Breathe in purple, and breathe out purple. As you do, feel the healing energy of crystal move into your sixth chakra, which primarily has to with your intuition and psychic abilities.

The seventh chakra connects you to your spiritual self and the divine. The reason you place clear quartz upon this chakra is because one of its main properties is clarity, something you need when becoming one with the divine. Position the crystal so that it makes contact with the top of your head. Breathe in white light, and breathe out white light. As you do, feel the healing energy of the quartz crystal move in through the top of your head and move downward, connecting with each of the other chakra stones.

Now imagine a thread of white light moving up and down through your chakras, harmonizing your energy to the key of life so that you can become healthier and more in tune with the movements of the divine. Spend as much time as you like, languishing in the healing chakra stream of energy. When you're done, remove the stones from your body, one at a time, starting with the crown chakra stone (quartz crystal) and finishing with the hematite (first chakra). Thank the divine, bid farewell to the elements, and pull up the circle. Keep the stones on your altar to use in other rituals and meditations.

Oracle of Health

Hold a book or magazine of paintings between your hands, close your eyes, and take a deep breath in and out. Breathe in deeply, still your breath for three heartbeats, and then exhale completely. Do this once more.

Now focus on a specific question about enacting your health empowerment plan in your mind. Turn your awareness entirely toward the question at hand. Next, take another deep breath in and out, and immediately open the book to a page without really thinking about it. Put your power hand on the page. Now open your eyes. What is the number of the page your hand is resting on? What are the images you see and how do they relate to the question regarding your health empowerment? Look within the painting at the colors, textures, and shapes to better understand the patterns in the painting and what they suggest about your future in terms of health. Do this two more times, for a total of three times. Each time, make a note in your empowerment journal of the page number as well as the names and artists of the three paintings. Also, list the helpful images, colors, or shapes. Often, these bits of information coalesce to form an answer to your question. Other times, the painting itself may be all you need to answer your question.

Prosperity

George Martin, producer of the Beatles, had a vision to record one last album before retiring. He wanted to produce a collection of Beatles songs performed by some people you wouldn't normally associate with either the Beatles or music. What Martin's vision showed is that one of his major qualities as a producer was the ability to focus on what people did well and expand his vision from there.

On the album *In My Life,* he brought a seemingly diverse array of people together and successfully demonstrated what they were capable of when pushed beyond their perceived boundaries. The results are surprising because they move beyond normal expectations, for example Jim Carrey sings "I am the Walrus," Goldie Hawn sings "A Hard Day's Night," and Robin Williams sings "Come Together."

George Martin's technique is to accentuate a person's strengths, thus bringing out his or her best qualities in terms of recordings and performances. It's a matter of letting people be themselves and working with what they do well. He suggests rather than forces.

Boundaries and expectations are continually being expanded, and as such they require a level of flexibility and adaptability. As you approach your prosperity empowerment plans, you have to be willing to adapt them to an ever-changing environment. You must forever be moving forward in your planning, or your prosperity plans become outdated and cease to reflect who you are. The important thing is to personalize your vision so it works for you and draws upon what you do well and hopefully enjoy.

The Fifth Empowering Step: Prosperity Meditation

Begin by sitting back or reclining in a comfortable, undisturbed spot. Take three deep breaths, inhaling for three counts, holding your breath for three counts, and exhaling completely. On your last exhale, feel yourself releasing all the tensions and worries of the day. Feel your neck relax and your shoulders drop and relax. Take another deep breath in and out and relax your body more and more, feeling your muscles loosen, relax, and grow warm as you meditate.

In your mind's eye, see or sense a single point of white light. Allow this light to flow into your third eye to expand throughout your entire being. From the top of your head to the tips of your toes, imagine you are the white light and the white light is you. As you become filled with light, you are now ready to begin your journey to empowerment.

Take another deep breath in and out and imagine floating gently down a river with your feet skimming the top of the water. Up ahead, you see the entrance to a cave, but instead of being dark, the entrance is brightly lit and inviting. As you approach the mouth of the cave, you can see that there are dazzling multicolored quartz crystals on every wall. Entering the crystal cave, you feel as though you are entering a gigantic crystal geode with light refracted from every facet. Looking up, you see a large clear crystal point blinking, once, twice, and three times, drawing you to it. You take a deep breath and merge with the crystal's natural light. It pulls you deeper and deeper still into its center. Now imagine being inside the crystal. As you shift into the crystal, you sense a slight inner energetic tug or clicking.

Bathe in the natural power of the crystal as you become one with it. Taking another deep breath in and out, you shift effortlessly into a fluid drop of water in the river, flowing out of the crystal cave and into the daylight. You shift effortlessly into a sea gull and find yourself flying high above the clouds. The sensation of flying frees and uplifts you, higher and higher. You can feel the soft downy feathers that cover your body and the air currents that flow under you. Your feathered wings spread out, caressing the breeze that carries you farther on your journey through the sky.

High above the cliffs you fly, slowly approaching the seashore. From your vantage point in the sky, you perceive the waves flowing back to sea from the shoreline, rolling up their strength and growing tall and powerful before finally flowing back into shore. Breath deeply, filling your lungs with the sea air as you fly even higher in your mind's eye, climbing ever upward toward your empowerment goals.

You sense your spirit soaring free, unencumbered by the laws of gravity, and you realize that everything is possible if you set your mind to it. You sense all of your prosperity goals easily within your energetic grasp. With this sensation firmly planted in your mind, take another deep breath in and out and begin shifting back into your human body. Take another deep breath in and out and move your toes and fingers, hands and feet. Then slowly open your eyes and stretch your arms as if they were wings. Take another deep breath and come back to the present time and place.

When you are done meditating, write your impressions of the meditation in your empowerment journal.

Prosperity Affirmation and Prayer

You can use a quartz crystal to affirm your prosperity plans by holding a quartz crystal in your power hand and repeating the following affirmation at least eight times a day for 28 days. Carry the stone on or with you. It will help to shape your perception of yourself and your potential:

Today and every day, I enact my plans for prosperity, and my goals crystallize before me.

When praying for assistance with your prosperity plans, it's always wise to say please and thank you, to show respect and love for the Goddess and God. For example, say this prayer before starting your day:

Dear Lady, I pray you
Please help me enact my prosperity plan
Each and every moment of the day
Thank you, kind and knowing Mother
For your blessings and guidance
Please help me draw prosperity
Into my life today naturally
Ayea! Ayea! Ayea!

Sacred Riches Space

Add a picture or figurine of an animal whose energy you would like to enlist to help you enact your prosperity empowerment plans and attain your goals. It can be a picture of an animal in the wild or of a favorite pet.

Also add a green candle and a picture or object that represents one of your prosperity goals to your sacred riches space, for example, a special coin for money, a picture of your dream house or dream car, a picture of a college diploma, or a seed catalog for a magnificent garden.

In addition, put the four clear quartz crystal points that you used in the love ritual on your altar. You don't have to clear them for this purpose, but rather you can build upon their positive energies.

Prosperity Ritual

In this ritual you are building a prosperity grid of magical energy. You will use your magic wand to help focus the energy on your prosperity goals. First, select one goal to work with in the ritual. Do this ritual on or just before a full moon for best results.

Begin by drawing a magic circle and empowering the elements. Next, set the candle in its holder in the middle of the altar. Then position the crystals around the candle in a clockwise circle, so that they are at the top, sides, and bottom of the candle. Point the crystals inward toward the candle. Now put the object or picture that represents your prosperity goal next to the candle in the middle of the crystal grid. Next, light the candle, dedicating it to your favorite Goddess and God of prosperity. Gaze at the candlelight for a few minutes and turn your mind toward enacting the plan to manifest your prosperity goal.

Hold your wand in your power hand and take a deep breath in. Point your wand toward the top grid crystal as you breathe out and imagine a powerful burst of energy flowing out of your wand tip, awakening the natural power of the stone.

Now take another deep breath in, and as you breathe out, point your wand toward the crystal on the right side of the candle. Again imagine a powerful burst of energy streaming out of the wand tip and awakening the natural power of the stone. Repeat this process with the crystal at the bottom of the candle, and then with the crystal at the left of the candle.

Next, use your wand to draw a thread of connecting white light in a clockwise circle, beginning with the top crystal. Do this three times. Now hold your wand over the crystal grid and empower the grid by saying:

Great Goddess of prosperity,
Please enrich this grid with your blessings,
Great God of fortune,

Please endow this grid with your favor,
May you empower my prosperity plans with success
And help me attain my goals
So be it! Blessed be!

Now take a few more minutes to gaze at the candlelight and imagine enacting your prosperity plan and naturally manifesting your goal. When you are done, thank the Goddess and God, bid farewell to the elements, and pull up the magic circle.

Leave the grid set up until the next full moon. Throughout the month, direct positive images and sensations of confidence and success toward the crystal grid. Hold your hands, palms down, over the grid and repeat the invocation as often as you like to add more energy. Once you take the grid apart, leave the crystals and the picture or symbol of your prosperity goal on your altar until you attain your goal.

Oracle of Wealth

Hold a book or magazine of paintings between your hands, and take a deep, complete breath in and out. Now focus on a specific question about enacting your prosperity empowerment plans. Turn your mind entirely toward the question.

Next, take a deep breath in and close your eyes. As you breathe out open the book to a painting. Put your power hand on the painting. Now open your eyes. What is the page number your hand is on? What images do you see and how do they relate to the prosperity question you asked? Look into the patterns of the painting. What do the colors, shapes, and images suggest to you about your future in terms of prosperity? Do this two more times, for a total of three times. Make a note in your empowerment journal of the three paintings and their artists as well as the page numbers you turned to in the book. Also note any helpful images that may provide clues to answer the question at hand.

Chapter Six

The Sixth Empowering Step:
Focusing on Your Path to
Empowerment

Every spring my family and I gather the seeds we want to plant for the season and bless them before we plant them in our garden. Last spring we blessed our hollyhock seeds with prayers that they would grow healthy and tall and have beautiful flowers. We planted the seeds in pots, and once they sprouted and the plants had started growing, we transplanted them along a garden wall in the backyard. We planted three hollyhocks just outside the back door so we would see them as soon as we came out the door. As we transplanted them, we again said a prayer that the plants would flourish.

This spring we were greeted by hollyhock plants that grew over eight feet tall with beautiful dark leaves that were healthy and vibrant. The giant buds on the plants started blossoming in florescent colors of white, pink, and purple. I was so awed by the splendor of the hollyhocks that I took pictures of the flowers, had the pictures enlarged, and hung them on my flower wall in the house. They remind me of what is possible, especially when we take the time and make the effort to bless the things in our lives with prayer.

In order for your garden to grow, you need to ready the space, plan ahead, select the seeds, and plant them. In terms of empowerment, your goals are your seeds. You fashion your goals and give them their appearance or seed coat. You nurture your goals as you do a seed embryo, and you feed your goals with your thoughts, actions, and efforts, just as a seed is fed with a supply of stored food within its coat. Like all seeds, your goals will grow stronger when you bless them with prayer.

The Seeds of Tradition

In terms of who you are, your seeds came directly from your biological parents and other immediate ancestors. Your parents and ancestors account for your DNA structure, which at least initially determines your basic physical makeup. Beyond that, your parents and the people who raise and influence you account for your socialization. They plant the seeds that grow into your belief system, attitudes toward the world, and your overall patterns of behavior. Because of this, people in therapy usually have to first work out any parental issues.

It may be that you are also a parent, meaning that you are taking the seeds that were given to you by your parents or caretakers and passing them along to your own children. In this sense, you are a conduit who is both affected by and affects the whole process of seed transmission from one generation to another.

Fortunately, most of us realize that we can choose to alter the course of some of our socialization patterns, and we go on to raise our children more in the manner we would have wanted to be raised. The idea with parenthood is to carry on the traditions and methods that work and improve the ones that don't by applying personal creativity and know-how. New Age Wicca stems directly from this concept.

For centuries, the art and craft of spiritual traditions, such as the Celtic and Egyptian traditions, were only kept alive because the seeds of knowledge were passed down through the generations—mothers teachings their daughters, fathers teaching their sons, and shamans teaching their apprentices.

Seeds create, and through rebirth, sustain traditions and knowledge over time. Applying this metaphor to empowerment goals, you grow up experiencing the goals of your parents, which you then modify so they work for you. You plant them and make them happen in your own life. For example, one of the traditional goals of people in the United States is to have a better life economically and educationally than their parents experienced. This was especially true after the mass emigration to this country by people looking for a better life and a new start, as well as after the Great Depression, when people naturally wished for something better.

As you progress in your empowerment process, it is important that you be aware of the seeds you are planting. In a metaphysical sense, your thoughts and actions are star seeds that spawn a multitude of reactions or constellations of energies, triggered by the initial thought or action. In terms of planting, strong, fine strains of seeds have a much better chance of growing into nice healthy plants, and it works the same way in your life. Positive actions and goals affect the patterns around you in positive ways, making for nice healthy empowerment plans that move toward fruition. Because of this, it's important to make every effort to be aware of the effects of your goals, actions, and plans in terms of the whole of your life and the whole of Oneness.

Planting Your Goals

Dr. Larry Dossey has devoted much of his professional life to showing that prayers have a positive effect on life that can be measured by scientific methods. In his book *Recovering the Soul: A Scientific and Spiritual Search*, he cites some of the more interesting experiments on the positive effects of prayer. One example is about the Spindrift organization that was set up to conduct scientific experiments in prayer. Originally, they were certified Christian Science practitioners who were later expelled for publishing their findings. In particular, the Spindrift experiments used rye and bean seeds as a means for observing the power of prayer. The assumption they went in with was that all humans are connected to the divine and as such have a universal Oneness with God.

The experiments of Spindrift on seeds produced results that proved the power of prayer influences life and in turn goals. Their findings showed that the prayed-for seeds grew faster and healthier, even when a salt solution was introduced to slow their development. They also found that more prayer resulted in a greater effect, practicing prayer helped, and invoking the divine also increased the results, sometimes twice as much. They concluded at the time that the effect was due to our ability to connect with the source of all life and energy.

New Age Wicca is a little more direct about connecting with the divine. We use this connection to empower all magic. Wiccan prayer is a process that is intended, expected, and directed to bring about physical results. Either way, it is your connection with the divine that matters and produces the greatest effect in your blessings and prayers. This is why you need to strengthen your connection with both your goals and the divine on a daily basis. The more you do it, the more comfortable you will feel doing it, and the more energy you can gather and direct toward your overall empowerment.

Dancing the Steps

The classic movies of Fred Astaire and Ginger Rogers have the distinction of being filled with beautifully choreographed dance sequences. The movements of the dancers look incredibly fluid, and they are completely in tune with each other. Much like your empowerment plans, dance routines are made up of a sequence of planned steps. You may not be able to make those steps look as effortless and artistic as Fred and Ginger, but you can certainly dance the dance, taking each step one at a time according to your personal pace and intention.

To put a little magic in your steps toward manifesting your goals, you need to truly believe in your abilities and learn to be at one with the experience, to be fluid like Fred and Ginger. There can be no negative internal dialogue disrupting your focus. When you stay focused, you build momentum, which is the positive energy that you have accumulated from your connection with the divine and the success of your goals. Often, they are one and the same.

What you need to do now is plant your goals. If the first step in buying your dream home is saving for the down payment, then you need to start doing that. Basically every goal, like every dance routine, has steps that you follow in order to manifest the desired result. Empowerment, like New Age Wicca, is based on the patterns of life. Each aspect is a reflection of every other aspect and in turn the whole.

Sometimes it is productive to set up a reward program so that you feel you're getting an immediate and physical reward for each step that you successfully take toward attaining your goals. This technique can be especially effective with long-term goals that require patience because you must wait for the beneficial outcome. Because of this, giving yourself positive rewards for taking the steps in your empowerment plans can be a great way to both give yourself positive reinforcement that you have made progress toward your goals, and also as a motivation for taking the next step in your empowerment plan.

When giving yourself rewards, be sure the reward doesn't negate the progress of your step. If you are rewarding yourself for staying on a healthy diet, the reward should not be splurging on something sweet and decadent, but more along the lines of buying a CD you've been wanting, going to a movie you've been thinking about seeing, or spending some time doing something you really enjoy, such as going to the beach. These are positive rewards that can help make you a more loving, healthy, happy, and empowered person.

The reinforcement of positive patterns is also a primary power behind meditations, affirmations, prayers, sacred spaces, rituals, and oracles. They are all ways for helping you make productive changes in your life. By taking the empowering steps you have planned, you move forward, and in the process, enrich your life.

Love

Cathy's first marriage ended in divorce, leaving it up to her to support both herself and her two-year-old son, Jake. Except for Jake, whom she adored, the experience left her feeling cautious about love and relationships, just like someone leery of bees after having been stung. Not only had her husband left her for another woman, but he also continued to harass her and make her feel disempowered and unsure about her worthiness as a human being.

When Cathy first saw the brochure from the travel agency advertising a Mediterranean cruise, she became excited at the prospect of finding someone new to love in an exotic new setting, but the possibility of finding another jerk made her cringe. So she stuck the brochure in her desk until the next time she happened upon it.

After repeatedly taking the brochure out and putting it away again, Cathy finally relented and signed up for the cruise, realizing that the only way she was going to get anywhere in terms of love was to start planting seeds. Going on this cruise was one of those seeds.

Starting out, she was nervous, but on the second night out of port, she met someone who turned out to be the man of her dreams. He was a hard-working dentist and a caring man who loved children. It wasn't easy, but she began to lose her distrust of love and relationships. After the cruise, they continued to see one another, eventually married after a short engagement, and now have a large, happy family.

Sometimes you have to be willing to take chances and move beyond your personal impressions of life in order to move forward. Planting seeds is one of the ways you can connect with the future and progress through your life, especially when it comes to love.

The Sixth Empowering Step: Love Meditation

First, turn on some soft instrumental music that evokes feelings of love and harmony within you. Then sit back or recline comfortably. Breathe in deeply to the rhythm of the music, still your breath, and then exhale completely.

Continue breathing to the soft music, relaxing more and more, feeling peaceful and calm.

Slowly close your eyes, and as you continue to breathe in and out, imagine breathing in pure white light, and breathing out any tensions or stress you may be feeling. Do this for a few minutes, until you feel filled with white light.

Now in your mind's eye, imagine being on a tropical beach. You watch as the ocean waves roll into shore, again and again. You can smell the salty sea air, and the bright sun warms your skin as you walk along the sandy shoreline hand-in-hand with your lover.

As you walk along, your body, mind, and soul are enveloped by euphoric sensations of love. Divine love cascades from you to your lover and back to you, completing an energetic circle that makes both of you feel at one with each other. As you continue walking down the sandy beach, you sense that for the moment you don't have a care in world. All that matters is the love between you and your beloved.

You come to a place along the beach where large boulders prevent you from going any farther. You notice a path to the left of the boulders. The path leads away from the ocean into the trees and lush vegetation. You and your beloved follow the path and quickly come to a round clearing in the surrounding jungle. From the moment you see it, you know there is something magical about it.

Once inside the clearing, you realize that it is a garden of some kind. On one side is a stone altar. As you and your lover approach the altar, you see that it is covered with numerous seed pods. On the right side of the altar, these words are carved into the stone:

This is the garden of wishes,
And these pods are the seeds of love,
Plant and bless them in the soil of this garden,
And all of your loving wishes will come to fruition.

Now imagine taking one of the pods from the altar. You and your beloved cup the seeds from the pod gently in your hands, and together you bless them with the love of the Goddess and God. Then you plant them in the garden. A warm rain suddenly begins to fall, and before your eyes, the seeds you planted sprout and begin growing into a magnificent natural staircase that continues growing until it reaches far up into the sky.

You take a deep and complete breath as you and your beloved begin ascending the magical stairway, moving upward step-by-step. With each step, you sense a feeling of empowerment that propels you to the next step. At the end of the first progression of steps into the heavens, you come to a brilliant star, and one of your love wishes comes true. You continue moving up the stairs, establishing a stronger rapport with your beloved. Each time you reach another star, another love wish comes true, until you realize that you have everything you could possibly desire.

Now take another deep and complete breath and delight in knowing that you have planted the seeds that can help your love wishes come true. Drink in this feeling of confidence and empowerment as you take in another deep and complete breath, feeling refreshed and revitalized.

Next, take another breath and move your awareness back to your physical body. Inhale deeply and feel your lungs expanding, and then exhale, becoming aware of your surroundings. Slowly open your eyes and rub your hands together a few times. Stretch your muscles and move around for a few moments.

While the meditation is still fresh in your mind, write down the date and any observations and feelings you experienced in your empowerment journal. For example, how did it feel to climb the natural stairway to the heavens? What did it feel like when your love wishes came true? Which part of the meditation did you most enjoy? In what ways did the meditation empower you?

Love Affirmation and Prayer

Like seeds, your love empowerment goals need to be nurtured and affirmed on a daily basis. Use this affirmation to stay on your love empowerment path:

Today, and every day, I focus on my path to empowerment by taking another step toward manifesting my love goals.

Say this prayer every morning for a month, or more, to request divine guidance:

Dear Mother Goddess and Father God
Of earth, air, fire, water, and spirit
I pray you, please guide me on my path to love empowerment
Shine your divine light so that I will know the way
Help me to take one loving and empowering step each day
I ask this in the Lady and Lord's name, blessed be!

Sacred Love Space

Add a package of daffodil bulbs to your sacred love space. (Daffodils are one of the first signs of spring and represent new beginnings.) Bless and empower them by saying:

Divine Mother and Father, please bless these bulbs with your divine love and light.

Also put either fresh or silk daffodils on your sacred love altar.

Love Ritual

In addition to the package of daffodil bulbs on your sacred love space, you will need a pot filled with potting soil for this ritual. The pot must be big enough to easily fit your daffodil bulbs so that they have room to grow.

Begin the ritual by drawing a magic circle of light and empowering the elements. Next scoop a handful of dirt out of the pot with your hands and hold it carefully as you ask for the blessings of a mother or earth Goddess (such as Gaea, Danu, or Innana) by saying:

Oh Great Mother Goddess,
Divine and loving Lady
Bless this earth,
So that it will be fertile.

Afterward, put the dirt back into the pot and take the daffodil bulbs out of their package. Now cup one of the bulbs between your hands and ask for the blessings of a goddess (such as Demeter, Bridget, or Coventina) by saying:

Oh Great Goddess of creation,
Bless this seed I hold in my hands,
So that it may grow strong and thrive,
With the light of your love.

Do this with each bulb until they all have been blessed with the loving light of the Goddess. Next, use your fingers to create a hole in the soil for each bulb. The hole needs to be about one inch larger than the bulb itself. Place each bulb in a hole and cover all of them with soil. After you are done planting and covering the bulbs, place your hands upon the surface of the soil. Take a deep and complete breath to center your mind, and then merge with the divine Goddess and say:

Divine Mother Goddess, as below, so above
These bulbs represent the seeds of love
As they blossom, so too do my love goals
I ask with my body, mind, and soul
Please bless these seeds with your divine power
And help them grow and bloom and flower.

Finish by thanking the Goddess, bidding farewell to the elements, and pulling up the circle.

Now take the pot outside and place it where you can easily see it from your bedroom window if you are doing this ritual during the spring. During cold weather, put the pot in a sunny window. At regular intervals, place your hands just above the surface of the pot and say an affirmation or prayer for the daffodils to flourish in the pot.

In time, the bulbs will sprout and flower in colors of white and yellow. After the bulbs bloom the first year in the pot, transplant them into your garden or yard. Each year their blossoms will serve as a reminder that your empowerment goals of love are renewed with the advent of spring. These lovely flowers will multiply every year, bringing more love and beauty into your life. Life and death are important influences, along with renewal. Like the tides, you move inward, you move outward, and then inward once again. In terms of New Age Wicca, it is life, death, and renewal, emulating the cycle and relationship of the Goddess and God.

When the first daffodil blossom appears, place your hands just above the surface of the flower and say:

First blossom of the year,
Empower me with your gift of love,
In the name of the Lady and Lord
So be it! Blessed be!

Oracle of Love

Since the beginning of time, numbers have been viewed as sacred symbols with mystic significance. Each number has a signature energy and traditional meaning. For this oracle, you will be using the power of seeds, plus the power of numbers to discover the answer to a question regarding your love empowerment path.

Begin by washing and drying an apple. Now take a deep breath in and out to center yourself. Next, hold the apple between your hands, merge with Oneness, and say:

I empower this apple as a naturally divine oracle.

Now pick one pressing question you have regarding your love empowerment path. Slowly eat the apple. As you do, turn your mind completely toward your question. Next, collect the seeds from the apple core and count them. Round off the number to the simplest number. For example, if you find 10 seeds, add 1 + 0 = 1. The oracle number is 1. If you find 14 seeds, add 1 + 4 = 5. The oracle number is 5. The two exceptions to this are if you find 11 or 22 seeds. You would then use the whole number, 11 or 22, because these are considered especially magical numbers.

Now match the number of seeds you find in the apple to the number in the following table to discover the meaning of the apple seed oracle. Record the date, love question, number of seeds, and the meaning of the number in your empowerment journal. Also, for the next week, keep an eye out for the same number appearing in your daily life—during work, while watching television, driving, reading, in conversations, and so forth. Notice its influence in your life.

Number	Meaning
1	Oneness, leadership, ambition, courage, independence, achievement, action, individuality, beginnings, initiation, creativity
2	Partnership, balance of polarities, the marriage of two elements into one, blending elements together, intuition, sensitivity to others
3	Unity of body, mind, and soul, the trinity of divinity, divine power, communication, flexibility, harmony, expansion, expression, optimism
4	Stability, loyalty, practical thinking, building foundations, the four elements, the four directions, the four seasons, construction, productivity, capability, organization
5	Freedom, adventure, travel, expansion, curiosity, change, magical power, resourcefulness
6	Imagination, intelligence, family matters and children, relationships, responsibility, love, compassion, beauty, the arts
7	Spiritual wisdom, the seven colors of the rainbow, the seven days of the week, the seven chakras, birth and rebirth, good luck, contemplation, meditation
8	Organization, practical application, business, success, reward, prosperity, the number of infinity
9	Compassion, understanding, tolerance, creativity, the arts, humility, modesty, completion, knowledge, humanitarianism
11	Insight, intuition, inspiration, joy, telepathy, spiritual healing, psychic abilities
22	Completion, perfection, visionary abilities, unlimited potential, personal mastery

Health

When the doctor told him he had a possibly cancerous tumor, George made an agreement with himself that if the surgery was successful, it would be a sign for him to move his family out of the city and begin a new way of life by putting health before wealth. The doctor gave him a 50/50 chance of survival as he went under the knife. George woke up after the surgery fully recovered and proceeded to move forward with his plan.

The disease and surgery helped George better understand what and who in his life empowered him. The experience provided a seed that after the surgery, George was determined to plant and help grow. He moved his family and business to the country where he felt it would be more healthy overall. He bought a place about 15 minutes commuting distance from town—five acres complete with horses, chickens, a swimming pool, and a garden that every summer grows bigger and bigger tomatoes.

The changes George made in his life have definitely empowered him. The cancer has not returned after 15 years, and he and his family have found a sense of belonging in the country and small town that had been missing in their lives in the big city. He no longer has to have metal bars on his windows and doors to feel secure. He and his family are free to walk down the country lane of their home any time of the day or night.

When you are faced with something that seems hopeless, make every effort to stick with it and keep hoping. Events, situations, and opportunities are forever changing from one state of being to the next (technologies demonstrate this on a daily basis). What seems hopeless one day seems achievable the next as you start to make a few changes. Continue believing in yourself and your empowerment goals through the thick and thin of it.

In terms of health, you can use change as an empowerment tool for personal transformation. Most likely you know what thoughts, actions (or lack of action), and eating habits you need to change to be healthier. Remember, take one step at a time down your path to health empowerment. By doing so, it becomes easier to take the next step, and the next, until you manifest your health empowerment goals.

The Sixth Empowering Step: Healing Meditation

Sit back in a comfortable place, close your eyes, and begin to relax by taking a deep breath. As you exhale, let all the stress and tension flow out of your body. Take two more deep breaths, each time sensing your body being cleansed of all negativity and unwanted energies. Continue breathing slowly and completely, relaxing more and more with each breath you take.

Now in your mind's eye, imagine moving slowly back in time, watching the events of your life as they move in reverse. You keep flowing backward to a week ago, a month ago, a year ago. You move back through the years to when you were a child; and then to when you were a baby. Now go to your moment of birth and be there for moment before you pass through an energetic doorway.

You sense that you are floating through the boundlessness, where time and space become one. All around you are other beings also floating in the boundlessness. This is a gathering place where energy beings wait to be blessed by the light before being born into a physical body.

Now move your awareness forward in time. You realize that the time has come to become you. Imagine floating into a circle of brilliant light that energizes and empowers you from every direction. The light emanates from the divine beings who form the circle all around you, and through their blessings you sense your spirit being reawakened and rekindled with the desire for life.

In this energetic state, just before you step into your physical body, you are in harmony with everything around you and at one with the divine. In this state you are divinely empowered and given a template for optimum health—a template that is always there for you to connect with and use to promote a healthier you. Now give yourself the suggestion to remember the template of divine light when you return from the meditation.

Now take a deep breath in and out, slowly move your awareness from the divine circle of light, and step into your present self. Carry the empowering light with you as you become you. Take another deep and complete breath and begin to stretch your muscles, becoming aware of your body. Take a third breath in and out and slowly open your eyes.

When you are fully present, write your impressions of the meditation in your empowerment journal. Also write down a brief description of the template of divine light, as well as the sensations and insights you experienced in the circle.

Healing Affirmation and Prayer

Write this affirmation on a white index card and put it on your refrigerator. Before you open the refrigerator, repeat the affirmation aloud:

Every moment of every day, I focus on my path to empowerment by thinking positive thoughts, doing positive actions, and eating healthy foods.

Staying on the path to better health takes effort and resolve. The rewards are well worth it, so use all your resources to remain focused. Say this prayer when you need some divine help to stay on your path:

Dear Goddess, I pray you
Help me stay on the path
To healing and better health
Strengthen my will and spirit
So that I make healthier choices
Today and every day of the year
Thank you Great Goddess
Blessed be!

Sacred Healing Space

Add a packet of hollyhock seeds to your sacred healing altar. Hollyhocks (Holy Mallow) are a biennial herb of the mallow family, originally cultivated in Europe for their nutritional and medicinal value. Each morning for three consecutive days before you use the seeds in the healing ritual, hold the package in your hands and bless the seeds by merging with the divine and saying:

Dear Mother Goddess and Father God
Dear helpful spirits of earth, air, fire, and water
Please bless these seeds with your powers
And fill them with divine love and life.

Healing Ritual

You can use the power of hollyhocks to renew your health. You can do this ritual any time of year. If you do it in the spring, you will have to wait until the next spring to get blossoms. If you do it in the summer or fall, you will have flowers the following spring. In addition to the hollyhock seeds from your sacred space, you will need a very large pot of soil, big enough to accommodate at least one hollyhock plant, which grows to the height of a person.

Begin by drawing your magic circle of light and empowering the elements. Next, bless the soil by placing your hands one inch above the soil and saying:

Great Goddess, bless this earth,
As you bless every part of yourself,
With the magnificence of life,
And the florescence of health.
So be it! Blessed be!

Next, carefully take the seeds out of the package and cup them in your left hand with your right hand flattened just above them. Take a deep breath in and out to center yourself and turn your mind toward thoughts of health and vitality, such as a row of hollyhocks gloriously in full bloom in your backyard. Say:

Mother Goddess of creation,
Please bless these seeds,
So that they may grow healthy and tall,
In the Lady's name, blessed be!

Plant the seeds in the pot according to the package directions. Poke several holes into the soil, and drop three seeds into each hole. Cover the holes carefully with soil.

Now fill a container with warm water. Hold the container between your hands and bless it by saying:

Mother Goddess of life,
Please bless this water,
With your divine powers.

Sprinkle the water over the seeds while focusing on images of emergence and vitality. Feel yourself breathing the breath of life into the seeds as the water seeps into the soil.

When you are done, thank the deity, bid farewell to the elements, and pull up the circle. Take the pot with the planted seeds and put it outside. It needs to go through the seasons in order to become empowered.

I started my hollyhocks in a pot and then transplanted them outside along a retaining wall where they could grow high. Depending on your situation, you can plant them in your garden, yard, or leave them in the large pot on a balcony or patio.

Oracle of Health

Simple oracles such as seed oracles can help you better navigate on your path to empowerment. Begin by taking a deep breath in and out to center yourself. Then hold an orange between your hands, merge with Oneness, and say:

I empower this orange as a naturally divine oracle.

Now select a question regarding your health empowerment path. Slowly peel the orange, eat it, and collect the pits. As you do, turn your mind completely toward your question. Next, count the orange pits. Add the number of pits like you did the apple seeds earlier in this chapter. Come up with the simplest number, with the exceptions being 11 and 22. Match the number of orange pits to the number listed in the earlier table to discover the meaning of the oracle.

When you are done, record the date, health question, number of pits, and the meaning of the number in your empowerment journal. Also keep an eye out for that particular number showing up during work, while you're watching television, driving, reading, in conversations, and so forth, for the next few days.

Prosperity

John Chapman, better known as Johnny Appleseed, traced his lineage back six generations to Edward Chapman, who originally came to Boston from Yorkshire, England, in the 1640s. The Chapman family had almost always made a living by growing things, and they had become quite prosperous from it.

John shared a love for growing things with his ancestors, and as he moved with the wave of people that were starting to spread westward across the United States, he found himself in Ohio, planting apple trees everywhere he went. This is why people started calling him Johnny Appleseed.

Johnny was constantly gathering seeds and making places for them to sprout and grow. He created planting beds using four logs as a makeshift raised box, placing mulch in the bed, and then planting the seeds. He would also make every effort to return when the trees started to grow, trimming and caring for them.

Johnny Appleseed became renowned for his love of nature and his belief in the divine. He was personally responsible for the spreading of particular varieties of apple trees throughout the northeastern parts of the United States. Some varieties stem from the original apple trees planted in this country.

In addition to planting and caring for the trees himself, Johnny Appleseed was also known to give seeds and young trees in pots to people, who then planted them in their own gardens. In exchange, he would take anything the person had to offer, including food, articles of clothing, or just about anything else. This idea of bartering was prevalent throughout the frontier at that time.

The idea of the gift is important in terms of seeds and prosperity because it denotes not only a physical exchange but also an energetic exchange with spiritual implications. A gift requires a gift in exchange. Seeds and life itself are gifts from the divine, which is why it is always important to thank the divine whenever you pray, say blessings, and perform rituals.

One of the findings of the Spindrift Organization in its studies on prayers demonstrated that prayers asking for divine help had a more powerful effect on the seeds and plants receiving the prayer, more than the seeds and plants that received no prayers and the ones receiving prayers where divine assistance was not requested. This shows a definite connection between the divine and your mind. You can use this connection to help you stay focused on your prosperity empowerment goals, to live a more joyful and abundant life, and to "phone home" through prayer in those times of personal need.

The Sixth Empowering Step: Prosperity Meditation

Begin by sitting back in a comfortable place, closing your eyes, and getting relaxed. Take a deep breath so that your lungs stretch and fill up with air like a balloon, and then exhale while feeling all the muscles in your body relaxing. Take another deep breath in and out and let go of all the tensions you may be feeling for a few minutes while you meditate. Take a few more deep breaths, each time feeling the muscles of your body becoming more and more relaxed.

As you become more deeply relaxed, you feel as though you are merging into the surface beneath you and with the air and light surrounding you.

Sense yourself becoming more fluid and light-filled as you continue to merge with everything around you until you reach a point where you imagine yourself as liquid light, flowing along streams that criss-cross and connect like a magnificent spider's web. The light streams move across the folds of time and space, which means in an instant you can be anywhere you want to be.

Now imagine flowing along the streams. You move across solar systems, universes, and through galaxies billions of light years away. You are divinely guided to a galaxy that has a solar system with 13 planets that orbit dual suns. You follow the stream that leads you to the fifth planet from the second sun, a planet that seems devoid of life.

In your mind's eye, imagine flowing along a light stream to the surface of the planet, splashing down in a pool of warm liquid light. You sense yourself changing shape and gradually becoming solid matter again. You take the shape of a seed with a coat that is hard on the outside, but inside you hold the embryo and food supply to sprout new life.

Now you sense yourself being carried on a breeze over the land until you reach a place where the soil seems abundantly fertile. Soon after you arrive and the breeze sets you upon the ground, you feel a light, warm rain begin to fall. You can feel the embryo inside of you coming to life, feeding off the stored light supply within the seed, and beginning to shoot to the surface and sprout.

Your tap root moves down into the soil and from it all your other roots emerge, giving you a strong base from which to grow. Now, your stem moves upward toward the light of the suns. From your stem, you send out branches that are soon adorned with an enormous number of leaves that act as solar collectors, filling your being full of warm, nurturing light. You sense yourself coming into florescence as beautiful flowers in all colors of the rainbow emerge from your branches.

As the flowers begin to fade, they are replaced by a seemingly infinite number of seeds. Again you feel the breeze as it comes to blow the seeds from your branches, spreading them everywhere across the once barren planet. Again the warm rain sprinkles down, and you watch as your seeds bring the entire planet to life. You sense a wave of satisfaction and joy move over you. You are the ultimate source of prosperity as you helped to create life itself.

You bring this sensation back with you as you enter the present time and place. Take a deep breath in, filling yourself with liquid light, and breathe out light. Gradually turn your awareness toward your surroundings as you take another deep breath, and begin stretching your muscles as you continue to move back into your body. With the third deep breath, slowly open your eyes, an then rub your hands briskly together.

When you are finished meditating, write your impressions down in your empowerment journal. What did it feel like to be liquid light? How did it feel to become the ultimate source of prosperity as you helped to create life on the planet?

Prosperity Affirmation and Prayer

Repeat this affirming statement several times a day for 28 days to keep you focused on your empowering path to prosperity:

Every moment of every day, I focus on my path to prosperity empowerment and draw divine riches into my life along the way.

Say this prayer whenever you need divine guidance, blessings, and protection to help you remain focused on your path to prosperity:

Mother Goddess and Father God
Please guide, bless, and protect me
On my empowering path to prosperity
Help me to stay focused and centered
Thank you divine friends, blessed be!

Sacred Riches Space

Add a packet of sunflower seeds (to plant, not eat) to your sacred riches altar. For three mornings before using them in the prosperity ritual, empower the seeds by holding them in your hands, merging with the divine, and saying three times:

Bless these sunflower seeds
With divine abundance and success.
By the Goddess, blessed be!

Also add a bowl or bag of raw or roasted sunflower seeds to use for the oracle of wealth. Empower them by holding them in your hands and saying:

Dear Goddess and God, please bless these seeds
With divine abundance and prosperity.

Prosperity Ritual

In addition to the package of sunflower seeds from your sacred riches space, you will need a pot filled with fertile soil and large enough to accommodate the sunflowers. (Use composted soil or potting soil with worm castings in it for best results.)

Begin by drawing a magic circle of light and empowering the elements. Now place both your hands over the pot of soil. Merge with the Goddess and bless the soil by saying:

Mother of all creation,
Please impart your blessings to this earth,
Grant it the divine power to grow life,
Let it be the medium to give birth.

Next, take the sunflower seeds from their package and bless them by cupping the seeds carefully between your palms and saying:

Goddess of flowers and nature
Lady of the guiding light
Please bless these seeds
With the divine power of the sun
Empower them so they may be born again
So be it! Blessed be!

Now make a hole in the soil with your finger, place a sunflower seed in the hole, and cover the seed with soil. As you are planting each seed, keep imagining the seed sprouting, growing strong, and flowering with large and brilliant golden sunflowers. Plant as many seeds as you feel the pot can handle without crowding the plants.

Next, fill a container with fresh warm water, and as you sprinkle it over your newly planted seeds, say the following:

Goddess of creation,
Please let your divine waters
Give these seeds the gift of life
So that they may grow abundant.

When you are done, thank the Goddess, bid farewell to the elements, and pull up the circle. Put the pot in a sunny location and bless and water the seeds regularly. If the season and weather permit, you can transplant them to a sunny location outdoors. Nurture your sunflowers as they grow and progress through the stages of their development from sprout to leafy plant, to flower, and finally back to seed again. Once the flowers have finished blooming, they will wilt away and eventually produce seeds in their centers. Collect the seeds and store them in a cool dry place until the next planting time. Both when collecting and replanting the seeds, be sure to thank the Goddess for her gift of abundance and prosperity.

Oracle of Wealth

You will need the bowl or bag of roasted or raw sunflower seeds from your sacred riches altar for this oracle. Begin by taking a deep breath to center yourself. Hold the bowl or bag of sunflower seeds in your hands and empower it as an oracle by saying:

I empower these seeds as a divine oracle.

Now turn your mind completely toward a question regarding your path to prosperity. With your question in mind, put your hand into the bowl or bag and pull out a handful of seeds. Count the seeds. Add the number up to the simplest number like you did with apple seeds and orange pits, with the exceptions being 11 and 22. Then match the number to the number list earlier in this chapter to discover the meaning of the oracle. In your empowerment journal, record the date, prosperity question, number of seeds, and the meaning of the number. Also keep an eye out for the same number appearing in your daily activities for the next few days and notice its influence.

Chapter Seven

The Seventh Empowering Step: Building Empowering Relationships

Now that you have planted your goals and they have started growing, it's time to care for and nurture them so they will continue to grow stronger. The Seventh Empowering Step, building empowering relationships, is an important part of this process.

When we are young, relationships are often simpler, more easy going, and filled with fun and laughter. We freely share confidences, thoughts, and feelings without fear of recrimination. As we grow older, relationships become more complex and are often built primarily on the idea of mutual use, such as our relationships at work.

No person can exist completely independent of all others. We all help each other to achieve both our individual and group goals. Collective groups, known as boundary groups—families, clubs, streets, towns, and countries—are examples of groups where people relate to one another.

When you relate to another person, you create a relationship. This relationship can be brief or long, positive or negative. You have a relationship with your family, with your co-workers, with your community, and with your country. You express these relationships in any number of ways, such as eating together, working and playing together, helping each other in times of crisis, worshiping as a group, and voting, to name a few.

The whole idea of building empowering relationships is to strengthen your connection with yourself and other people, as well as build your rapport with the divine. The best relationships are loving, healthy, and beneficial to everyone involved. These are the kinds of relationships that will empower and sustain you as you work toward manifesting your goals.

Transforming Relationships

A few years ago, I found myself looking for practical ways to reduce my levels of stress and anxiety. Things were constantly going from bad to worse, and nothing seemed to be getting any better. Finally, after much soul searching, I decided to make some long overdue personal and professional changes.

First, I distanced myself from those people who were constantly disempowering me. These were the folks who kept telling me that I couldn't make a living writing books at home, couldn't live in the country, couldn't be a vegetarian, couldn't homeschool my son, and couldn't really be interested in God, Goddess, the New Age, or Wicca. Not for one moment did I go along with their nonsense, but at the same time, I was having to use a lot of energy shielding myself from their negativity. I knew it was time to positively transform these relationships.

Because some of the disempowering folks were relatives and old friends, I didn't want to cut them completely out of my life. What I did was to shape my daily life in such a way that those disempowering people had much less influence and impact. Most importantly, I stopped seeing them as much. Instead, I kept in touch by phone, e-mail, and short notes. I let them know I cared, but I didn't let them blow holes in my goals.

Then I worked on creating some new empowering relationships by finding people with common interests. I took a series of vegetarian cooking classes being offered at a local health food store. I also began getting involved in the local Audubon and gardening clubs. From these activities,

I have met several like-minded people who are empowering and fun to be with. In turn I feel uplifted by these associations rather than drained.

I also let go of the working relationships and jobs that were draining my time and finances. I took a few days to meditate and rethink my writing career and business dealings. I decided to work smarter, not harder, and began applying the 80/20 rule to my work and working relationships. First I identified the 20 percent of things in my life that provide me with 80 percent of my income and enjoyment. Then I deliberately started doing those 20 percent of things, 80 percent of the time. This helped me get rid of the unrewarding jobs, relationships, problems, and trivia. As a result, my workload was much lighter, and I was able to spend more quality time crafting my writing. My finances also greatly improved by applying the 80/20 rule. Accordingly, my anxiety and stress were significantly reduced.

Creating Empowering Relationships

Relationships by their very nature imply a mutual exchange of energy that can simultaneously exist on many levels. In disempowering relationships, the exchange drains you. It feels as if your energy is being sucked right out of you. In contrast, both parties mutually benefit in an empowering relationship. Both are fortified by the positive exchange of regard and energy. This mutually positive energy that each participant receives from the relationship is what makes it empowering.

The exchange of energy that happens in a relationship must be positive in order to be empowering. The people you choose to surround yourself with need to have a positive influence in your life. They should help you to realize your empowerment goals rather than obstruct you from them. To this end, some people are nice to be around, but when you are around them, you never get anything done. When they leave, you feel yourself overwhelmed by a list of things to do. These types of people might be fun to share good times with now and again, but they may not be all that helpful in your quest to achieve your empowerment goals.

When building empowering relationships, make every effort to look toward people you think are successful and are doing what you want to do. Examine how they live their lives and conduct their affairs with reference to their relationships with other people. All people have things they do well, and you can learn from them by observing their actions, patterns, and basic techniques. Make sure your examples are people who are worthy of your admiration, those whose lifestyle and practices are ones you truly want to emulate and include in your life. Be selective! It's the quality of the relationship that's important here, not the quantity.

Two primary empowering relationships you need to cultivate are with yourself and the divine. To manifest your empowerment goals, you need to know who and what you are and believe in yourself and your abilities. This is the key to self-confidence, giving you an important edge toward making things happen according to your plans.

It's also essential to create a positive, empowering relationship between yourself and the divine power of creation. Gain rapport with divine energies and beings who are positive and will nurture your seeds of empowerment. Like a divine parent who is always lovingly present, divinity will guide you on the path to realizing your empowerment goals.

Love

The first time I saw Elsa, she seemed nervous and unsure of herself, particularly when around her husband, Bob, who was a traditional, old-school dominant male. Bob was focused on controlling everything in his life. He especially liked to intimidate everyone, including Elsa, by continually barking out commands like a marine drill sergeant. I felt sorry for her as she flitted about trying to please Bob, who, in return, seemed to enjoy disempowering her. That's basically what intimidation is all about—completely disempowering the other person.

About six months ago, I heard from a friend that Elsa had finally mustered enough courage to leave Bob and start a new life. Recently, I saw her at a local bookstore, and I was amazed at the changes. She looked brighter and was smiling. She was much more confident and at ease with herself. She attributed the change to her young son and her support group of a few close friends, who not only helped her through the hard times after her divorce, but also helped empower her sense of self-worth. She commented that who she had been before now seemed like another person.

You are a reflection of your relationships with the people around you— your beloved, your children, your parents, your siblings, your peer group, people at work, and even the supermarket checkout person. If the relationships are empowering, you are in turn empowered and uplifted. You are filled with positive power that will help you take on those daily challenges and effectively deal with them. This is why it's so important to surround yourself with people who empower you.

The Seventh Empowering Step: Love Meditation

Turn on some pleasing New Age or instrumental music such as classical or soft jazz. Sit or lay back comfortably and close your eyes. Slow your breath by taking a deep breath in, holding it for three heartbeats, and exhaling completely. As you exhale, feel the stress and tension in your muscles being released as you become more and more relaxed, yet peacefully aware. Breathe from your diaphragm as you take another deep breath in, lightly holding your breath for three heartbeats, and exhaling completely, letting go of any residual tension and worries you may have. Take another deep breath in, still your breath for three heartbeats, and then completely exhale. After the third breath, allow your breathing to go back to normal.

In your mind's eye, imagine walking along an earthen path that is lined with large white rocks. The path winds in and out through a forest of trees. The air is alive with the aroma of cedar, and because of the many layers of humus on the forest floor, the ground is soft and spongy. You can hear your footsteps softly thudding as you continue along the path.

As you reach the middle of the forest, you meet your beloved, who takes your hand. Together you continue down the path. Among the surrounding rocks lush ferns are growing, their long green fronds stretching out as if to greet you. The light under the canopy softly shimmers as you and your beloved continue walking hand-in-hand along the path.

You approach a giant redwood tree standing straight and tall in the middle of the magnificent cedars. The closer you walk toward the redwood, the bigger it seems to get, until you stand with your beloved before the tree in awe of its greatness. You both reach out to touch the tree trunk and stroke the rough texture of its bark. When you touch the tree, you sense an ancient energy, an energy that seemingly connects back to the original seeds of life.

As you continue to touch the tree, you sense in its roots a connection with history, tradition, and your past. In the trunk, you sense a centeredness and strength that acts as a foundation of everything else. The branches are like different paths and aspects of yourself as you continue to move up through the tree canopy. The leaves are things that people choose to dress up their lives, and the tree seeds are expressions of the beauty of creation, eventually providing the seeds for your offspring and your future.

While still in contact with the tree, your beloved's hand covers your hand, and you sense a loving connection with your past, present, and future. You also feel a loving connection with all the beings, mortal and divine, who are a beneficial part of your life. You sense the strong connection you have with your beloved, both within this lifetime and others. You sense the love that emanates from the very core of creation, spreading out like a giant tree across the infinite cosmos. You sense every cell in your body tingling with this love as you feel the warm caress of your beloved's hand holding yours. In this moment, you sense complete empowerment.

Now bring this blissful and loving image back with you as you begin returning to the present time and place. Take three deep breaths and begin stretching your muscles. Slowly open your eyes. Rub your palms briskly together for one minute. Now take a few minutes to write down your impressions during the meditation in your empowerment journal. In particular, note how you felt when you connected with the ancient energy of the redwood tree and your beloved. Also note any sensations of love and empowerment that you experienced while meditating.

Love Affirmation and Prayer

Affirm your empowering relationships by repeating these affirmations several times a day for at least 28 days. If you prefer, create your own empowering relationship affirmations by altering those I have provided to better suit your individual needs:

- Today and every day, I am creating and cultivating loving and empowering relationships that help me manifest my goals.
- Right now, I reaffirm my loving connection with Mother Earth and the empowering people I know that encourage and uplift me.
- Today, in every way, I feel divinely empowered by the positive and loving relationships in my life.

Use prayer to ask that divine love and peace flow into your relationships. For example, say this prayer every morning as you begin your day:

Dear Mother Goddess of perfect love
Dear Father God of perfect peace
I ask you, please hear my prayer
Help me to create empowering relationships
This blessed day and every day
So that I might know and share the divine power
Of perfect love and perfect peace
By the Lady and Lord, so be it!

Sacred Love Space

Add a green candle, a red candle, and amber-scented oil to your sacred love altar. Then put a few photographs of the people who most empower you in your sacred love space, such as your beloved and your children. If you like, add a few photographs of your most cherished pets as well. Also place an uplifting birthday or holiday card, a personal note, or a letter from someone you care for on your love altar. The photographs and cards serve as reminders of your empowering relationships. Now further empower the photographs, notes, cards, or letters by holding your palms over them and saying:

May these reminders of my empowering relationships
Fill me with love, light, and positive energy
By the loving power of the Goddess and God, so be it!

Love Ritual

Perform this ritual with your partner or a close friend to help you determine which relationships are empowering with regard to your love goals and plans. The ritual is based on the concept of muscle testing, which tracks your body's natural response to foods, situations, and people. You will use the green and red candles from your sacred love space, the amber oil, photographs, a pen, and a piece of paper.

Begin by drawing a magic circle of light and empowering the elements. Rub the candles with a thin film of amber oil and also anoint your wrists with a few drops of the oil. Wipe the oil from your hands and then light the green candle. Dedicate it to a favorite love goddess. Next, light the red candle and dedicate it to a favorite love god. After lighting both candles, place the photographs of your loved ones on the altar so the candlelight illuminates them. On the piece of paper, write the names of at least 10 people you know, including family and friends. Then take a few minutes to gaze at the candlelight and center your awareness. Merge with the light and say:

Goddess and God of love,
Please grant me divine wisdom
So that I might now know
Who empowers me. Blessed be!

Place the list of names where you can easily see it. Take a deep breath to center yourself. Then put your left palm just above your heart area (called the witness spot) while extending your right arm and hand outward in a straight line from your body. Now in your mind's eye, imagine the first person on your list of names. Fix this person in your mind. If you have a photograph of the person, focus your attention on it and ask your partner to push down on your extended arm. Most likely, your arm will remain firm and stationary. To test the process, fix your mind on someone who disempowers you, someone you don't like, and have your partner push down on your extended arm. You will find that your arm can easily be pushed down. Now go through the people you have written down on your list, one by one, and make a note of your response next to the name—whether your arm remains firm or is easily pushed down.

After you are finished going through the names on your list, thank the Goddess and God for their help, bid farewell to the elements, and close the circle. Allow the candles to safely burn down. Use the information you gained during the ritual to further your network of empowering people that can help you make your love goals a reality. Focus on those people on your list who empower you with positive energy and politely distance yourself from those that disempower you.

Oracle of Love

You will use dowsing rods for this oracle. Traditionally, dowsing rods are used to divine water, but they are also ideal for divining questions regarding your empowerment goals. You can purchase rods from Internet sites and New Age catalogs offering dowsing equipment, or you can make a pair. To do so, use two 17-inch pieces of thin copper wire (welding wire works best) and two 5-inch pieces of hollow copper tubing. You can find these items at most hardware stores. You can also use two wire coat hangers and two straws in a pinch.

First, bend the two wires into "L" shapes, with the main extended rod arm measuring twelve inches and the handle measuring five inches. Insert the five-inch handles into the copper tubing and bend the end of the wire to keep the handles in place. The rod arm should swing freely. If you are using straws and coat hangers, cut the straws to fit the handles and then insert the handles into the straws. Again, bend the ends of the handle wires to keep the straws in place.

Next, hold the handles of the rods waist high, one in each hand, with the rod arms straight out in front of you. Say:

May the Goddess and God bless these dowsing rods as divine oracles.

Take a deep breath to center your awareness. Focus on one specific yes-or-no question regarding your love empowerment goals, particularly about your empowering love relationships. State the question aloud three times and watch the rods. Do they swing outward or inward? If they swing outward, it indicates a positive response to your question. If they swing inward or cross, it indicates a negative response. For best results, ask no more than three questions each time you use this oracle. Make a note of your questions and the answers you receive in your empowerment journal for easy reference.

You can also use your dowsing rod oracle to check out new people. Just take a deep breath, hold the rods in your hands, and state the person's name three times aloud. Notice how the rods respond. It takes a little practice to learn how to work the rods properly, so be patient and have fun!

Health

Shortly after moving to a new town, Jane began experiencing sharp pains in the upper part of her stomach in conjunction with lower back spasms that were at times disabling. Not knowing anyone in town, she went to the local natural foods co-op, and after talking with one of the people working there, she obtained the number of a good massage therapist. After several sessions with the therapist, Jane's back pain began to ease. During one of the sessions, she mentioned the shooting pains in her upper stomach, and the therapist recommended an acupuncturist who had helped her friend with a similar problem. Having an aversion to needles, Jane was reluctant to take the recommendation, and only relented when faced with the idea that the needles couldn't be as bad as the shooting pain.

At the first visit, Jane was apprehensive as the acupuncturist inserted the fine, thin needles along her body's meridians, the physical pathways of energy. She was surprised that she barely felt the needles as they were inserted and twirled. Through a combination of treatments and herbs that the acupuncturist gave her, the shooting pains in Jane's stomach went away completely. In addition, the acupuncturist recommended a chiropractor, who was able to adjust the disk in Jane's lower back so that it felt better than it had in a long time.

Jane's story shows how one health empowering relationship can lead you to another health empowering relationship. Often like stepping stones, these relationships can help you to realize your empowerment goals for better health. When the need arises, it's important to have a network of health care practitioners whose healing abilities you trust. Ask healthy people who they recommend and do some research to check out the practitioner before making an appointment. This will make the process more effective and pleasant.

The Seventh Empowering Step: Healing Meditation

Turn on some soft healing music and sit or lay down in a comfortable place. Close your eyes and make sure your hands and feet are uncrossed so the energy can flow freely through your body. Also loosen or remove any clothing, jewelry, or shoes that may be binding you.

Begin by using your finger to close your right nostril. Breathe normally through your left nostril for a few minutes. This is called left nostril breathing and naturally helps reduce stress in your body, mind, and spirit. As you breathe in, imagine breathing in white light. As you breathe out, imagine your stress diminishing with your exhalation. Breathe in bright white light, and breathe out stress and any toxins in your body. As you breathe this way for a few minutes, imagine the parts of your body becoming more and more relaxed as they are filled with white light. Imagine breathing the healing white light into your toes and feet, up through your ankles, legs, and up your thighs, pelvis, and lower back.

Allow the healing white light to flow into and fill your stomach as you breathe in, and then imagine it flowing into your chest, upper back, neck, and finally to your face and the top of your head.

Now imagine the radiant white light energetically connecting all the parts of your body, filling them with healing energy. You sense a balance where each part complements the others, bringing a healthiness to the whole of your body.

You begin to sense the healing energy moving from your body to your mind. A wave of positive contentment moves across the various parts of your mind from your conscious to your subconscious. Imagine any feelings of anger, fear, or disappointment completely evaporating as the positive healing energy softly flows across the totality of your mind, which is now in a state of diffused focus, where your mind flows into the whole Oneness. Your mind feels healthy and in harmony with your body.

Next you sense the healing energy moving higher in your being to your spirit. Like a gentle breeze through the trees, it begins blowing over the many parts of your spirit from past lives to this life to future lives, filling them all with healing energy. Ancient, present, and future wounds heal in the breath of an instant as the breeze of healing energy continues moving through your spirit. Your spirit becomes one with the divine and, in the process, becomes immortal. Like the fabled phoenix, your spirit is reborn so that it may once again fly on the breeze. Your spirit now feels in healthy harmony, at one with your mind and body.

As you become one with your body, mind, and spirit, you also become aware of yourself as energy, and as such you become aware of aware of other energies around you. Imagine fine tuning your senses so that you continue to become more acutely aware of the energetic beings that are around you. Particularly become aware of the spirit guides and helpers around you. As energy, you can communicate with them and ask them questions. Sense an energetic light that streams between you and your guides and helpers, making a connection that seems to complete a circle of health that moves through every part of your being.

Bring this healthy sensation from the healing energy back with you as you begin returning to your body by taking three deep breaths and stretching your muscles. Open your eyes and clap your hands three times to return your awareness to the present time and place. Place your hands on the various parts of your body, for example, the top of your head, your heart area, and feet. As you touch your body, remember the state of well-being you experienced as the healing energy filled your body, mind, and spirit during the meditation.

Before doing anything else, write your impressions during the meditation in your empowerment journal, especially those about the healing link you sensed between your body, mind, and spirit. Also make a note of what it felt like to meet your spirit guides and helpers around you.

Healing Affirmation and Prayer

Say the following healing affirmation aloud several times a day for at least 28 days:

Each and every day, I am filled and empowered with the divine healing friendship of the Goddess and God.

Say the following prayer to draw more healing relationships to you:

Divine Lady and Lord,
Thank you for uplifting me.
Dear ones, I pray you
Please fill my life with empowering people
With kind and helpful friends
Each and every day and night
In the name of the Goddess and God,
Blessed be!

Sacred Healing Space

Add green and gold candles, a vial of lavender essential oil, and your magic wand to your sacred healing altar. Bless the items by holding them in your hands one at a time and saying three times:

By the power of the Goddess and God
Please bring healthy, empowering relationships to me
Blessed be, blessed be, blessed be!

Healing Ritual

Use this ritual to encourage healthy and empowering relationships in your life. Use the green and gold candles on your sacred healing altar, as well as the wand and lavender essential oil. Begin by drawing a magic circle of light and empowering the elements. Dress the candles with a thin film of lavender essential oil and then anoint yourself with the oil. Wipe the oil from your hands, light the green candle, and say:

Great Goddess of well-being and good health,
I ask for your help in this ritual,
So that I might have healthy relationships
That bring empowerment into my life.

Next, light the gold candle and say:

Great God of strength and vitality,
I ask for your help in this ritual,
So that I might make healthy choices
When choosing empowering relationships.

After lighting the candles, move to the middle of the circle and with your magic wand draw a small clockwise circle of bright green light on the floor before you. Next, begin visualizing a cone of bright green light emanating from the circle as you continue moving your wand around and around, tracing the outline of the small circle. Feel the energy increasing until the cone is a spiral reaching from the floor to the ceiling. Raise your wand in the air and say:

Great Goddess and God of healing,
Please speed this cone of light outward,
So that it may brighten my path
And draw healthy, empowering relationships to me.

Then build the cone of light even brighter so that it fills the room, the area around your home, your community, state, country, and the Earth. When the cone seems so bright that you can't build it any brighter or stronger, imagine pulling the cone up with your wand and releasing it to Oneness with a loud, resounding, "GO."

When you are done, thank the Goddess and God for their help, bid farewell to the elements, and pull up the circle. Allow the candles to safely burn down. For the next 28 days, anoint yourself with the lavender essential oil. As you anoint yourself, imagine drawing healing and empowering relationships to you each and every day.

Oracle of Health

Hold in your hands the dowsing rods that you made for the oracle of love and take a deep breath to center your mind. Now focus on one specific yes-or-no question regarding your health empowerment goals, particularly a question about your healing relationships. State the question aloud three times and watch the rods. Do they swing outward or inward? If they swing outward, it indicates a positive response to your question. If they swing inward or cross, it indicates a negative response. Remember, you can ask a maximum of three questions each time you use this oracle. Make a note of your questions and the answers you receive in your empowerment journal for future reference.

Prosperity

In one of my first jobs, I worked for a man who believed the key to networking was to establish a relationship with 10 new people every day. He sold insurance, something that he not only made a living from, but believed in wholeheartedly. He felt if he made the effort to talk to 10 people each day about the value of insurance his ideas and sales would spread out accordingly. As he figured, in one year he would have connected with 3,650 people, and in 10 years 36,520 people.

This concept is important when establishing a network for the empowerment of your prosperity goals. These numbers only reflect people directly contacted; they don't include all the people that the first group pass the information to, and so forth down the line. Known as word of mouth, this can often be a potent force when establishing prosperity relationships. If you use it effectively, you have the potential to realize any prosperity goal that you can imagine. Modern tools, such as mass media and the Internet, can lend even more potential to this process, depending on how you use them.

The Seventh Empowering Step: Prosperity Meditation

Turn on some meditative music and sit or recline in a comfortable place. Close your eyes and take several deep, complete breaths, feeling yourself becoming more relaxed each time you inhale and exhale. Return your breathing to normal; imagine breathing in golden light and breathing out any stress or anxiety you may be feeling. As you breathe in, roll your eyes upward behind your eyelids. As you breathe out, roll your eyes downward. Continue doing this for a few minutes. As you relax more and more, your mind naturally flows into an alpha state. The alpha state is most associated with waking relaxation, where you are peacefully calm, yet alert. As a result you become more focused in a meditative sense.

Now imagine you are gliding down a long dark tunnel, moving toward a bright light that shines before you. As you glide closer and closer, the light becomes brighter and brighter, until it's like the beacon of a lighthouse, guiding you through turbulent seas to safety. When you reach the light, you sense yourself passing through a doorway into another realm of being, a realm filled with light.

You now sense yourself in a giant circle of light beings like yourself. You are all connected to each other and to Oneness by a latticework of light beams like a giant radiant web. As a circle, you have no beginning or end; you are simply a continuity of being. Waves of energy move around the circle, empowering everyone in a continuous cycle that constantly renews itself.

As the energetic wave of light moves through you, you feel revitalized and reborn, both in terms yourself and your connection to all the other beings who make up the circle. Because of this connection, you sense that on a grander scale the circle is a living entity with wants, needs, and desires of its own. For a moment, allow your perception to easily flow back and forth between you as an individual being and you as part of a much larger being that at some point extends out into infinity and even further.

Move to that vortex where the circle and infinity intersect, a pocket of tranquility where everything comes together and, at least for the moment, you understand why things happen the way they do. Turning your perception toward your own life, you understand the reasons why you've done certain things and met certain people. Like the pieces of a puzzle, all the events fit together seamlessly in a way that helps you view them for what they are in terms of the whole of your life.

Take a snapshot of that perception for future viewing before starting to move yourself back to the present time and place. Take three deep breaths and stretch your muscles. Open your eyes without really focusing on anything in particular and rub your palms briskly together for one minute.

Before doing anything else, write your impressions of the meditation in your empowerment journal. What did it feel like to be in the circle of light with the other light beings? What was it like to view your life in terms of Oneness? Did you gain any insights into your past, present, or future? Write down the images in the snapshot you took where everything in your life seemed fit together seamlessly.

Prosperity Affirmation and Prayer

Use the following prosperity affirmation as a way of reinforcing the idea of creating relationships that are beneficial and from which everyone becomes prosperous:

Today and every day, my connections and relationships with other light beings are positive, beneficial, and help me manifest my prosperity goals.

In terms of the prayer, ask for the help of the Goddess and God in your quest for more empowering and prosperous working relationships:

Hear me, divine friends,
Dear Mother Goddess and Father God,
Please help me be in the right place at the right time
To meet empowering and prosperous people
Who will encourage me to manifest my prosperity goals
By the Lady and Lord, blessed be!

Sacred Riches Space

Add an orange and apple to your sacred riches altar. Also add patchouli-scented oil. Bless the orange and apple by holding them in your hands, one at a time, merging with the Goddess and God, and saying:

Dear Lady and Lord
Please fill this fruit with divine blessings
Of abundance, wealth, and prosperity
So be it! Blessed be!

Next, gently roll the vial of patchouli oil between your palms to warm it and then say:

Dear Lady and Lord,
Please bless this oil with your divine grace
May it draw empowering prosperous people to me
So be it! Blessed be!

Prosperity Ritual

Use the orange, apple, and the patchouli-scented oil from your sacred riches altar. This ritual is preferably done with a group of people, such as your family—people with whom you have a close energetic bond.

The expectation is to strengthen and empower the connection among all of you. If you do the ritual solitary, call upon favorite Goddesses and Gods to complete your circle.

Begin by drawing a circle of light and empowering the elements. Then anoint yourself with the patchouli oil. When working with others, also have them anoint themselves with the oil. Face the north point of your circle and say:

Divine and shining Ones, rulers of the North,
We ask that you come into this circle,
And empower all of those within it.
Please honor us with your divine presence
And shower us with prosperity and abundance.
So be it! Ayea, Ayea, Ayea!

(Note: When working solitary, change "we" to "I" or "me" accordingly.) Next, move to the east, south, and west points respectively, and repeat the invocation, changing the directional names accordingly.

Then have everyone in the circle join hands. As a group, select three Goddesses and Gods to help create a cone of wealth and prosperity power, for example, Danu, Odin, and Demeter. Now slowly move in a clockwise circle and chant the names of the Goddesses and the Gods you have selected. For example, chant:

Danu, Danu, Danu
Odin, Odin, Odin
Demeter, Demeter, Demeter.

Continue chanting the deity names over and over as you move faster and faster around the circle. Let your voices rise a little higher and stronger, all the while imagining a divine, brilliant white cone of prosperity and wealth emanating up from your circle and flowing outward. This cone is symbolic of your eternal connection to one another, meaning that all prosper from the relationship that extends out into the infinite circle of the divine.

Once you have amassed enough light energy, release the cone of power by shouting "Ayea!" three times while raising your hands high in the air. Sense the wealth and prosperity cone of power moving outward through your arms and hands into the universe and the many realms of being. Realize your innate connection with those around you and sense the cone of prosperous power flowing through you and into the universe, further empowering your relationships and connections to one another.

When you have released the cone, sit back and share the apple and orange with the group. When working solitary, share the fruit with the Goddess and God by putting a portion of it outside on the ground as a divine offering.

Complete the ritual by thanking the Goddesses and Gods that helped you. Then bid farewell to the elements and pull up the circle. For the next 28 days, anoint yourself with a bit of the patchouli oil to draw more empowering and prosperous working relationships to you.

Oracle of Wealth

Hold your dowsing rods in your hands and take a deep breath to center yourself. Now focus on one specific yes-or-no question regarding your prosperity empowerment goals, particularly a question about your business and working relationships. State the question aloud three times and watch the rods. Do they swing outward or inward? If they swing outward, it indicates a positive response to your question. If they swing inward or cross, it indicates a negative response. Make a note of your questions and the answers in your empowerment journal. Use the information you received to build more empowering and prosperous working relationships.

Chapter Eight

The Eighth Empowering Step: Understanding the Empowerment of Persistence

Without the inspiration and persistence of two people, Thomas Edison and Nikola Tesla, it would have taken much longer to brighten up the world with electricity. As an inventor, Nikola Tesla had the uncanny ability to envision his goals and then manifest them. This ability was aptly demonstrated in his development of the component parts used to generate and transmit "alternating current," which at the time was unheard of, but today is universally used in households throughout the world. The motors he built were exactly as he imagined them; he made no attempt to improve their design. He simply reproduced the images in his mind and the motors operated just as he expected.

Unlike Tesla, Thomas Edison, who was the inventor of the electric light bulb and the phonograph, was known to spend long arduous hours of trial and error to make his goals a reality. Inventing the electric light bulb proved to be such a struggle that he almost gave up before discovering that carbon in the bulb's filament gave it longevity and thus practical usage. Because of this and other experiences, Edison coined the phrase "Genius is 1 percent inspiration and 99 percent perspiration."

Like Edison, many of us come to realize that mundane tasks and practical steps often take the most time when bringing a goal to fruition. Unlike Tesla, most people don't have the uncanny ability to bring their goals into reality without at least some tweaking and lots of work. The "99 percent perspiration" to which Edison referred is what the Eighth Empowering Step, understanding the empowerment of persistence, is all about. Inspiration and creativity often initiate goal-setting, but work, conscious reason, and dedicated persistence are what manifest inspiration and creativity into reality.

The Positive Benefits of Persistence

Persistence will help you stick with your empowerment plans until they and your goals become reality. Often this requires a lot of patience, experimentation, hard work, and a few hard knocks—all which act as motivating factors for you to adapt your overall plan accordingly. Sometimes the odds seem insurmountable and you feel like giving up just to escape the madness, but if you are persistent, you'll discover that things are continually changing. Keep in mind that what once seemed out of bounds, for example, alternating current and electricity, is lighting the world today.

Persistence is about maintaining your focus on your goals and cultivating your ability to merge with divine Oneness. Change often seems to happen very slowly, but nonetheless it is continually happening on many levels simultaneously. For success, it's vital to continually reinforce your belief in your abilities and the eventual realization of your empowerment goals. After all, being successful is what empowers you. It's also your best weapon against negativity.

Keep in mind that being pushy, intimidating, and belligerent is not the same as being persistent. Those characteristics are about being controlling and manipulative, whereas persistence is all about having the ability and faith to keep trying until you're successful.

I have a little beagle named Lady Liberty who is the model of persistence. Through observation, I have learned a lot from her about the art of persisting. I have yet to put her in an enclosed yard without her eventually finding a way out. She digs under or climbs over fences, and quite often it's a complete mystery how she finally gets out. Sometimes it takes her a few hours, other times a few days, and once in a while even several weeks, but she keeps trying and is ultimately successful in her goal of escaping the yard. I call her my little Houdini dog because of her amazing amount of persistence and ingenuity and her seemingly magical ways of attaining her goal.

Persistence propels you. It moves you forward into the future. As you move forward, it's important to believe in yourself, to keep trying, to keep the faith in your divine connection with Goddess and God, and to never underestimate your abilities to succeed at what you put your mind to. These positive beliefs, attitudes, and actions form the backbone of persistence, which ultimately helps you attain your goals.

When setting up, planning, and working toward your empowerment goals with persistence, make every effort to stick with what works in your life, while phasing out the things that don't. This will help you continue to persist. Rather than beat your head against the proverbial brick wall when things don't go as planned, be willing to adapt your plans and goals so they do work for you.

One successful method I have found to diminish self-flagellation, banish self-defeating thoughts, and eliminate destructive attitudes is to say aloud to myself, "I transform that negative thought to a positive one, right now. I expect the very best. I expect success!" Then I take a few moments to imagine myself persisting toward my goal, manifesting it, and succeeding.

As you work through the empowerment process, you may find yourself changing your ideas of what you want. That's perfectly normal; most of us change our minds from time to time as we gain knowledge and experience. That's why it's important to look over the empowerment goals you wrote down in your empowerment journal and update them from time to time. The fact that your goals are changing is positive in that it denotes forward movement in your life, meaning that you're moving closer toward personal empowerment.

In terms of persistence, remember that simple goals are often easier to attain than more complex ones. Small miracles can happen everyday, but larger miracles often take time and require more work and "perspiration." As Miss Frizzle always says in the popular children's series *The Magic School Bus*, go ahead and take chances and make messes and mistakes. Just make certain that they aren't too extreme and you and others are not harmed by your actions. Also make an effort to look ahead and see the consequences of your choices. Experienced gamblers often say, "Never bet more than you're willing to lose."

Taking chances to bring about change in your life is most definitely a gamble. The nature of your gamble depends on your particular situation and how much you are willing to risk to make what you want happen. Often, you will need to keep your risk-taking in check so that it works to advance your empowerment goals and not hinder them. Be careful and intelligently cautious. Use your inner wisdom and intuition and be sure to persist, persist, persist.

A Story of Empowering Persistence

Pat Croce, owner of the Philadelphia 76ers basketball team and author of the book *I Feel Great and You Will Too* was taking a cross-country trip in 1999 when his motorcycle spun out of control and he found himself laid out on the wet pavement in bad shape. One of his legs was ripped to shreds and had to be operated on several times. In the end, he had pins holding his leg together and was told he would not walk again.

A firm believer in positive thought and never one to quit, Pat decided immediately that his goal was to prove the doctors wrong, that he would indeed walk again. He laid out an empowerment plan that included rigorous therapy and exercising. From the outset, he amazed his doctors with his progress. Several times during his recuperation, Pat wanted to give up because of overwhelming pain and depression, but instead he used his persistent determination to move forward in the healing process. Finally in a visit to the doctor, an x-ray on his leg showed that new tissue was beginning to form. Pat took that as a sign and continued his efforts until he once again could stand on his leg without crutches and walk on his own. Regarding the achievement of goals, he said, "Every day I work toward the completion of my goals. Little by little. Chip away here, bang away there, with my goals and dreams always in sight."

Sometimes manifesting your empowerment goals can seem overwhelming, especially when the people around you keep telling you it can't be done. But as my father used to tell me when I was growing up, "Can't never did anything."

Taking persistence a step further, you have to believe in your abilities, and you have to ask for what you want. In the words of Pat Croce, "It never hurts to ask. The worst thing they can do is say 'no.' And as my pop said, If you don't ask, then the answer is always 'no'."

I guarantee you will reap wonderful results when you apply Pat Croce's example of the power of persistence. Make every effort to keep trying and keep asking. It's important to always ask for what you want, otherwise the answer is automatically "no." Even when you ask and the answer is still "no," often you can persist and change that "no" to a "yes." Avoid badgering people, however, because that may irritate them and make them dig in their heels more. Instead, gently persist, keep asking in positive, polite, and creative ways, and be sure to point out how both parties can benefit by a "yes."

Persistence is how you eventually get what you want in life, otherwise your goals can become as elusive as butterflies. When persisting, be sure to keep your thoughts positive, and you will most definitely move forward and succeed.

You have to be willing to keep trying, to keep fine-tuning your timing and actions, and to learn from both your triumphs and mistakes. You must be willing to think and work in new ways to make your goals a reality. Persistence combined with ingenuity, creativity, and experimentation is the cornerstone of victory.

Love

Two of my close friends, Catherine and Francisco, have been in a relationship for more than 30 years. They are still together because they are a couple whose persistence and loyalty to one another sees them through good times, bad times, and the intrusion of other people. Recently Catherine told me, "Most couples make it through the good times. It's the bad times and the intrusion of other people that often make or break a relationship. You have to really persist and work at making an empowering relationship."

When you are in a long-term relationship, the important thing is to focus on the empowering aspects of the relationship. Make every effort to avoid letting outside influences, especially disempowering circumstances and people, split you apart. This requires persistence, focus, and a little creativity.

Time is what gives the relationship depth. Time also creates repetition and boredom, which is why you always need to find new elements to make your relationship alive and fresh. This is why you must be creatively persistent in your approach to relationships if you want them to be lasting and empowering.

The Eighth Empowering Step: Love Meditation

Begin by sitting or reclining in a comfortable spot where you can easily see a ceiling corner in the room, preferably an easterly ceiling corner that corresponds to the air element. Now fix your eyes on the ceiling corner and breathe in for three heartbeats, still your breath for three heartbeats, and then exhale for three heartbeats. Breathe this way for a minute or two, all the while focusing your gaze on the ceiling corner. Place your awareness up there at the ceiling corner. As you do this, you may find that the ceiling corner seems magnified, much larger than it usually does. Continue breathing deeply and focusing your awareness in the ceiling corner until your eyes begin feeling heavy. As they get heavier and heavier while you breathe in and out, finally just allow your eyes to naturally close and relax.

Now in your mind's eye, imagine you are lighter than air and can float. Like a balloon filled with helium, you float through the air, up past the ceiling and outward. As you float, you feel as though you are swimming through the air, using your arms and legs to propel and guide you. You are weightless, sensing the pulling constraints of gravity lifted from your being. You are now free to go anywhere you want, unencumbered by walls and boundaries.

As you float upward, you meet your beloved. You join hands, and together you continue floating through the sky, high above the clouds. As you continue your journey, you magically bond with your beloved and float as one into the universe. The love that connects you propels you both higher and higher as you float into unknown realms of existence. Everywhere you go, you fill the space with bright love and joy, lighting your path as you move forward.

Together you effortlessly float for what seems like eternity. Even though everything seems nebulous and without form around you, you hold a vision of your empowerment goals in your mind's eye. You move forward toward this vision, toward a world where all of your dreams and empowerment goals are realized.

By keeping your expectations and focus intact, you manage to traverse a great expanse, until up ahead you see your destination, a world where expectations and dreams become reality. You sense that all of your efforts have been rewarded, your plans activated, and your goals realized.

Now take a deep breath in and out and bring this realization back with you. Imagine floating down through the air, into the room and back to your comfortable meditation spot. Take another deep breath and slowly open your eyes, once again focusing on the ceiling corner for a few moments. Now stretch your body and clap your hands three times to come fully back to the present time and place.

When you are done, write your impressions of the meditation experience in your empowerment journal. Make specific notes about what it felt like to float outward beyond the ceiling into the universe, and what it felt like when all your efforts were realized and your expectations manifested.

Love Affirmation and Prayer

Affirmation and prayer can help you persist, even when the odds seem insurmountable. Say this affirmation aloud to yourself in a mellifluous voice several times a day for 28 days to reinforce your efforts of persistence:

Each and every moment of each and every day, I persist in attaining my love goals, and the divine love of the Goddess and God help me ever move toward personal empowerment and Oneness.

Say the following prayer to empower your love persistence, both earthly and divine:

Dear Goddess and God of Earth
Please bless me with the power of worldly persistence
So that I may know earthly love.
Dear Goddess and God of the heavens
Please bless me with the power of divine persistence
So that I may know divine love.
By the loving bond of the Lady and Lord, blessed be!

Sacred Love Space

Add five candles—green, white, yellow, blue, and purple—and five holders to your sacred love altar, plus a vial of honeysuckle oil and three sticks of jasmine incense. Bless these items one at a time before putting them on your altar. Cleanse the candles by rinsing them in cool salt water and dry them. Then hold each candle between your hands, merge with the divine, and say:

Bless this candle with the divine loving persistence of Oneness.

Next, gently roll the vial of honeysuckle oil between your palms to warm it, merge with the divine, and say:

Bless this oil with the divine loving persistence of Oneness.

Then hold the incense in your hands, merge with the divine, and say:

Bless this incense with the divine loving persistence of Oneness.

Love Ritual

This three-day ritual stresses the importance of persistence when actualizing your love empowerment goals. Choose one of your love goals and five-step plans to work on for this ritual. You will also need the five colored candles, the honeysuckle oil, and jasmine incense from your sacred love altar.

Begin by drawing a magic circle of light and empowering the elements. Next, dress the candles with a thin film of the honeysuckle oil and anoint yourself. Wipe the oil from your hands and light the incense, dedicating it to the divine love of the God and Goddess. Now go to the north point of the circle and light the green candle. Raising the candle holder with the lit candle high in the air, say:

Powers of Earth,
First step of my plan,
Help me to start,
And do all I can
Ayea! So be it!

Place the candleholder with the green candle on the altar and pick up the candleholder with the white candle. Light the white candle from the green candle flame and move to the east point of the circle. Holding the candleholder upward with the lit white candle, say:

Powers of Air,
Second step that I take,
Help me to flow,
In every move I make
Ayea! So be it!

Place the white candle back on the altar. Then light the yellow candle from the white candle. Move to the south point of the circle, and raising the candleholder with the yellow candle up high, say:

Powers of Fire,
Third step of action,
Help me to light
A path to the Sun
Ayea! So be it!

Set the yellow candle down and light the blue candle from it. Move to the west point of the circle, hold the candleholder with the blue candle up high, and say:

Powers of Water,
Fourth step of success,
Help me continue
And do my best
Ayea! So be it!

Now set the blue candle down on the altar and light the purple candle from it. Move to the center of circle. Hold the candleholder with the purple candle high in the air and say:

Powers of Oneness,
Fifth step through the door,
Help make my love goal real,
Now and forevermore
Ayea! So be it!

Remain in the middle of the circle for a few moments, visualizing your love goal happening in all its many aspects. Like a beautiful dream, relish the moment. See it, feel it, be it, and make it real for yourself. Finish by thanking the Goddess and God, bidding farewell to the elements, and pulling up the circle. Snuff out the candles.

Repeat this ritual for three days or nights in a row for best results. When you are done with the ritual on the third day or night, allow the candles to safely burn down.

Oracle of Love

Runes are a potent tool for self-discovery. As a channel to the divine, they represent one of the oldest divination systems known to humankind. Runes were given to the Norse God Odin when he hung upside down from the Yggdrasil (World Tree) for nine days. Heroic deeds were recorded in runic writing and runes were carved on stones throughout Northern Europe.

Used primarily by the Norse, Germanic, and Celtic peoples in Europe, runes were employed in magic and divination and carved on magical wands called gandrs. For thousands of years runic symbols have been carved into wood, stone, metal, and bone, and used as family marks ("hof" marks), hex signs, and in building construction. They have been carved on caskets, gravestones, coins, musical instruments, marked on livestock, trade goods, saddles, boats, amulets, and talismans, among other things.

The Vikings took the runes with them where they traveled, and so runes can be found throughout the world. They are inscribed on crosses and used to decorate stained glass windows, on churches, castles, carved on large marker stones, and on bridges.

Rune rows, called "futharks," begin with the runes Fehu, Uruz, Thurisaz, Ansuz, Raidho, and Kenaz—"F," "U," "TH," "A," "R," "K." The earlier runes and oldest known full rune row, the Elder Futhark, are considered to be the most powerful of all rune rows. Each of the runes of the Elder Futhark is a storehouse of knowledge. Like the Greek alphabet, the Elder Futhark has 24 rune symbols that are in a specific sequence. There are only uppercase runes, and no curves, only straight lines. This makes them very easy to learn and write.

For this oracle of love, you will need a set of rune stones or rune cards. You can purchase these at most New Age shops, or you can make your own rune cards by drawing one rune symbol on each of 24 3 × 5-inch index cards. For more about runes and a listing of rune symbols and names, refer to my book, *The Little Giant Encyclopedia of Runes* (see the Bibliography at the end of this book).

Begin by holding your rune stones or cards in your hands. Take a deep, complete breath and then say:

In the name of the Goddess and God, I bless these runes as divine oracles.

Now close your eyes and focus on a specific question regarding your love empowerment goals. With your mind turned toward your question, and with your eyes still closed, select three runes from your rune bag or shuffled deck of rune cards. Put the three runes upright in front of you, in a row from left to right. Runes are traditionally read upright with no reversed meanings. The rune on the left represents the past influences to your love question, the middle rune symbolizes the present, and the rune on the right signifies the future, with regard to your love question. Refer to the following rune meanings to understand the rune symbols you have selected.

Rune	Meaning
Fehu	Money, prosperity, wealth, good luck
Uruz	Stability, healing, offering
Thurisaz	Conflict, road blocks, pitfalls, change
Ansuz	Spiritual love, communication, transformation
Raidho	Movement, journey, adventure, action, union
Kenaz	Creative fire, new opportunities, insight, passion
Gebo	Gifts, presents, partnerships, sexuality, love
Wunjo	Joy, happiness, wishes come true, attaining goals
Hagalaz	Change, disruption, constraint, self-growth
Naudhiz	Restriction, fear, anxiety, necessity, bad luck
Isa	Crystallization, stagnation, limbo, social conditioning
Jera	Harvest, accomplishment, achievement, persistence
Eihwaz	Transcendence, motivation, inspiration, change
Perdhro	Good luck, material gain, intuition, personal power
Algiz	Protection, defense against negativity
Sowilo	Faith, divine light, success
Tiwaz	Honor, justice, leadership, victory, celestial wisdom
Berkana	Intuition, fertility, birth, family, new beginnings
Ehwaz	Action, change, cooperation
Mannaz	Relationships, social position, humanity
Laguz	Emotions, imagination, clarity, psychic ability
Ingwaz	Security, fruition, planting seeds, fertility
Dagaz	Balance, initiation, new love, new job, new beginnings
Othala	Inheritance, completion, wisdom, rebirth

When you are done, write your question and the runes you selected in your empowerment journal for easy reference.

Health

When I was young, my family vacationed at a small lake called Sand Pond, which was located 7,000 feet up in the Gold Country of Northern California. In the lodge located near Sand Pond, there was a newspaper article that had been clipped out years ago, framed, and hung on the wall. The article described how the man who originally built the lodge had suffered from a terminal disease and whose health was rapidly fading. He couldn't walk and his doctors had given him only a short time to live. After moving to the mountains and regularly swimming in the waters of Sand Pond, he not only could walk, he was completely healed of his disease and went on to build the lodge with his own two hands. This story shows that if you persist in believing you will get well, you often will. Indeed, some waters are indeed filled with natural healing powers that really do have a healing effect on those who bathe in or drink them.

At age 39, Franklin D. Roosevelt was diagnosed with polio and given little chance of ever doing much in life, except being a paraplegic. He was not one to give up, though, and after finding the healing waters of Warm Springs, Georgia, he started working on his goals of health and power that eventually lead him to the presidency of the United States. Franklin Roosevelt was not about to let his infirmities stop him from realizing his dream of becoming a politician, even though there had never been a handicapped president who could not walk without assistance. Not only did Franklin succeed as a politician, but he became the thirty-second president of the United States and the only President to serve four terms. Through his persistence, he hid his disability so well that most people never realized he was disabled. He is a true testament to show how courage and persistence can propel one forward toward personal empowerment on several levels. He is also someone whom people can emulate in terms of their health goals.

The Eighth Empowering Step: Healing Meditation

Sit or recline in a comfortable place where you will not be disturbed. Take a deep breath in through your nose as you silently say "OM." As you do this, imagine your body, mind, and spirit being filled with life-force energy. Still your breath for four counts and then exhale quickly and completely through your mouth. Imagine every part of your being revitalized as you breathe in and silently say "OM." Release any tension, worries, or discomfort you may be feeling as you exhale. Breathe this way three times with your eyes open, and then close your eyes and breathe this way three more times.

Now in your mind's eye, imagine standing before a pool of water that on one side has a mountain stream flowing into it. As you immerse yourself in the clear cool water, you sense its purity cleansing your body. Like a crystal, you sense all the negative energy, discomfort, and pain being washed from your being. Effortlessly, you glide across the water, making your way toward the other side of the pool. As you reach the other side, you feel refreshed and your energy is renewed.

Stepping out of the first pool, you see a second pool of water. The edges of the second pool are lined with different types of stones. You move over to it and again immerse yourself in the cool water. You sense the energy of the stones resonating healing energy into the water. The fabric of your being has the sensation of being harmonized with the resonance of the healing energy of the stones. You glide across the pool and as you reach the other side, you feel a new sensation of healing fill your body, mind, and spirit that revitalizes you.

Climbing out of the second pool, you see a third pool of water with a mist of steam cascading across its glassy surface. As you move slowly into the water, you feel its warmth soothing and healing every cell of your body. A calmness caresses each part of your being, and you feel at one with everything. You glide across the warm pool, and as you reach the other side, you feel in harmony with who you are and who you are becoming.

Rising out of the third pool, you see a fourth pool of water. As you move into the warm pool, you can smell the scent akin to an herbal mineral bath. Moving into the water, you sense it healing any pain and disease that your body may be harboring. Your entire being releases all pain and illness, opening up all the places in your body, mind, and spirit where the energy has become blocked. Reaching the other side of the pool, you feel a sensation that you are becoming more and more healthy, free from pain and illness.

Floating out of the fourth pool, you see a fifth pool of water that seems like an endless ocean whose opposite shore is not clearly visible. When you look, there is nothing but an endless expansion of blue in every direction. As you move into the water, it seems to welcome you like an old friend. You flow into its divine expanse and feel yourself buoyed up with a power from its depths. You feel a new resolve to continue your quest of becoming healthier and happier, to manifest your health empowerment goals. Through persistence and by focusing on your expectations, you reach the other side of the boundless fifth pool. As you do, you come home to the present as a healthier person.

Now bring this healing image with you wherever you go. Take a deep breath in and out, knowing you can return to the healing pools whenever you like.

Take another deep breath in silently saying "OM," still your breath for four counts, and then quickly exhale through your mouth as you say "OM" aloud. Open your eyes and breathe in, silently saying "OM." Hold your breath for four counts and then exhale quickly through your mouth, saying "OM" aloud once again. Do this once more. Slowly stretch your muscles and come fully back to the present time and place.

When you are done, record your impressions in your empowerment journal. Note how you felt as you floated and glided across the five healing pools, especially when you used resolve and persistence to move across the fifth pool to home.

Healing Affirmation and Prayer

Strengthen your powers of healing persistence by saying the following affirmation aloud several times a day until you actualize your goals for good health:

Every moment of every day, I persist with my healing empowerment goals in every way. Each cell in my body is filled with divine power and strength.

Say the following prayer in the morning to enlist the powers of divine persistence:

May the persistent healing powers
Of the blessed Goddess and God
Fill my body, mind, and spirit
With divine love and light
Every day and every night
Thank you dear Lady and Lord
Blessed be!

Sacred Healing Space

Place a bowl of earth, sandalwood incense, a white candle and candle-holder, and a chalice of water on your sacred healing altar.

Empower each of these items by blessing them with the divine energies of the Goddess and God. Hold each of them in your hands and say:

Bless this magical item with divine healing powers.

Healing Ritual

Use this ritual to resolve any problems that may be persisting with your health empowerment goals. You will need the bowl of earth, sandalwood incense, white candle, and chalice of water from your sacred healing altar. You will also be using your athame.

Begin by drawing a circle of light and empowering the elements. Light the candle, dedicating it to a favorite Goddess and God. Then light the incense from the candle flame, once again dedicating it to the Goddess and God of your choice. Now take the bowl of earth from the altar and go to the north point of the circle. Sprinkle three pinches of earth in front of you. Merge with the earth element and call out:

Gatekeeper of the stones of ancestry,
Please let me enter through your gate,
May I be worthy of your blessings
To manifest my health empowerment goal.

When you're finished, imagine all you hear is the silent strength of the earth. Set the bowl of earth on the altar and carefully pick up the lit incense. Move to the east point of the circle and slowly wave the incense back and forth three times. Merge with the powers of air and call out:

Gatekeeper of the winds of knowledge,
Let me enter through your gate.
May I be worthy of your blessings
To manifest my health empowerment goal.

When you're finished, imagine all you hear is the whistling of the wind. Place the incense on the altar and carefully pick up the lit candle. Move to the south point of the circle and slowly wave the candle back and forth three times. Merge with the powers of fire and call out:

Gatekeeper of the fire of life,
Let me enter through your gate.
May I be worthy of your blessings
To manifest my health empowerment goal.

When you're finished, imagine all you hear is the crackling of the fire. Put the candle down on the altar and pick up the chalice of water. Move to the west point of the circle and use your fingers to sprinkle a few drops of water in front of you three times. Merge with the water element and call out:

Gatekeeper of the waters of Oneness,
Let me enter through your gate.
May I be worthy of your blessings
To manifest my health empowerment goal.

When you're finished, imagine all you hear is the babbling of the water. Set the chalice of water back on the altar and move to the center of the circle. Focus your mind on manifesting your health empowerment goal. Pick up your athame from the altar and draw an energetic door for yourself toward the north point of the circle. Walk through the door, and as you do, aim your athame at the north point and spin around, connecting all the points and elements together as one. You have completed the circle of light. Now spend some time savoring the energy of all the elements and imagine them powering the successful completion of your health goal. Remind yourself to call upon the power of the elements whenever you need them. They are always there to help you.

When you are done, thank the deity, bid farewell to the elements, and pull up the circle. Allow the candle and incense to burn safely down. Spread the bowl of earth and pour the water outside under a tree.

Oracle of Health

Hold your rune stones or cards in your hands and take a deep complete breath to center your awareness. Now close your eyes and focus on a question regarding your health empowerment goals. With your eyes closed and your mind turned toward your question, select three runes from your rune stones or the shuffled deck of rune cards.

Place the runes in front of you upright and in a row from left to right. The rune on the left represents the past influences to your question, the middle one symbolizes the present, and the rune on the right signifies the future, with regard to your health empowerment question. Refer to the rune meanings presented in the oracle of love to understand the rune symbols you have selected. Record your health empowerment question and the runes you selected in your empowerment journal.

Prosperity

Popular New Age author James Redfield had a vision to write a book that would change the way people approached their spirituality. Rather than writing a how-to book, he decided to write a fictional story that included his spiritual ideas as its foundation. The idea was novel, but that did not deter James from writing his manuscript, *The Celestine Prophecy*, and submitting it to a number of publishers.

After being rejected by every publisher, he decided to self-publish the book. Loading the copies in the trunk of his car, he began to visit bookstores around the country. His persistence paid off, and the book began selling well. It eventually caught the attention of Warner Books, who purchased the book for several million dollars. *The Celestine Prophecy* landed on all the bestseller lists, including *The New York Times*, breaking many records. Through persistence, James made his book a phenomenal success that still has not been equaled.

The Eighth Empowering Step: Prosperity Meditation

Turn on some soft New Age, instrumental, or classical music and sit back or recline in a comfortable spot. Close your eyes and take a deep breath through your nose to the count of three. Still your breath, curl your tongue backward until it touches the roof of your mouth, and then exhale thrusting your tongue quickly forward and letting out a throaty growl. Breathe in this manner for a minute or so and then return your breathing to normal.

Now in your mind's eye, imagine you are in a spaceship moving through the infinite reaches of space. By peering through a portal in your ship, you see an array of lights as they dot the dark landscape that spans out before you. Picking up a map of the cosmos, you begin to chart your course to the star system where your prosperity resides, a place where your riches are waiting for you to claim them. You set the ship's controls and begin your magical journey to the star system and your prosperity empowerment goals.

To pass the time as you move through space, you begin focusing on and imagining your prosperity goals. You envision what it will be like when you reach the star system. Like a beautiful dream, you savor the images that you know will become part of your life in the near future. These images keep you moving forward in anticipation of the outcome of your magical journey.

Through the ship's portal, you watch a meteor shower that slowly becomes more intense. From a distance, the shower looks magnificent, like fireworks that shoot in every direction, lighting up the darkness of space. As you move closer to the shower, the meteors begin bombarding your ship, making it more difficult to navigate. For a moment, it seems like it will knock you off course, but through your persistence, you are able to navigate out of the meteor shower and stay on course toward your prosperity goals and the star system where they dwell.

As you approach the star system, you note through your instruments that the brightest star is a sun with 13 planets revolving around it. Further investigating your instruments, you discover that your prosperity resides on the eighth planet from the sun, a place that is like a magical garden, always in bloom. Touching down on the eighth planet, you move down the ramp of your ship to the ground. In front of you, all of your prosperity goals come to fruition. You are surrounded by abundance, prosperity, and incredible wealth. You smile as you realize that through your persistence and efforts, abundance and prosperity fill your life.

Now take a deep and complete breath, knowing that you can return to the eighth planet any time you desire. Take another complete breath and slowly open your eyes without really focusing on anything in particular. Then take another breath in and out and move your toes and fingers, coming back to the present time and place. Rub your palms together briskly for one minute.

When you are done, record your impressions of the meditation in your empowerment journal. Note how you felt moving through space, watching the meteor shower, landing and touching your feet upon the ground of the eighth planet, and seeing your prosperity goals manifested there.

Prosperity Affirmation and Prayer

Write this prosperity affirmation on the back of your business card or something similar and put it in your wallet, purse, top desk drawer, or next to your computer monitor. Read it aloud at least eight times a day for 28 days to increase your powers of persistence:

Today and every day, I am continuously increasing my persistence and awareness of abundance. Divine prosperity showers upon me from everyone I meet everywhere I go.

Say the following prayer to cultivate divine persistence with regard to your prosperity empowerment goals. Make every effort to be persistent in prayer because it truly makes a positive difference when manifesting your goals:

Dear God and Goddess,
I am one with you
As you are one with me.

Please help me persist
In attaining my goals
Of abundance and prosperity.
Thank you dear ones
For once again empowering me
By earth, air, fire, and water
By divine grace and goodness, blessed be!

Sacred Riches Space

To your sacred riches altar, add your magic wand, checkbook or bank-book, a golden-colored bell, a green candle, and your ritual bowl filled with uncooked barley. Place your palms about an inch above these items on your altar and imagine energy flowing from your hands and into them. Say three times:

I empower these magical focals with the abundant power and wealth of the Goddess and God.

Prosperity Ritual

Through ritual, the divine powers of the Goddess and God and the natural powers of the elements can all be tapped to help you persist in manifesting your prosperity empowerment goals. You will need a sheet of white paper and a green felt or gel pen, plus your wand, the bell, your checkbook, the green candle, and the bowl of uncooked barley on your sacred riches altar.

Begin by drawing a magic circle of light and empowering the elements. Take the bowl of uncooked barley and scatter it clockwise around the outline of the magic circle. Put the bowl on the altar. Use the green felt or gel pen to write the words, "PERSIST, PERSIST, PERSIST," in large capital letters on the sheet of white paper. Go over the words three times with the pen to make them even bolder. Open your checkbook and place it next to the paper. Ring the bell once and return it to the altar. Hold your wand in your power hand and softly tap the words on the paper three times with the wand tip. With your wand still in hand, move to the north point of the circle. Point the tip of your wand toward the north, merge with the powers of earth, and say:

God and Goddess of the north,
Please bless my goals with your power.
Make them solid, make them real
Like the stones, trees, and flowers.
Ayea! So be it!

Feel the energy of the God and Goddess of Earth coming in through your wand. Take the power in as long as you can and then pick up the bell in your receiving hand and ring it once. Set the bell down on the altar and, with your wand in hand, again softly tap the words on the paper three times with the wand tip. Move to the east point of the circle, point the tip of your wand eastward, merge with the powers of air, and say:

God and Goddess of the east,
Please bless my goals with your power.
Make them move, make them fly
Through the seconds, minutes, and hours.
Ayea! So be it!

Feel the energy of the God and Goddess of air flowing through the wand into your body, mind, and spirit. Absorb the divine power as long as you can. Now pick up the bell in your receiving hand and ring it one time. Set the bell down on the altar and, with your wand still in hand, tap the words three times with the wand tip. Move to the south point of the circle and point the tip of your wand toward the south point. Merge with the powers of fire and say:

God and Goddess of the south
Please bless my goals with your fire,
Spark and kindle them with light and life
And with the feeling of endless desire
Ayea! So be it!

Feel the energy of the God and Goddess of fire flashing through your wand into your body, mind, and spirit. Absorb the divine power as long as you can. Pick up the bell in your receiving hand and ring it one time. Set the bell on the altar and, with your wand in hand, tap the words "PERSIST, PERSIST, PERSIST," three times with the wand tip. Move to the west point of the circle and point the tip of your wand toward the west. Merge with the powers of water and say:

God and Goddess of the west,
Please bless my goals with your grace
Make them fluid, make them flow,
With every movement and in every space
Ayea! So be it!

Feel the energy of the God and Goddess of water flowing through your wand. Take in as much divine flowing power as possible.

Next, move back to your altar. Ring the bell once and set it on the altar. Tap the words on the paper three times with your wand tip, then grasp your wand with both hands and imagine absorbing the powerful divine abundance of the Goddess and God from north, east, south, and west, by the powers of earth, air, fire, and water. Do this for at least five minutes.

When you are done, ring the bell three times, close your checkbook, and snuff out the candle. Thank the Goddess and God, release the elements, and pull up the circle. Tack or tape the paper with the words "PERSIST, PERSIST, PERSIST," in clear view where you can easily see it in your sacred riches space. Read it several times each day to effectively encourage your natural powers of persistence. Also, relight the candle the day after the ritual and allow it to burn for a while before snuffing it out. Then relight it again the following day and allow it to safely burn down. Each time you relight the candle, chant the words on the paper several times.

Oracle of Wealth

Hold your rune stones or rune cards in your hands. Close your eyes and take a deep breath to center your mind. Focus on one specific question regarding your prosperity empowerment goals. With your mind focused on your question and your eyes closed, select three runes. Put them in front of you upright and in a row from left to right. The left-most rune signifies past influences with regard to your prosperity question, the middle rune signifies the present influences, and the right-most rune represents the future. Refer to the rune meanings listed in the oracle of love to understand the symbols you have chosen.

Chapter Nine

The Ninth Empowering Step:
Using the Empowerment
at Your Fingertips

Although born in the ghetto of East St. Louis, Jacqueline
Joyner-Kersee was bound for glory, particularly when her
grandmother named her after Jacqueline Kennedy and noted
that someday her granddaughter was destined to be the first
lady of something. Always full of determination and the will
to survive, Jackie lived up to her grandmother's expectations
by becoming one of the greatest female athletes in history. She
won six Olympic medals, holds the American record for the
long jump, and holds the world record for the heptathlon.

The heptathlon is a grueling two-day contest. On the first
day, athletes run the 100 meter hurdles, high jump, shot put,
and run a 200 meter race. On the second day, they participate
in the long jump, javelin throw, and 800 meter race. This
event requires great endurance and flexibility to succeed.
Jackie lived up to this expectation; she became the beautiful
and powerful rose that grows up through the cracks in the
sidewalk.

In terms of empowerment, determination means giving your goals the proper attention and effort they need to be realized. This involves making that last push toward your empowerment goals just when you didn't think you had any push left. Much like the last lap of a race, you are tapping your reserve and nourishing your goals in order to go the distance. Ultimately, you empower your goals and they, in return, empower you.

Nurturing Your Goals to Fruition

In terms of the garden analogy, plants need a lot of attention and care during their many growing stages before they bloom and come into florescence. Often what this means is fertilizing the plants in your garden and keeping the pests away so they can realize their full potential.

With regard to the ninth empowering step, this means nurturing and feeding your goals so that they come to fruition. In addition, you need to stay focused and coalesce your powers so that you can meet any challenges that may arise. Like running a race, sometimes the last few steps before empowerment involve calling up all of your reserves so that you can reach your goals. Part of nourishing your goals to fruition is staying focused on them and remaining determined with your intentions and expectations.

When you formulated your empowerment goals and plans, you created a template for success that requires you to follow through with what you started. Empowerment is not a random process, but one in which you learn directly from your triumphs and mistakes. Adapt your empowerment goals and plans as needed. You live in world that is moving, and as such it is constantly changing, even if the change seems slow at times. The important thing is to continue moving forward in terms of your love, health, and prosperity goals.

The Will and the Way

The incredible blues singer Bessie Smith embodied the will and determination it takes to manifest your goals. The Ku Klux Klan tried to break up a concert she was giving, and rather than being daunted by their threats, Bessie, through pure determination, courage, and will, literally chased the disruptive members of the KKK away from the concert. She did not let them deter her from what she set out to do.

Bessie's story is a true story of empowerment. It serves as a magnificent reminder that you should never allow others to deter you from what you have set out to do, regardless of the situation and circumstance. You may be a woman, you may be black, and you may grow up on the wrong side of the tracks, but never allow these circumstances to discourage you from setting your empowerment goals and making them happen. You can overcome whoever and whatever gets in your way with courage and determination.

Bessie used her strength of character and her drive to overcome negative events that were obviously meant to derail her from empowerment and prevent her from achieving her goals of being a great blues singer. Sometimes strength of character and drive is what you need when pursuing your love, health, and prosperity empowerment goals. Don't let people and events intimidate you, knock you off course, or derail your empowerment plans. Focus on your goals and the people who empower you and limit your exposure to the people who are always telling you that you can't do something.

When you have strong determination and willpower, you can always find a way to make your empowerment goals become reality. You need to believe in your abilities to be successful, believe in your inner vision, and believe in your goals. Whether you are running a race or chasing off the "bad guys" like Bessie Smith, you have to remain focused and realize that nothing will stand in your way. You can be anyone you want to be, because after all, you're on a divine mission of the Goddess and God.

Love

The end of the movie *The Graduate* has a beautiful sequence where the character played by Dustin Hoffman decides at the last moment to follow his heart and pursue the female character played by Katharine Ross, even though everyone is against him. He races around to find the church where she is marrying someone else to please her parents. He storms into the church and rescues her at the last minute as the preacher is about to complete the wedding vows. Together they escape with everyone screaming and running after them. The last scene is of the two of them sitting in the back of a bus with everybody on the bus staring at them.

The idea worth pointing out here is to avoid bending your will according to social pressure. This is generally much easier said than done. It's essential that you believe in yourself and what you are doing enough to follow through and make it happen. When you are working on your empowerment goals, people may belittle your efforts and try to make you believe that you will fail. Often that is merely projection on their part. They actually feel like failures and want you to join them in their misery. An example is someone who's overweight belittling the efforts of someone else who's trying to lose weight. Stay away from this pitfall by avoiding these people as much as possible as you are working toward manifesting your goals.

By contrast, once you attain your empowerment goals, people can't seem to say enough nice things about you and how successful you are. As with most things, it's a matter of perception. Once you are successful, that's the image people perceive. This is why the ninth power step can sometimes be difficult because you are changing not only who you are as a whole, but also the way people view you.

The Ninth Empowering Step: Love Meditation

Begin this meditation with a walking exercise. In a quiet room or outdoors, stand comfortably. As you take a slow and deliberate step forward with your right foot, breathe in completely, and as you take the next slow and deliberate step with your left foot, breathe out completely. Walk the length of the room or area in this manner, paying close attention to your breathing and walking.

When you have completed the walking exercise, sit or recline in a comfortable chair and close your eyes. Breathe normally, in and out. As you breathe in, imagine breathing in white light. As you breathe out, release any tension or stress you may be feeling. Do this several times to relax more and more.

Now in your mind's eye, imagine yourself walking out the door of your house and down the path to your love empowerment garden. Slowly you descend the hill that leads to your garden, and as you do so, the garden comes into view. Upon reaching the bottom of the hill, you stop for a moment to savior the sight of thriving plants ready to bloom.

Entering your love empowerment garden, you greet your beloved, who is already there busy tending a row of giant sunflower stalks topped with enormous flower buds that are ready to burst open. Grasping the handle of your water pail, you pick up the green container with a curved spout and begin filling it full of water from a nearby hose. After it fills, you pour a little fertilizer into the pail and swish it around with your hand. You bless the water by putting your hands over it and saying a short prayer to the Goddess and God, asking for their blessings.

As you move around the garden giving each of the plants some of the nourishing liquid that will help bring them into florescence, you sense your being becoming one with the essence of the plants. You encourage each of them to grow to their fullest potential. They respond to you by continuing to grow healthy and abundant. Each plant is adorned with either large flower buds about to blossom or enormous green fruits and vegetables beginning to ripen.

Taking your beloved's hand, you walk over to a thriving stargazer lily in the middle of the garden. The stalk stands high as if trying to connect the earth with the heavens above. It is covered with pointed leaves, and its branches and top with large pink and white fragrant flower buds. Taking your beloved's hands in yours, together you form a circle around the budding lily. Using your intention and expectation, you direct nurturing energy toward the plant, and as you do so, you become one with the essence of the plant. As you become one with the lily, it blossoms completely as if by magic.

You sense that the plant embodies your relationship with your beloved. You sense your relationship growing strong and healthy under the nurturing care of both of you. You sense that your relationship is ready to move to the next level of development, where you enter the florescence of empowerment. You now know that it is there at your fingertips, ready to happen. You can feel it with your entire being.

Now take a deep breath in and imagine breathing in the power and beauty of your love empowerment garden. Breathe in the growth, strength, and florescence and allow the garden's energy to fill you to the brim. Now as you take another breath in and out, imagine once again that you are breathing in pure white light. As you breathe in again, begin to move your hands and feet and slowly open your eyes without focusing on anything in particular. Stretch your body and slowly stand up. Repeat the walking exercise once more for a few minutes to bring you completely back to your body and the present time and place.

When you are done, record in your empowerment journal your impressions of the walking exercise, both before and after the mediation, as well as how you felt walking in your love empowerment garden with your beloved.

Love Affirmation and Prayer

Say this affirmation aloud several times a day to manifest your goals more quickly:

Every day with the help of the God and Goddess, I have the strong will and steady determination to nourish my love empowerment goals to fruition.

Say the following prayer just before you go to sleep every night to empower your love goals:

Hear my prayer this night Great Goddess. Please grant me the hope and power to keep moving forward in my effort to manifest my love empowerment goals every moment of every day. Thank you dear Lady. Blessed be!

Sacred Love Space

Add a clean three-foot piece of green string or cord and a clean three-foot piece of red string or cord to your sacred love space. These two strings symbolize you and your beloved. Bless the strings with divine love by holding them in your hands and saying:

Bless these cords with the power of the loving Goddess and God.

Also add a vial of grape seed oil. Hold the vial in your hands until it warms up and then say:

Bless this oil with the power of the loving Goddess and God.

Love Ritual

You will need the two pieces of string from your sacred love altar and the vial of grape seed oil for this ritual. It is most powerful when done on a full moon after sunset.

String magic is an art and craft whose origins stem from the fishing nets of ancient mariners and from the spinning and weaving of string into cloth. They are both symbolic of the web of Oneness that connects us all. This relates to the "web of the wyrd," which in the Norse tradition is the string or thread of the three Norns. Urd gathers and spins the thread of existence, Verdandi weaves it into its present pattern, and Skuld unravels the thread and throws it back into the unmanifested. In the Greek tradition they are known as the "Fates" or the "Three Sisters." Our connection with both our physical and divine mother, the umbilical cord is the cord or string that connects us to our present incarnation.

Begin by drawing a circle of light and empowering the elements. Rub a few drops of grape seed oil on the length of the two strings and then anoint yourself with the oil. Take the green string and from one end, measure out one foot (12 inches). At that point in the string, tie a knot while saying:

Blessed God and Goddess,
Weaver of all Oneness,
Let this knot come to be,
The physical bond between my beloved and me.
Ayea! So be it!

Now take the red string and tie a knot one foot from the end while repeating:

Blessed God and Goddess,
Weaver of all Oneness,
Let this knot come to be,
The physical bond between my beloved and me.
Ayea! So be it!

Next take the green string and measuring from the same end you used before, measure two feet from the end. Again tie a knot while saying:

Blessed God and Goddess,
Weaver of all Oneness,
Let this knot come to be,
The mental link between my beloved and me.
Ayea! So be it!

Take the red string, tie a knot two feet from the end, and repeat:

Blessed God and Goddess,
Weaver of all Oneness,
Let this knot come to be,
The mental link between my beloved and me.
Ayea! So be it!

Take the green string and tie the two ends together, forming a circle. As you do so, repeat the following:

Blessed God and Goddess,
Weaver of all Oneness,
Let this circle come to be,
The spiritual love between my lover and me.
Ayea! So be it!

Now weave the red string through the green circle and knot the end. The two strings are like two links in a love empowerment circle. As you do this, repeat:

Blessed God and Goddess,
Weaver of all Oneness,
Let this circle come to be,
The spiritual love between my lover and me.
Ayea! So be it!

When you are done, thank the Goddess and God, release the elements, and pull up the circle. Afterward, place the two knotted circles of string on your sacred love space as a reminder of the divine love between you and your beloved, between the Goddess and the God.

Oracle of Love

Tarot has gone far beyond its fortune-telling origins. Now it is primarily used as a visual tool for divination, for getting in touch with the divine, and in turn, yourself. It acts as a magic mirror you can look through to better understand yourself.

Tarot was a popular 52-card game with four suits in Europe around 1370 C.E. The cards originated from Egypt and were considered a collection of nature's secrets that were the very essence of the universe.

For the purposes of this oracle, you can use a traditional tarot deck or select one of the New Age tarot decks that are available, such as "The Shapeshifter Tarot." If you don't have a tarot deck and you don't want to purchase one, you can get a free tarot reading on the Internet by clicking on one of these suggested Internet sites:

- www.tarotmagic.com, an ideal site that provides several tarot decks and readings from which to choose
- www.dreampower.com, author R. J. Stewart's "Dreampower Tarot" site
- www.facade.com, a site with several tarot decks from which to choose
- http://thenewage.com, home of the Matrix Oracles

Before beginning the oracle, take a few deep, complete breaths to center your awareness. Then bless the tarot deck or computer as a divine oracle by saying:

I bless this tarot deck as a divine oracle.

Or

I bless this computer and Internet site as a divine oracle.

Now focus on your love empowerment question and gently shuffle or mix the cards. When using the Internet, click on the tarot reading while you focus on your question.

Now turn three cards over in a row from left to right. The left-most card represents the past influences, the middle card signifies the present, and the right-most card symbolizes the future, with regard to your love question. Use the book that accompanies your tarot deck and read the meanings of the cards. When using the Internet, click on the reading format you like, and the site will provide the meanings of the cards for you. For best results, ask only three questions each time you use the tarot deck or cyber tarot site.

In your empowerment journal, record the date, your question(s), the tarot cards and their meanings that appeared in the reading, and in what position they appeared.

Health

Soon after being named the top-ranked cyclist of 1996, Lance Armstrong began experiencing soreness in his body, blurry vision, and severe headaches. He also began coughing up blood. After consulting a doctor, he was diagnosed with an advanced form of testicular cancer and was given a 50/50 chance of survival.

Lance responded by finding the best doctors he could, keeping a positive mental attitude, and spending a lot of time with family and friends. During treatment, he continued to ride his bicycle and never gave up hope on his goals as a cyclist. In 1997, he was diagnosed as cancer free, and by 1998 he was back to racing again. In 1999 and 2000, he overcame any skepticism of his return to top form by twice winning the Tour de France, the premier race for cyclists. This race requires an inordinate amount of endurance—something that was thought impossible for an ex-cancer patient. Returning to the United States after winning, Lance received a welcome usually reserved for astronauts coming back from an expedition in space.

In addition to winning cycling races, Lance has gone on to set up the Lance Armstrong Foundation for Cancer Research and Awareness to help other cancer victims, and he has written a book with contributing author Sally Jenkins, entitled *It's Not About the Bike: My Journey Back to Life* detailing his extraordinary efforts to beat cancer and become well again.

Lance Armstrong's healing experience serves to remind us that no matter what the odds are against you, anything is possible when you wholeheartedly focus your thoughts and actions toward empowering your health. Also, his story shows that it is important to utilize the resources available at your fingertips by getting the best doctors, keeping a healthy state of mind, and reaching out to helpful family and friends for support. All these elements can help you to actualize your health empowerment goals.

The Ninth Empowering Step: Healing Meditation

Do this meditation after sunset. Turn on some soft New Age or instrumental music. Sit or recline in a comfortable spot, holding a clear quartz crystal in your receiving hand. Close your eyes and take three deep, complete breaths. As you breathe in, imagine your lungs being filled with a bright green light. As you exhale, see and sense the light moving throughout your body, making you feel relaxed and healthy. After the third breath, imagine feeling lighter than air and floating magically out the window into the night sky. Like a firefly you float freely upward amongst the branches of a giant tree, and then upward, higher and higher, until you become a bright star in the night sky.

The stars around you fill every part of the sky. Looking upward, you see the three stars that are the belt of Orion the Hunter, the star constellation that is just coming up over the horizon. Moving even higher into the night sky, you see the Milky Way, beckoning you into its depths. At this point, you sense yourself being uplifted on a moving carpet of light, like an escalator to the heavens, transporting you to a distant universe.

Once you reach your destination, you find yourself on a planet that is part of a circle of planets, all revolving around the cosmic light of the divine. Each planet derives its life, warmth, and nourishment from this divinity. Your sense that all movement in this place revolves in a circular motion. Every circle is part of an even larger circle, reaching all the way to Oneness, which by virtue is a circle of holistic and infinite proportions.

Now imagine yourself part of a gigantic healing circle of starlight energy filled with positive, helpful beings. Everyone nurtures and empowers each other. Each being is holding hands with those on either side of it, and the healing energy cycles around and through the many participants who make up the circle. Everyone prays for himself or herself, everyone else, and to the divine. This prayer moves into the circular energy of the circle, empowering everyone involved, and increasing the overall energy.

Sense your body, mind, and spirit becoming healthier with each moment you are in the circle of starlight energy. Any blockages in your health goals fill with light and magically dissolve as you move closer toward health empowerment. You sense that you have the knowledge and power to heal yourself with the help of these divine beings and the starlight energy. You understand that you can become as healthy as you desire by just putting your mind to it, and by accepting the healing energy of the divine star circle of light. You realize that anything is possible as long as you believe you can do it in your heart, head, and spirit.

Now take a deep breath, breathing in the power of the healing circle, and breathing out any tension, discomfort, or illness you may be experiencing. Take another deep breath in and imagine floating downward this time, slowly and lightly descending to earth. You transform into a firefly and float back through the window into your room. Breathe in again, breathing in the knowledge that you are successfully manifesting your health empowerment goals and breathing out any tension, discomfort, or illness. Now take another deep breath, feeling relaxed and calm, yet peacefully alert. Slowly open your eyes and come back to the present time and place. Stretch your muscles like a cat, feeling the healing effects of the starlight circle in your body, mind, and spirit.

While the meditation is still fresh in your mind, write your impressions and experiences in your empowerment journal. Note your impressions of floating upward, entering and participating in the healing circle of starlight energy, and how you felt when you floated back down to earth.

Healing Affirmation and Prayer

Say this affirmation several times a day to manifest your health empowerment goals more quickly:

Every day I move steadily toward attaining my health empowerment goals. Nothing can deter me from manifesting my most cherished healing goals.

Say the following prayer in the morning to enlist divine determination and power to help you attain your healing goals:

Great Goddess I pray you, please give me the strength and determination to be healthy and fill me with your divine healing light. I am a reflection of your greater good, of your bright nature, now and forevermore. Thank you Dear Lady, blessed be!

Sacred Healing Space

Add a three-foot blue string, representing your physical self; a three-foot green string, representing your mental self; and a three-foot white string, representing your spiritual self to your sacred healing space. Bless the strings by holding them in your hands and saying:

Bless these cords with divine healing power.

Healing Ritual

In the Hawaiian tradition, "Huna" is the hidden secret that lies within each one of us, waiting to be realized. String magic is used to break up blockages and bring divine blessings. "Mana" is the power that comes from within our being as we weave our patterns that connect our body, mind, and spirit to the whole of Oneness.

Begin by drawing a magic circle of light and empowering the elements. Lay all three strings from your sacred healing altar out side by side. Using a yardstick or measuring tape, measure one foot (12 inches) from one of the ends, and using all three stings, tie a knot while saying the following:

Blessed Goddess and God,
I tie healing energy to me.
This knot represents my potential,
Someone I shall come to be,
When I naturally realize my destiny.
Ayea! Blessed be!

Now from the first knot, measure another foot, two feet from the end. Again using all three strings, tie a knot and say:

Blessed Goddess and God,
I tie healing energy to me.
This knot represents who I've become,
Moving through my health empowerment process,
Merging further into the greater Oneness.
Ayea! Blessed be!

Last, tie all the ends of the strings together into one great circle. As you do this, say:

Blessed Goddess and God,
I tie healing energy to me.
This knot represents my full circle.
I realize who I want to be,
And I am becoming more and more healthy.
Ayea! Blessed be!

When you are done, thank the Goddess and God, bid farewell to the elements, and pull up the circle. Put the knotted strings on your sacred healing altar as a reminder that your health empowerment goals are now at your fingertips. You just need to keep working toward successfully manifesting them, one day at a time.

Oracle of Health

Use a deck of tarot cards or navigate to an Internet site that offers cyber tarot readings (see the earlier list in the section "Oracle of Love"). Focus your mind on your health question and gently shuffle or mix the cards. When using the Internet, click on the tarot reading while focusing on your question.

Turn three cards over in a row from left to right on the surface in front of you. The left-most card represents the past influences, the middle card the present, and the right-most card the future, with regard to your health empowerment question. Use the book that accompanies your tarot deck and read the meanings of the cards you have selected. When using the Internet, the site will provide the meanings of the cards for you on the screen.

In your empowerment journal, record the date, your question(s), the tarot cards that appeared in the health empowerment reading, brief meanings of the cards, and the position in which they appeared.

Prosperity

At age 19, actress Jodie Foster received unexpected and unwanted media attention with regard to the attempted assassination of President Reagan. The would-be assassin indicated that he styled his attempt from the movie *Taxi Driver*, for which Jodie had received an Academy Award nomination for Best Supporting Actress. After the incident, she shunned media attention and wrote an article for *Esquire* magazine entitled "Why Me?"

Jodie Foster was not one to give up, and through her dedication and determination, she went on to graduate from Yale University with honors and a B.A. in literature. She won two Academy Awards for Best Actress before the age of 30, and went on to become one of the most successful directors and producers in Hollywood.

Known for balancing artistic integrity with commercial success, Jodie Foster is a shining example of how to keep your determination and belief in yourself alive, even in moments when it would be easier, and safer, to give up and quit. Her determination and will to rise above adversity remind us that the empowerment process is not about giving up, it's about realizing and actualizing your prosperity goals. As you get closer to actualizing your own goals, things don't always get easier, but instead the challenges are sometimes greater, especially as you make it over the last few hurdles that stand in your way.

To help you over those final hurdles, read inspiring stories like Jodie Foster's and Lance Armstrong's. More important, continue to use the meditations, affirmations and prayers, sacred spaces, rituals, and oracles in this book to move beyond these hurdles and manifest your prosperity goals.

The Ninth Empowering Step: Prosperity Meditation

Begin by sitting back or reclining in a comfortable, undisturbed spot. Take three deep breaths, inhaling for three counts, holding your breath for three counts, and exhaling completely. As you exhale, let go of any tension, worry, or anxiety. Allow your neck to relax and your shoulders to drop and relax. Take another deep breath and relax your body even more, feeling calm and peacefully aware.

Say these words silently, "Great Goddess, send me to the place where I can find my prosperity empowerment." Then, imagine you are drifting in a mystical haze. When the haze lifts, you find yourself walking on a narrow cobblestone street lined with shops of all kinds and sizes. You can buy anything you want in these shops for a price. When you reach into your coat pockets, you find them filled with plenty of money.

You enter the shop closest to you and smell the scent of frankincense and myrrh lingering in the air. The shelves are lined with an assortment of books containing the knowledge of a thousand lifetimes. As you sort through the volumes that endlessly cover the shelves, you pick the ones that pertain to realizing your prosperity goals. These particular books help you maintain your focus and understand what you need to do to be empowered. You leave the shop with the books you need to read to help you manifest your goals.

Entering the next shop, you are greeted with beautiful music. You see musical instruments of every kind, records, cassette tapes, and CDs on the seemingly endless shelves, tucked into every nook and cranny of the shop. You are magically drawn toward music that inspires you and helps you continue on your path to prosperity empowerment and abundance. You leave the music shop with the music you need to listen to in order to manifest your goals.

You enter the next shop, and you are fascinated by the assortment of magic tools, such as cauldrons, chalices, swords, athames, candles, and magical wands. Picking up the wand closest to you, you recite a simple incantation and nothing happens, so you put the wand back down. From the dozens of wands on display, you finally select one that truly resonates with you. As you recite the simple incantation again, the wand tip fills with bright white light that streams out across the shop walls. With your wand in your hand, you realize the basic tenet of magic—anything is possible as long as you believe it's possible. You leave the shop of magic tools with your wand in hand.

As you enter the next shop, you notice its name printed above the door in large script letters, "Empowerment at Your Fingertips." This shop contains the remaining bits of things you need to successfully manifest your prosperity empowerment goals. Sorting through the things, you find several items to help nurture, feed, adorn, and coalesce your goals. You leave the shop with everything you need to achieve your prosperity empowerment goals.

As you stand outside the shop called "Empowerment at Your Fingertips," a thick haze suddenly flows toward you and engulfs you. You take a deep breath in and find yourself floating back to the present time and place. You take another deep, relaxing breath in and out, and you realize that all of your prosperity goals are easily within your grasp, right at your fingertips. With this knowledge, you take another deep breath and begin to move your fingers and toes. Slowly open your eyes. Stretch your body and then clap your hands three times.

When you are done meditating, write your impressions of the meditation in your empowerment journal. Record how it felt as you discovered the many things you needed to manifest your prosperity goals. How did it feel to have your goals at your fingertips?

Prosperity Affirmation and Prayer

Say this affirmation at least 10 times a day for 28 days for best results:

Each and every moment of each and every hour, I move closer to prosperity empowerment and abundance. My goals are now at my fingertips.

Say the following prayer in the morning to help your prosperity goals come true:

Dear Goddess and God of prosperity and abundance, today please grant me the will, determination, and courage to successfully attain my prosperity goals. Thank you divine ones. Blessed be!

Sacred Riches Space

Add a green candle and a three-foot gold-colored cord to your sacred riches space. Cleanse the candle by rinsing it in cool salt water and then dry it. Bless the items by holding them in your hands and saying:

Bless these tools with divine empowerment.

Now tie a fairly loose knot in the middle of the cord.

Prosperity Ritual

Best done on a new moon, this magic string ritual can be used to clear any blockages you may have in actualizing your prosperity empowerment goals. Before starting, select one goal to work on in the ritual.

Begin by drawing a magic circle of light and empowering the elements. Light the green candle and dedicate it to a favorite prosperity Goddess. Next, while gazing at the candle flame, state the blockage or problem you want to clear up. Take the gold cord with the knot and hold it up in your right hand while saying:

Dear Goddess, I ask for your help,
So that my path will become clear,
And bless me with the knowledge,
That my empowerment is near.
So be it!

Lower the cord, and with your fingers, begin untying the knot in the cord, all the while imagining the blockage in your prosperity goal being cleared with the help of the Goddess. Smooth out the cord where the knot used to be, making it so energy flows unimpeded from one end of the cord to the other.

Now take both ends of the cord and tie them together to make a circle. As you do this, say this blessing:

Eternal Goddess,
Whose energy is endless,
Bless my prosperity,
So that it may forever be.
I am unto you
As you are unto me.
So be it!

Finish by thanking the Goddess and bidding farewell to the elements. Then pull up the circle. Loop the gold cord on your sacred riches altar as a focal to help remind you that any blockages can be cleared up so that you can successfully attain your prosperity goals.

Oracle of Wealth

Use your deck of tarot cards or navigate to an Internet site that offers free tarot readings (see the earlier list under oracle of love). Focus on your prosperity empowerment question and shuffle or mix the cards. When using the Internet, click on the tarot reading while focusing on your question.

Turn three cards over in a row from left to right on the surface in front of you. The left-most card indicates the past influences, the middle card the present influences, and the right-most card the future influences regarding your prosperity question. Use the book that comes with your tarot deck and read the meanings of the cards you have selected. When using the Internet, the meanings of the cards will appear onscreen.

Take a few minutes to record in your empowerment journal the date, your prosperity question(s), the tarot cards that appeared in the reading, their meanings, and also the position in which the cards appeared.

Chapter Ten

The Tenth Empowering Step: Manifesting Your Empowerment Goals

Wilma Rudolph was diagnosed with polio as a young girl and was told by her doctors that she would never walk. A strong, intelligent, and determined woman, Wilma's mother began taking her young daughter to physical therapy. Her mother carefully watched the therapist and then taught Wilma's many brothers and sisters how to massage Wilma's legs. Up to the age of 11, Wilma had worn a leg brace, but when she turned 11, she discarded the brace and started walking without it. At age 13, she started running track, a sport she began to aggressively pursue. In 1956, while still in high school, Wilma Rudolph competed in the U.S. Olympic Trials. Although she didn't make the team, the stage was set for the 1960 Olympics. During those games she became the first woman to win three gold medals, and she also set the record for the 200 meter race.

In another story of empowerment, Alice Paul and the National Women's Party picketed the White House in the winter of 1917. They wanted to persuade President Wilson to support their goal and give women the right to vote—a goal that women had been working toward for almost 70 years. President Wilson and both houses of Congress refused to support the idea.

Alice Paul and the women picketing were harassed and arrested for their efforts, but they were undaunted as they continued their quest. Trying to silence the protesters once and for all, the police arrested Alice Paul, and she was sentenced to seven months in prison. Once in prison, she immediately went on a hunger strike. The authorities retaliated by placing her in a psychiatric ward, and when that didn't work, they began force-feeding her. Still, she refused to eat on her own. When the story attracted media attention, Alice was released after five arduous weeks.

For women, the media attention of Alice Paul was the push needed to help manifest their goal of achieving the right to vote. Shortly thereafter, President Wilson relented and gave his support. Congress passed a resolution giving their support, and finally, on August 26, 1920, with the Nineteenth Amendment to the constitution, women were given the constitutional right to vote.

The empowering stories of Wilma Rudolph and Alice Paul represent two contrasting approaches to the Tenth Empowering Step, manifesting your empowerment goals. In Wilma's case, she aggressively approached her goals by first going through rigorous physical therapy so she could walk, then by rigorously training so that she realized her goal of winning Olympic gold. In Alice's case, she chose passive resistance as a means for achieving her goal, although she was just as strongly focused on her goal as Wilma. Even though they had two contrasting approaches, both women were successful at manifesting their goals.

When choosing your own approach to manifesting your empowerment goals, be aware of your own circumstances and choose accordingly the best approach to make them happen. Sometimes you may find that you have to be more aggressive; other times you may find you need to be more passive. Still other times, you may find blending both approaches works best. Most of the time, the situation dictates which approach to take. The important thing is to be aware and stay in tune not only with your own abilities, but also with the totality of the situation, your environment, and the larger picture. As you make your decisions, be sure to ask for help when you need it, both from empowering people and the divine.

Change Your Perspective

One day I woke up and with my first step out of bed, my foot encountered something wet, undoubtedly left there during the night by our six-month-old puppy. As I went to wash off my foot, I realized there wasn't any hot water because my water heater wasn't working properly. After waiting most of the morning and afternoon for a tardy repair person, I was starting to think there was a chance I was having a bad hair day.

At that point, I remembered something a friend of mine always says, "If you find that you are digging yourself into a hole, the first thing you need to do is stop digging." I took a deep breath and said aloud, "Cancel those negative thoughts and experiences and transform them into positive ones."

I meditated for about 30 minutes and then listened to some soft music. I asked for the guidance and blessings of the Goddess and God. My disposition quickly changed, and I heard the doorbell ring, signaling that the repair person had arrived. A couple hours later, I was releasing the tensions of the day with a warm and soothing bath.

Part of empowerment is dealing with adversity at every level—the big problems and little nuisances. Although sometimes it feels the world is chucking dirt clods at you, you need to keep focused, be sure to duck, and deliberately turn things around for the better. Make every effort not to get stuck in the moment where you feel as though you can't get out of it. The best way to get unstuck is to change your perspective.

Asking for the help of the Goddess and God is your most powerful tool for changing your point of view and, ultimately, for personal transformation. Remember that the divine is always there to help you 24 hours a day. All you have to do is ask!

Love

By the time John Lennon and Yoko Ono met, each had already achieved their basic goals. As a member of the Beatles, he was a successful songwriter and musician, and she was a respected avant-garde artist. From the beginning, they moved past adversity, even as people tried to split them apart.

Their relationship empowered both of them in terms of love. Rather than compete with each other, they helped each other rise to new levels of awareness and empowerment. Through their ups and downs, they ultimately stayed together and continued to help each other manifest their empowerment as evidenced by the album, "Double Fantasy." They shared a spiritual bond that went beyond the physical. Today, Yoko continues to champion their shared causes and protect the way people view John and his music.

Empowering relationships are almost always built on cooperation, not competition. The benefits of cooperation and the pitfalls of competition become more obvious as you begin manifesting your love empowerment goals. Although competition can initially be useful in motivating you to excel, eventually it creates animosity. Someone wins and someone loses. As a result, competition eventually breeds contempt, whereas cooperation often provides that extra boost you need to help you attain your goals.

The Tenth Empowering Step: Love Meditation

Use your empowerment stone (see Chapter Three) for this meditation. Turn on some soft New Age or instrumental music and sit or recline comfortably. Use the pulse-breath technique to clear your empowerment stone, and then pulse the color rose into the stone three times. Hold the stone in your receiving hand as you close your eyes and take a deep breath in and out. Take another deep breath and imagine breathing the rose color of the stone into your being.

Take another deep breath and imagine breathing in feelings of love and joy. Sense the love spreading outward through all parts of your body, mind, and spirit, bringing a sense of soothing joy. Feelings of love and joy resonate throughout your being as you breathe in and out. You feel relaxed and peacefully aware.

In your mind's eye imagine standing before a wooden garden gate. On both sides of the gate are solid rock walls made from stones that have been carefully fitted together. You open the latch on the gate and step into the garden. As you do, your senses are filled with a multitude of fragrances and colors. You are surrounded by flowers of every kind and green grass. In the center of the garden, you see your beloved waiting for you.

Imagine slowly walking through this empowering garden, hand-in-hand with your beloved. You sense a magical energy that moves with you wherever you go. It is an energy that helps you to manifest your empowerment goals of love. As you walk through your garden, you sense that energy present between you and your beloved and between you and the elements. You sense that something wonderful is about to happen.

Your whole body begins to glow with anticipation as you and your beloved move toward a magnificent rosebush that is covered with red buds about to bloom. Standing in front of the rosebush, you feel a connection with the Goddess that moves in a circle from you to your beloved to the rosebush and back to you.

You and your beloved focus your awareness on one of the buds. As you do, the bud begins to open up and flower. The deep red petals shine with extraordinary brilliance and divine radiance.

You walk hand-in-hand to a second rosebush covered with yellow buds. As you focus upon a perfect bud, it opens and blossoms with a radiance that shines divinely upon its yellow petals. You sense the love and the bond between you and your beloved increasing in strength as you both gaze upon the splendor of the two roses. Side by side, they empower each other, and in turn empower you and your beloved, enlarging your circle of light.

Feeling the warmth of your beloved's touch, you walk over to a third rosebush covered with white buds. You both begin gazing with expectation on a third rosebud that at first seems not to respond, but as you continue moving your thoughts toward it, the rosebud begins to open. The petals are creamy white and its divine fragrance soon fills your nostrils, leaving you with a feeling of enchantment as the bud transforms into a magnificent blossom. From the corner of your eye, you sense movement, and taking your eyes off the blossom, you notice that all the buds are now opening in a splendor of different colors.

The brilliance is overwhelming, much like a tree being lit up at Yule, as you and your beloved stand cradled in each other's arms. Your senses are in awe as if being filled to capacity with divine love that creates a circle to encompass all of Oneness. In the moment, your awareness expands and you realize that anything is possible as long as you focus your expectations on it; magic is matter of perception. You find the thought extremely empowering.

Now take a deep breath in and out, once again breathing in the rose color from the stone in your hand. Breathe in again, feeling refreshed and empowered. Move your hands and feet. Slowly open your eyes and come back to the present time and place. Stretch your body for a few moments, and then record your impressions of the meditation experience in your empowerment journal. Note what you thought and how you felt as the rosebuds bloomed, and how you felt as you were filled with divine love. When you are done, put the stone on your sacred love altar.

Love Affirmation and Prayer

Hold your empowerment stone in your power hand and repeat this affirmation several times a day for at least 28 days:

Every moment of every day is like a beautiful rose opening. With each blossom, I realize my love empowerment goals and rejoice in manifesting them.

Hold your empowerment stone in your power hand as you say the following prayer each morning:

Dear Goddess and God, please let each day be empowering, and help me to maintain my focus and inner balance as I manifest my love empowerment goals. Thank you dear friends for your guidance, blessing, and protection. Blessed be!

Sacred Love Space

Add a picture of you and your beloved, two red silk roses, a vial of rose oil, and a red candle to your sacred love altar. Bless the items by holding them in your hands, merging with the divine, and saying three times:

Blessed be the divine love of the Goddess and God.

Love Ritual

Perform this ritual with your beloved on a Friday evening, if possible just before a full moon. I suggest you take a warm bath before the ritual and add a few drops of rose oil to the bath water. You will need the two red silk roses, the red candle, the rose oil, and the picture of you and your beloved from your sacred love altar, as well as a ballpoint pen.

Draw a magic circle and empower the elements. Use the ballpoint pen to write "I love you" on the candle. Then have your beloved write "I love you" on the candle as well. Dress the candle with rose oil, anoint your beloved with the oil, and then have him or her anoint you with the oil. Wipe the oil from your hands and light the candle, dedicating it to your favorite God and Goddess of love. Then say to your beloved:

I love you with my body, heart, mind, and soul.
Have your beloved repeat to you:
I love you with my body, heart, mind, and soul.

Next, set the picture by the candle in such a way that the candlelight illuminates it. Then each of you hold a red silk rose in your power hands and say together:

Sacred roses, sacred fire
Blessed be our loving desire
Two as one, and one as two
You love me, and I love you.
Blessed be, blessed be, blessed be!

Now hand the roses to each other and embrace. Sit together for a few minutes as you gaze at one another in the candlelight. For a while, become like the Goddess and God and express your divine love for one another. Allow the candle to safely burn down.

When you are done, thank the Goddess and God of love, bid farewell to the elements, and pull up the circle. Put the silk roses next to your bed to remind you of the sacred love you have manifested. Frame the picture of yourself and your beloved and set or hang it in a special place in your sacred love space to remind you of the love you share each and every day.

Oracle of Love

The I-Ching is a Chinese divination system. The symbols are over 5,000 years old. I-Ching, more than any other divination system, paints a complete picture to answer your question, plus it shows you several other options. Get a free I-Ching reading on the Internet by clicking on one of these suggested Internet sites:

- www.tarotmagic.com
- http://thenewage.com
- www.facade.com

Before beginning the oracle, take a deep, complete breath to focus your mind. Bless the computer site as a divine oracle by saying:

By the grace of the Goddess and God, may this Internet I-Ching site be a divine and clear oracle for me right now.

Focus on your love empowerment question and type it or a few words that describe it into the space provided. Click on the reading and follow the instructions. Remember to note the date, your question, and the basic meaning of the reading in your empowerment journal.

Health

Ingrid Bacci seemed to have everything she ever wanted. She had a Ph.D. from Columbia University, and at the age of 27, she was an assistant professor of philosophy at the State University of New York. She married her college sweetheart who was from a wealthy family, so she had plenty of money. But instead of being happy and healthy, Ingrid's life was falling apart. Her problem started as a soreness in her legs after being active. It continued to get worse until one morning her legs gave out on her and she had problems walking. The condition worsened until there was a burning sensation in all her muscles and joints, making it hard to even move. This went on for three years with each doctor's visit less illuminating than the last. All the best physicians were confounded and offered no medical explanation for what was happening to her. In desperation, Ingrid reached beyond the boundaries imposed on her and began seeking alternative methods to turn the tide that was destroying her health.

Ingrid gave up cigarettes and coffee, consulted a naturopathic doctor, and became a vegetarian. These changes made a difference, and she started getting better. Then Ingrid began a journey of self-discovery that meant reading self-help books and doing daily meditations. As she explains in her intriguing book, *The Art of Effortless Living*, when she started to experiment with her lifestyle and consciousness, her body chose to live again and her life began to positively transform.

If things don't work for you, like they didn't for Ingrid, dare to experiment and try different things until you can manifest your health empowerment goals. Keep trying even when things don't seem to work out at first. Empowerment is a process that must be approached on a daily basis. Give yourself realistic time frames in which to expect results. Ingrid is the first to admit that trying new things and alternative therapies wasn't a panacea and it didn't change her life overnight. But day by day, the incremental changes that meditation brought into Ingrid's life completely transformed her. Specifically, she credits the daily meditation that over time taught her how to release anxiety, depression, anger, tension, and pain and live joyously again.

The Tenth Empowering Step: Healing Meditation

Sit or recline in a comfortable spot. Hold a key in your power hand. Close your eyes and take a deep breath. As you breathe in, imagine breathing healing energy into your being. As you breathe out, release any tensions or pain through your exhaled breath. Breathe in this manner for a few minutes and then allow your breathing to return to normal.

In your mind's eye, imagine you are walking down a staircase that has 10 stairs. One by one you descend the staircase, and with each step, you move closer to a large wooden door just beyond the tenth step. In front of the wooden door that now has a visible lock is a table covered with what seems like an infinite assortment of keys—from ancient skeleton keys to modern keys made with numerous patterns of teeth.

At first, the task of finding the right key to open the door seems overwhelming, but soon you find yourself sorting through the keys. Once you are finished sorting, you still find you have a number of keys to choose from. Spreading the sorted keys out on the edge of the table, you begin moving your palms about one inch above the keys while opening your senses to any energy coming from the keys. After a few minutes, you sense a stronger power in one of the keys and it keeps drawing you back to it. Picking up a golden-colored skeleton key, you sense it is the correct one, and you insert it into the lock. The key fits perfectly, moves the tumblers, and the door opens with a soft click.

Moving through the open doorway, you sense that your physical body is healthy and empowered. Fine-tuning your senses, you become aware that you are in a room that to one side has a giant copper-covered door. In front of the door is another table that has a magnificent assortment of musical pitch pipes. Like the keys, you begin moving your palms over the pipes, searching for the correct one, the one with the strongest energy that seems to call to you. You ask for the confirmation of the Goddess and God, and then you pick up the pipe and blow into one end. The pitch pipe sounds with a series of five notes with divine resonance. You sense a rumbling and the copper covered gate opens, allowing you entry into the next chamber. As you pass through the door, your body and mind feel even more healthy and empowered.

In the chamber beyond the door stands a massive stone wall that seems to stretch endlessly on both sides. The wall is solid and there doesn't seem to be any way of getting past it. There is no visible doorway or key. Touching the wall, you sense its strength and solidness. Standing back from the stone wall, you survey it and conclude that there is no way you can climb over it. You ask for the help and blessings of the Goddess and God, at which point you become aware of a light that moves around and through your body. The light increases in intensity like a halo of energy moving inward and outward from the many levels of your being.

Moving over to the wall, you extend your arms and hands outward toward it. As you do, a bright white light shimmers from your hands to the wall. At first nothing happens, but then, little by little, the wall begins to crack and crumble with white healing light emanating from the next chamber. As you walk through the remaining rubble to the other side, your body, mind, and spirit become one. You are filled to the brim with the white healing light. You know that each step you take moves you closer to your health empowerment goals until they are easily within your grasp. As you manifest your goals, the bright white light within you and emanating around you becomes even brighter. You know that the Goddess and God are with you at all times, guiding your continual forward movement to empowered health.

Now breathe in the white healing light as you take a deep and complete breath in and out. Know that you are now manifesting your health empowerment goals with intelligence, diligence, and grace. Take another breath and begin moving your fingers and toes. Then slowly open your eyes. Rub your palms briskly together several times until they are warm to the touch. Then clap your hands three times to bring you back to the present time and place. Put the key on your sacred healing altar to use again later.

While the meditation is fresh in your mind, record your impressions in your empowerment journal. Make a note of how you felt as you walked through the doors, when the wall came down, and when you were able to easily walk through the rubble to good health and physical empowerment on the other side.

Healing Affirmation and Prayer

Say this affirming statement each time you walk through a doorway. Repeat this process for at least 28 days to help you more readily manifest your goals:

Each and every day, I step through the door to health empowerment and manifest my goals with intelligence, grace, and deliberate effort. With each step I take, my inner awareness and health grow strong and capable.

Hold the key from your sacred healing altar in your hand as you say the following prayer to enlist divine power when manifesting your goals:

Blessed Goddess and God, please guide me through the divine door toward health empowerment. I pray you, please show me the key, take my hand in yours, and lead me to a healing place where I am strong and vibrant. I ask this with my body, mind, and spirit. Thank you dear Lady and Lord for your divine guidance and help. Blessed be!

Sacred Healing Space

Add a blue candle, a white candle, a green candle, three 9-inch sticks, a yard length of green string or cord, and a vial of lavender oil to your sacred healing altar. Bless these items with the divine healing power of the Goddess and God by holding them in your hands, one at a time and saying:

May the divine healing power of the Goddess and God flow into me right now. So be it!

Healing Ritual

In this ritual, you bind yourself to good health and create a simple health empowerment charm at the same time. Do this spell during the waxing moon phase. You will be using the key, the blue, white, and green candles, the three sticks, the green string, and the lavender oil from your sacred healing altar.

First draw a magic circle and call in the elements. Then use the tip of the key to inscribe the words "Old Self" on the blue candle, "Divine Healing" on the white candle, and "New Self in Good Health" on the green candle. Place the candles in a row, with the blue candle on the left, the white candle in the middle, and the green candle on the left. Also, put the key on the altar in front of the candles. Dress the candles with lavender oil and anoint yourself. Wipe the oil from your hands, light the blue candle, and say:

Divine light, blessed be
This is my old self
The self I used to be.

Light the white candle from the blue candle and say:

Divine light, blessed be
This is my spiritual self
The self I will always be.

Now light the green candle from the white candle and say:

Divine light, blessed be
This is my new self
The healthy self that is now me.

As the candles burn, merge with the divine for a few minutes. Then hold the three sticks in your receiving hand and wind the green string around them several times with your power hand. As you do this say three times:

Goddess and God bless my healthy and peaceful body
Goddess and God bless my healthy and peaceful mind
Goddess and God bless my healthy and peaceful spirit
May the divine bind good health to me. Blessed be!

When you have wound the string around the sticks, tie a knot so the string is tight and secure. Then tie the key to the string ends with three knots. As you do, repeat three times:

Goddess and God bless my healthy and peaceful body
Goddess and God bless my healthy and peaceful mind
Goddess and God bless my healthy and peaceful spirit
May the divine bind good health to me. Blessed be!

Next, carefully drip nine drops of wax from the green candle onto the bundle and the key. Hold the bundle in your hands and repeat three more times:

Goddess and God bless my healthy and peaceful body
Goddess and God bless my healthy and peaceful mind
Goddess and God bless my healthy and peaceful spirit
May the divine bind good health to me. Blessed be!

Now hold the bundle in your hands for several minutes while focusing your awareness on images and sensations of good health. Know that your body, mind, and spirit are healthy and peaceful. Know that you have now manifested your health empowerment goals.

When you are done, thank the Goddess and God, release the elements, and pull up the circle. Allow the candles to safely burn down. Put the stick bundle and key in a safe place.

Oracle of Health

Think of a question about manifesting your health empowerment goals. Click on an Internet I-Ching site (see the earlier list in the section "Oracle of Love").

Before starting the reading, take a deep and complete breath to center yourself. Next, bless the Internet site as a divine oracle by laying your hands on the computer and saying:

By the grace of the Goddess and God, may this Internet I-Ching site be a divine and clear oracle for me right now.

Take a few moments to focus on your health empowerment question and type the question or a couple of words that describe it into the space provided. Then click on the reading and follow the onscreen instructions. Remember to note the date, your question, and the basic meaning of the reading in your empowerment journal.

Prosperity

Joanne K. Rowling began her professional career as a secretary. She quickly realized her disorganized nature would soon make her the worst secretary ever, and besides, what she really liked to do was write stories. Giving up on office jobs, she went to Portugal to teach English as a foreign language. In the meantime, she started writing a story about a magical boy who would meet his calling as a wizard. Eventually, she returned to England, divorced and with a young baby, where she lived on assistance. Later, she moved to Edinburgh and set a goal to finish the book before going back to work.

Between her daughter's naps, she began to craft the book, and soon thereafter she garnered a grant from the Scottish Arts Council that helped her finish the book. This led to her acceptance by a publisher, winning the British Book Awards Children's Book of the Year, and landing on the best seller list. She has reported that the period when she was writing *Harry Potter and the Sorcerer's Stone* was the lowest point in her life and that it was the challenge of the book that kept her from going stark raving mad.

After four best selling books and two popular movies, J. K. Rowling has established herself as one of the world's greatest fantasy writers. As a good author, she culminated her information and ideas from many sources, coalescing them into one cohesive artistic statement. Unfortunately, with success came more stress as some claimed she stole her ideas for her books from published sources. Fortunately, these claims were found to be without merit. By applying persistence, effort, and creativity, J. K. Rowling successfully manifested her prosperity goals and empowered herself through her books.

The Tenth Empowering Step: Prosperity Meditation

Turn on some soft, instrumental holiday music and sit or recline in a comfortable spot where you will not be interrupted. Also, burn cedar incense or put a few drops of cedarwood oil on a handkerchief and keep it close by. Be sure to loosen or remove any clothing, belts, or shoes that may be binding you. Uncross your hands and feet. Now take a deep breath and let go of any tension or stress you may be feeling as you exhale. Do this several times, feeling more and more peacefully relaxed with each breath you take.

In your mind's eye, imagine walking down a long hallway that leads to an elevator door. As you press the down button, lights begin blinking until the door opens and you enter the elevator. After the door closes behind you, your finger presses the button for the bottom floor, and you begin to sense the movement of the lift, generating a tingling sensation that travels up and down your spine. You watch as the indicator above the door lights up the number of each floor as you descend downward: 10-9-8-7-6-5-4-3-2-1.

As it reaches the first floor, the elevator comes to a halt, and the doors slowly open. Exiting the elevator, you enter a room filled with a woodsy cedar fragrance. In one corner of the room is a giant Yule tree whose branches magically change color every few seconds. As you move closer to the tree, you see presents of every size and shape stacked under it. You suddenly realize that the magnificent tree and the presents underneath represent your prosperity empowerment.

At the very top of the tree is an exquisite image of the Goddess, lit from behind. As you gaze upon her, she asks you for your wish list of prosperity gifts. Reciting your prosperity goals to her, she smiles. As she does so, the tree turns a bright golden color. You notice that there are even more presents under the tree than there were previously, and many of them have tags with your name written on them.

Sitting before the tree, you wait with anticipation for the moment when you can open your presents. You're eager to open your empowering gifts, things that you have asked for and worked toward with all your efforts. Your excitement continues to mount as the cuckoo clock on the wall sounds 10 cuckoos, signaling that now is the moment to open your divine gifts.

You burst with excitement and sing with glee as you move over to the base of the tree and begin gathering your presents. You rip off the ribbons and wrapping paper to reveal the gifts inside. Each one fills you with joy as you realize you have received exactly what you asked the Goddess for. Looking up to the top of the tree, she smiles at you. As she smiles, you sense a magical wave of divine empowerment flowing through you. You feel as though every part of you is smiling with joy and wonderment.

You thank the Goddess for her gifts and the joy she has shared with you. She has helped you to realize your prosperity goals and the empowerment that goes with them. You become aware that she is always with you as you take your gifts and move back into the elevator. You press the up button, and the elevator doors open. You enter the lift and press the button to the tenth floor. You feel divinely empowered as the elevator travels upward: 1-2-3-4-5-6-7-8-9-10. When the elevator doors open on the tenth floor, you step out of the elevator and walk down the hallway. As you do, you take a deep, complete breath, rejoicing in the fact that you have manifested your prosperity goals. Now take another deep breath in and out as you continue down the hallway, knowing that you can take that uplifting, empowering feeling with you wherever you go. Take another deep breath and start moving your feet and hands. Slowly open your eyes and rub your hands briskly together several times. Stretch your body like a cat and come fully back to the present moment and place.

Record your impressions of the meditation in your empowerment journal. Note how it felt entering the elevator, going down, addressing the Goddess, receiving your prosperity gifts, and going back up the elevator.

Prosperity Affirmation and Prayer

Affirm your prosperity goals by repeating this positive saying at least nine times a day for 28 days:

Each and every day of life is a divine gift placed before me. As I open it, I watch my prosperity goals come to fruition with eager anticipation and joy.

Say the following prayer of thanks when you successfully manifest your prosperity goals:

Dear Goddess of abundance, thank you for your many divine gifts of prosperity and wealth. Thank you for your guiding light and loving grace. Dear Lady, thank you for helping me manifest my prosperity goals. In the name of the Goddess, blessed be!

Sacred Riches Space

Add a small living tree in a pot; red, white, and green ribbon; three white candles; three green candles; three red candles; and cedarwood essential oil to your sacred riches space. Bless each item with divine abundance by holding it in your hands and saying:

May the divine prosperity of the Goddess and God manifest right now and empower me.

Prosperity Ritual

Perform this ritual just before or on a full moon. You will need a ballpoint pen, a pair of scissors, the small living tree, cedarwood essential oil, the three colors of ribbon, the three white candles, three green candles, and three red candles.

Begin by drawing a magic circle and empowering the elements. Use the ballpoint pen to write the words "Prosperity Now!" on each of the nine candles. Dress the candles with a thin film of cedarwood oil and place them at a safe distance around the small potted tree in a clockwise circle. Start at the north point with a white candle, then place a green candle by the white candle, a red candle by a green candle, and so forth around the circle. Next, cut several eight-inch strips of white ribbon. On these, use the ballpoint pen to write your prosperity goals, one goal per ribbon. Then anoint the ribbon ends with cedarwood oil and tie the ribbons onto the branches of the small tree. As you tie on the ribbon, read out loud the prosperity goal that is written on it.

Next, cut eight lengths of eight-inch red ribbon and eight lengths of eight-inch green ribbon. Anoint the ends of the ribbons with cedarwood oil and also tie them onto the tree branches. As you do, chant:

Blessed be, divine abundance and prosperity.

Wipe any remaining oil from your hands and light the white candle at the north point of the circle. As you light the candle, merge with Oneness and say:

By the guiding light of Oneness,
I am manifesting my prosperity goals right now!

Light the green candle from the white one, merge with the divine Goddess, and say:

By the guiding light of the Goddess
I am manifesting my prosperity goals right now!

Light the red candle from the green one, merge with the divine God, and say:

By the guiding light of the God
I am manifesting my prosperity goals right now!

Repeat this process until all the candles are lit. Then sit before the prosperity tree and notice how the candlelight illuminates its branches and the ribbons you have tied on them. Imagine your prosperity goals coming to fruition in the candlelight. Know that you have been successful in attaining your goals. Do this for several minutes.

When you are done, thank the Goddess and God, release the elements, and pull up the circle. Allow the candles to safely burn down.

Put the tree in a sunny place of honor (where you can easily see the tree and praise its beauty and magical power) for 28 days, watering and fertilizing it. Each day, place your hands softly on the tree branches and say:

Sacred tree of prosperity, blessed be.
I am manifesting my goals
By earth, wind, fire, and sea!

After the 28 days are over, plant the tree in your garden or backyard, weather permitting. If you prefer, put it in a larger planter with plenty of drainage and place it on your patio. When you plant the tree, leave the ribbons on it to remind you of successfully manifesting your goals. As you plant the tree, gently whisper to the tree over and over:

Sacred tree of prosperity, blessed be
Thank you for sharing your abundance with me.

Oracle of Wealth

Think of a question about manifesting your prosperity goals. Then click on an Internet I-Ching site (see the earlier list in the section "Oracle of Love").

Take a few deep and complete breaths to center yourself before beginning. Bless the Internet site as a divine oracle by laying your hands on the computer and saying:

By the grace of the Goddess and God, may this Internet I-Ching site be a divine and clear oracle for me right now.

Take a few moments to focus on your prosperity question and type in the question or a few words that describe it in the space provided. Then click on the reading and follow the simple instructions. When you are done, record the date, your prosperity question, and the meaning of the reading in your empowerment journal.

Chapter Eleven

The Eleventh Empowering Step: Enjoying the Rewards of Personal Empowerment

Empowerment is much like a fine meal that you prepare. Once you have prepared the food the way you want it and have set the table, it's time to enjoy the rewards of your efforts. Rather than gobble down the meal in five minutes, it's always more enjoyable to take time to savor each delicious mouthful.

Once you have attained your goals, give yourself an opportunity to sit back and savor the rewards. This process can be the most empowering part of manifesting your goals. After all, it's the spiritual, mental, and physical rewards that empower you and motivate you to continue toward realizing your full potential.

Every time you manifest one of your empowerment goals, pat yourself on the back. Take some quality time to appreciate your success. Celebrating your success reinforces your successful nature. Be aware of and enjoy the benefits of your hard work, whether that be a closer relationship with your beloved, losing weight and feeling healthier, getting a large bonus for a job well done, or planting five acres of wildflowers for pleasure and to attract butterflies.

Many people are very successful at achieving goals, but they have problems relaxing and enjoying the rewards of their efforts. They feel compelled to continually strive for more than they have with a drive that never lets up. On some level, this is commendable, but unfortunately, in the long run, it is draining and leads to health and other problems.

Within the cycle of empowerment, it's important to make time for the Eleventh Empowering Step, enjoying the benefits of manifesting your personal empowerment goals. These times of celebration are as important as the work times, if not more important because of their motivating power. Go ahead and reward yourself by celebrating your accomplishments. Dare to have some fun and enjoy a few magical adventures. You deserve it!

Love

In New Age Wicca, traditionally, a feast is held after the Sabbats and Esbats. The feast celebrates the blessings of the God and Goddess. The first harvest festival by tradition is Lughnassad, named for the Celtic sun god Lugh. The last part of the name, "nassad," means "to give in marriage." This refers to the marriage of the sun and earth, a union that produces the food of the harvest. "Nassad" also refers to an ancient rite where couples went to "the Hollow of the Fair," where they were joined in marriage.

In the context of love empowerment, it is the joining, the union of your goals with reality, that produces empowerment. Each success gives you more confidence to move forward. This forward movement is what empowerment is all about. You continue to realize your full potential step-by-step.

The Eleventh Empowering Step: Love Meditation

You will need a flashlight for this meditation. At night in a quiet room, stand comfortably and take a few deep breaths in and out to center yourself. Begin by taking a slow and deliberate step forward with your right foot. Turn the flashlight on and off as you breathe in completely. Next, take a slow and deliberate step with your left foot, turn the flashlight on and off as you breathe out completely. Walk a few steps in this manner, all the while focusing on your breathing, walking, and the flashing light.

Now sit or recline in a comfortable spot with the flashlight in hand. Turn off the lights in the room. While inhaling, flash the light of the flashlight three times, still your breath for three counts, and then exhale for three counts. Breathe in again and flash the light three times, still your breath for three counts, and breathe out for three counts. Repeat this several times.

Put the flashlight down and close your eyes. In your mind's eye, imagine walking down a path lined on both sides with milky white crystals. The sun shines on the crystals, lighting them up like natural flashlights. It's a beautiful day, and in your hand is the handle of a large empty wicker basket. You veer off the path and move toward a grove of trees that is on your right side. Approaching the grove, you see a tree whose branches are loaded with beautifully ripened red apples. You pull several apples from the lower branches and place them into your basket. After thanking the tree for its fruit, you go from tree to tree, picking other ripe fruits and placing them into your basket. Then you return to the crystal-lined path and continue on your journey.

As you travel on, you discover a large vegetable garden. Reaching the rows of ripe corn, you begin picking the golden ears and placing them in your basket, which is now beginning to fill up. After thanking the Goddess and corn spirits for your bounty, you move through the rest of the garden, filling your basket to the brim with the fantastic harvest. You move back to the crystal-lined path and continue your journey.

In the distance is a small gathering of busy people focused on their tasks. Some are cooking food; others are preparing additional fresh foods and placing them on platters on a large round wooden table. Moving closer, you greet the people, and they take your basket and add the contents to the ever-growing array of foods gracing the table.

Everyone sits down around the table. A symbol of the Goddess and God serves as the table's centerpiece. Before eating, all the people join hands and give their thanks for the bountiful feast that sits before them. Each person feels a connection with everyone else in the circle, as well as a connection to the divine. Each person has given to this elaborate feast, and now each is about to receive the fruits of their labors.

As you begin to eat and enjoy the feast, you realize that all the people you love are sitting there around you. That thought makes the food taste even better. Each bite seems to confirm the love around the circle of people. You savor each moment of the magical meal, thanking the Goddess and God for their guidance and blessings.

Now take a deep breath and imagine breathing in the enjoyment of the divine feast. Breathe in knowing that you have successfully manifested your love goals and fill yourself to the brim with that delightful energy. As you breathe in again, begin to move your hands and feet and slowly open your eyes, without focusing on anything in particular. Stretch your body and slowly stand up. Turn on the lights and repeat the walking exercise once more for a few minutes to bring you back into your body.

When you are done meditating, record your impressions of the divine feast in your empowerment journal.

Love Affirmation and Prayer

To affirm your faith in yourself and your success, repeat this affirmation several times a day:

Today and every day, I celebrate manifesting my love empowerment goals, and I fully enjoy the rewards of my success.

Say the following prayer of thanks at night before you go to sleep:

Dear Goddess and God, thank you for your divine guidance, blessings, and empowerment. I pray that you will ever guide and shower me with divine love and light. I ask that you bless me with helpful, loving, and magical dreams. By the Lady and Lord, blessed be!

Sacred Love Space

Add a vial of edible vanilla oil to your sacred love altar. Bless the oil by gently rolling the vial between your palms until it gets warm. As you do, chant "Blessed be" several times.

Love Ritual

Enjoy this celebration ritual on a full moon with your beloved and close family members and friends. You will need music, a votive candle and holder for each person present, the vanilla oil from your sacred love altar, and plenty of tasty beverages and delicious food prepared especially for the celebration feast. For this candlelight supper, try chocolate or cheese fondue with fruits, breads, and cakes. Put a couple of drops of the edible vanilla oil into some of your foods such as the chocolate fondue or the cakes. Stir the sweet oil in the fondue or cake batter clockwise. As you do, chant "Blessed be" several times.

Turn on the music and set the table with a nice tablecloth and napkins, your best dishes, crystal, and silverware. Also put a vase or pot of flowers on the table. Then anoint yourself with the vanilla oil and drip three drops of oil on top of each of the votive candles.

Next, draw a magic circle around the room you will be dining in and empower the elements. When your guests arrive, hand them their votive candle and a long stick to light it with. Have them each light their votive candle upon arriving. As each person lights her or his candle, say together:

Bright blessings to everyone here.

Put the lit candles on the tabletop until everyone is done lighting their candles. Then join hands and say a simple prayer such as:

Goddess and God, bless, guide, and protect us always!
By earth, wind, fire, and sea, blessed be!

Put the candles on the table where they can safely burn down and enjoy your candlelight supper. Make empowering toasts and enjoy the rewards of manifesting your goals. Empower each other.

When the celebration is over, thank the Goddess and God, bid farewell to the elements, and pull up the circle. Return any uneaten food to the earth. As you do, say.

Blessed be the Lady and Lord.

Oracle of Love

Choose one question regarding manifesting your love empowerment goals. Write the question and date in your empowerment journal. Go over to the radio or television, place your hands above the appliance, and say:

Bless this machine as a divine oracle, right now!

Take a deep, relaxing breath and let go of any tensions you may be feeling. Turn on the appliance and write down in your journal the first few words you hear or images you see. Look for any messages in the words and images. Circle any meaningful ones.

Health

Once you have manifested your health goals, it's time to congratulate yourself. Reward yourself by doing something healthy and healing in the next few days or weeks.

Health empowerment is a continual process, and it's hard work. When you are successful, it's important to relax and reap the rewards. The rewards can be anything—walking in the park; buying yourself a new bike; purchasing a membership at the local health club; having a therapeutic massage; contributing to your favorite charity; planting new bulbs, bushes, or trees in your garden; watching an uplifting movie; purchasing new clothes; having a picnic; or going on a dream vacation.

The Eleventh Empowering Step: Healing Meditation

Turn on some healing New Age or soft instrumental music. Sit or recline in a comfortable spot, close your eyes, and breathe in and out to the rhythm of the music. Become one with the music. Do this for a few minutes.

Now imagine the notes of the music sounding inside of you, soothing your body, mind, and spirit. As the music continues, you sense your being start to resonate with the healing music until you feel in tune with it.

The musical melody weaves through your body, mind, and spirit. The music becomes like a magic carpet that carries you through the air. Your senses tingle and you notice that you suddenly feel better than ever before as you glide through the air. You are guided by the soothing music that resonates through your every cell, connecting you as one to yourself, the world, and the universe.

The music guides you to many different realms of being, places magical and mystical, places of healing, good health, and celebration. Moving through the air, the rhythm of the music sends you dancing through the sky on your magic carpet of melody. Each note of the music heals and invigorates you.

You fly to a mountain home where friends gather to celebrate good health with a feast of healthy foods and good music;, to a rooftop where people celebrate the birth of a new baby; to a country field with families who are celebrating life, the harvest, and the Earth Mother's bountiful gifts.

Now take a deep breath in, breathing to the rhythm of the music. Allow the healing power of the celebrations of health and healing to flow through you like the music. Enjoy your health empowerment and everything that goes with it. All your efforts are finally coming to fruition, and you are reaping the benefits of following your health empowerment plans.

Take another deep breath in and out and allow the divine healing energy of the Goddess and God to flow into your body, mind, and spirit just like the melody of the music. Take another deep breath in and out and imagine floating slowly down to earth on your magic carpet. Breathe in the pleasing knowledge that you have manifested your health empowerment goal and breathe out any residual tension or stress. As you breathe normally now, you feel relaxed, yet peacefully alert. Slowly open your eyes and stretch your body to the rhythm of the music for a few moments.

When you are done meditating, turn off the music. Record your impressions in your empowerment journal. How did it feel to become one with rhythm and melody of the music? What sensations did you experience when flying up and down on your magic carpet?

Healing Affirmation and Prayer

Say this affirming statement several times a day to reap the empowering benefits of attaining your health goals:

I am healthier and happier every hour as I am continually showered with divine healing power. Every moment, I enjoy the empowering benefits of attaining my health goals.

Say the following prayer of thanks every night before you go to sleep:

Dear Mother Goddess and Father God, I thank you for your healing strength and power. Thank you for your helping hands, for guiding me toward better health. I pray you, please continue to guide, bless, and protect me and those I love, now and forevermore. Thank you dear friends. Ayea! So be it! Blessed be!"

Sacred Healing Space

Add fruit juice, bottled water, a couple loaves of whole grain or sourdough bread, and a bowl of fruit with apples, grapes, oranges, and peaches to your sacred healing space one day before you take a healing picnic. Bless these items with divine healing power by putting your palms about an inch above them and saying three times:

Blessed be the divine healing power of the Goddess and God!

Healing Ritual

Spending a pleasant day in the country or in the park on a picnic is a great way to celebrate your healing success. Plan a picnic feast with your immediate family and a few special friends, or plan a peaceful picnic by yourself to celebrate attaining your health empowerment goal. Pick a favorite picnic spot or a place recommended by a reputable person. In bad weather, have the picnic in a room of your home.

Fill your picnic basket or bag with cups, plates, silverware, and napkins. Bring your camera, sunscreen, hats, blankets, and folding chairs. Bring the fruit, loaves of bread, fruit juice, and bottled water from your sacred healing altar. Add other healthy foods and extra water to your picnic basket or bag.

When you set up your picnic area, draw a magic circle around the spot. Start at the north point and drag the heel of your shoe around the area in a clockwise circle. Then invite the Goddess and God into your picnic circle by softly saying:

Dear Lady and Lord, I invite you to this picnic of good health. Come, I call you. Blessed be.

Before eating the food, make a toast with the juice or water from your sacred healing altar. Pour the drink into the cups and hold your filled cups upward with everyone saying several times:

Blessed be our good health!

Before eating your healthy picnic feast, bless the food by holding your palms above it, merging with the divine, and saying:

Blessed be the healing power of the Goddess and God
May their divine healing energy now fill this food
We are about to eat. So be it! Blessed be!

When you are done picnicking, return any leftover food and drink to the earth. As you do this, say:

I thank the divine healing spirits for their blessings.

Leave the picnic area in its natural, healthy, trash-free state.

Oracle of Health

Select one question about manifesting your health empowerment goals. Write the question and date in your empowerment journal. Go over to the radio or television, place your hands above the appliance, and say:

Bless this machine as a divine oracle, right now!

Take a deep, relaxing breath to focus your awareness. Then turn on the appliance and write down in your journal the first few words you hear or images you see. Look for any messages in the words and images. Circle those you find meaningful.

Prosperity

At some point, prosperity empowerment is about the integration of love, health, and wealth together into a working and empowering whole, which I call Oneness. Even the term "wealth" has many aspects, and riches come in many forms. Wealth may mean spiritual abundance, material possessions, real estate, business investments, a keen and inventive mind, talent in the creative arts, or a happy and healthy family and good friends.

Prosperity is open-ended, and you deserve the rewards you have worked so hard for. Once you discover and mine your vein of gold, it's time to take a moment a savor your good fortune. Celebrate your experience and enjoy your achievement. This is a good time to spread a little of your wealth around and share your good fortune with others. So enjoy your prosperity and celebrate!

The Eleventh Empowering Step: Prosperity Meditation

Turn on some meditative instrumental music and light a votive candle in a glass holder. Sit comfortably where you can easily see the candlelight. Focus your awareness on the candle for a few minutes. As you breathe in, imagine breathing in warm, white light, and as you breathe out, imagine breathing out any unwanted tension and anxiety you may be feeling. Do this for a few minutes. Focus on breathing in warm white light and exhaling any unwanted energy from within you as you relax more and more.

Now close your eyes while still imagining that you are breathing in warm white light. In your mind's eye, see the words, "LET ME BE LIGHT." As you slowly read the words, you find yourself on a platform where a multitude of trains sit waiting to take you to your desired destination. Instinctively, you move toward a particular train. As you do, a door opens, beckoning you to enter. As you move into the train car, the door closes and the train whisks you away at a very fast speed.

Through the window, you can see the images of the many steps you took to manifest your prosperity goal. As the images pass quickly by, one-by-one, a sense of accomplishment fills you. Inside and out, you are one big smile. You are completely filled with a warm joyful glow that lights up your whole being.

You become aware that the train is slowing down and gently coming to a stop. Once again the door opens, and you step through it into a beautiful, magical city that shimmers with golden light. You follow a ruby-colored path leading you to the gates of the city. Above the massive crystal gates rests a brilliantly colored sign reading "Celebration of Empowerment." As you state the steps you took toward prosperity empowerment to the gatekeeper, the doors swing open, and you are free to enter the golden city.

A festive celebration is underway, and you can hear the music and laughter and sense the excitement around you. As you take a deep breath in, you can smell the aroma of food cooking. Knowing you have now manifested your prosperity goals, you taste the thrill of success, see the many possibilities for continued achievement, and feel divinely empowered.

Realizing, accepting, and enjoying your empowerment, you become like a candle of radiant light. You transform into a bright star, into a constellation of stars, then into planets in solar systems, suns, and universes. The evolution continues into infinity, changing on endless levels like concurrent spheres of a circle wrapped around one another, until the whole thing weaves into a cosmic web of Oneness. Eventually the beginning meets the end, and together they move to the next level.

Having achieved physical prosperity, you then achieve mental prosperity, and at last, you reach the ultimate goal of spiritual prosperity, a point where you are at one with yourself and everything around you. You savor the moment with an image of all things coming together at all times. Like blowing out all the candles on a birthday cake, your wish has come true. It's a moment that lives with you forever.

Each time you recall your success, you are filled with light and experience personal empowerment all over again. You know you are continually drawing abundance and riches into your life each and every day. You effortlessly envision the many different roads that ultimately lead to abundance and prosperity. These many roads stretch out before you, waiting to be traveled. Take a few minutes to look down, and energetically walk down, some of the more attractive roads to abundance and riches. Make a mental note of what you see and sense. Are there any road signs? Are there any buildings? If so, what kind? Are there any people, music, laughter, or modes of transportation? Are there any trees and gardens along the road?

Take these sights and sounds with you as you begin to come back to the present time and place by breathing deeply in and out. Feeling refreshed and revitalized, take another complete breath and begin to move your hands and feet. Now slowly open your eyes and stretch your body for a few minutes. Gaze at the candlelight for a few moments and then clap your hands three times to focus your awareness.

Record the date and your impressions of the golden city and the celebration party in your empowerment journal. Also make a note of what you saw or sensed when you looked down the roads of abundance and riches. Allow the candle to safely burn down.

Prosperity Affirmation and Prayer

Say this affirmation several times a day to celebrate manifesting your prosperity goals:

Today and every day, I successfully manifest my prosperity empower-ment goals and joyfully celebrate the divine rewards of my worthy efforts.

Say the following simple prayer of thanks when you attain you pros-perity empowerment goals:

I thank you dear Lady and Lord of earth, wind, light, and water for helping me to successfully manifest my prosperity goals. I am divinely rewarded by your loving grace and goodness. I pray you, please continue to guide, bless, and protect me and those I love, now and forevermore. Blessed be, bright and shining Ones!

Sacred Riches Space

Add a golden candle, a star symbol, a wooden box, citrus oil, and a compass to your sacred riches altar. Bless these items by holding them in your hands one at a time and saying three times:

Blessed be divine abundance and prosperity.

Prosperity Ritual

Perform this ritual during a full moon for best results. You will need the candle, star symbol, wooden box, citrus oil, and compass from your sacred riches altar.

During the day, take a walk, collect a few small things from nature that you are drawn to, and put them in the wooden box. Examples are small stones, shells, leaves, twigs, seeds, feathers, and flower petals. Put the box on your altar.

After dark, use your compass to find the directions of north, east, south, and west. Mark them for easy reference. Then draw a magic circle and empower the elements. Dress the candle with citrus oil, and anoint yourself. Put the candle in the center of your altar and the star symbol next to it. Take the things you collected out of the wooden box and put them around the candle and star symbol in a stellar pattern. Rub the outside of the wooden box with the citrus oil and also anoint the star symbol with a few drops of the oil. Wipe any remaining oil from your hands and light the candle, dedicating it to your favorite Goddess and God of prosperity and abundance.

Now face north, merge with the powers of earth, and say:

Enriching powers of earth
I thank you for helping me
To manifest wealth and prosperity.

Face east, merge with the powers of air, and say:

Enriching powers of air
I thank you for helping me
To manifest wealth and prosperity.

Face south, merge with the powers of fire and with light, and say:

Enriching powers of fire and light
I thank you for helping me
To manifest wealth and prosperity.

Next face west, merge with the powers of water, and say:

Enriching powers of water
I thank you for helping me
To manifest wealth and prosperity.

Face center, merge with the divine, and say:

Divine and enriching powers that be
I thank you for helping me
To manifest wealth and prosperity.
Blessed be! Blessed be! Blessed be!

Now spend at least 15 minutes focusing on the candlelight and bask in the many ways you benefit by attaining your prosperity goals. Think about the rewards your efforts have make possible. Decide how you would like to celebrate your success and make a few notes in your empowerment journal as to your personal empowerment celebration.

When you are done, thank the Goddess and God, bid farewell to the elements, and pull up the circle. Put the star symbol and the things from nature into the wooden box. Drip eight drops of wax from the golden candle onto the box contents and then close the lid. Put the box in a special place to remind you that you have successfully manifested your prosperity goals and now can enjoy the enriching rewards of your success.

Oracle of Wealth

Pick one question about manifesting your prosperity empowerment goals. Write the question and date in your empowerment journal. Put your hands over the radio or television, palms down, and say:

Bless this machine as a divine oracle, right now!

Take a deep, relaxing breath and let go of any tensions you may be feeling. Turn on the appliance and write down in your journal the first few words you hear or images you see. Look for any messages in the words and images and circle those you find meaningful.

Chapter Twelve

The Twelfth Empowering Step: Reviewing Your Empowerment Goals

In terms of your magical garden, you have now harvested your goals and have celebrated your success. The time has come to reflect upon your achievements and determine ways to make next year's garden even better.

As with the seasonal cycles of the Goddess and God, the empowerment process is circular. As such, empowerment is naturally ongoing and ever-changing. Even when you achieve all your empowerment goals the first time you try, you can still move forward by fine-tuning your process and thereby enter a deeper level of empowerment.

In the final Twelfth Empowering Step, you review your empowerment process and reflect on the impact it has had on you and your life. Your vision of the future becomes more clearly defined through achievement, reflection, and review. It's important to take stock of where you have been and reflect upon this information to establish new empowerment goals and plans. Each time you set, plan, manifest, celebrate, and review your goals, you become more adept at empowering yourself.

Taking Stock of Your Empowerment Goals

The best way to review your empowerment goals is to read back through your empowerment journal to discover what worked and what didn't. Begin by reading everything you have written in your journal. The idea is to find the things that worked and writing them down in the back of your journal or highlight these items so you can easily refer to them. If you like, you can start a new journal, listing the things that worked for you, the divine energies you feel a strong rapport with, and your favorite methods for personal empowerment.

The final step in empowerment, reviewing your goals, is also the first step of your next level of empowerment. In this sense, it is a rebirth. The idea is to take what you have learned the first time through and do the process again, becoming even more empowered the second and third time, and so on. Most of the time, practice does facilitate better results.

It's important for you to set your own level of excellence by which you measure success. When reflecting on your achievements, measure by your own standards and not by those around you, because empowerment is a very personal process.

Love

Begin by reviewing your love empowerment goals and plans that you have written in your empowerment journal. What were your strong points? What were the things that you did well? The idea is to move forward, so you must be honest with yourself. Make a few notes on how you can change your approach and integrate more effective ways of doing things. That's the beauty of empowerment. Goals are stepping stones to other goals that lead you further on your path to empowerment. As with anything, each time you do it, you become better at it, until you eventually attain your goals.

In this chapter, I have combined the meditation, affirmation, prayer, sacred space, and ritual into one for each of the three sections of love, health, and prosperity. The purpose for doing this is to show you how you can integrate these empowering techniques into your daily life as a seamless whole.

Reflecting on Love

You will need a small surface in your bathroom to serve as a temporary sacred love altar. You need to see the altar when you are in the tub. Set your candles (green and red) and a lighthouse figurine or picture, ballpoint pen, and vanilla oil on this altar. Place the lighthouse figurine between the candles so they will illuminate it when they are lit.

Now draw a magic circle around the entire bathroom and empower the elements. Slowly fill the tub with warm water. As the tub is filling, hold the green candle in your hands and center your awareness by taking several deep, slow breaths in and out. When you are centered, your body, mind, and spirit flow in harmony. Also when you are centered, it becomes easier to focus on what you are doing. As you breathe in and out, reflect on your love empowerment goals. Think about what worked. Focus on your success. Then merge with Oneness and use the ballpoint pen to write in your empowerment journal or on a piece of paper the first few words that come to mind. Then write the words on the candle body. These words may not make sense to you, and that's okay. Just write them down. The important thing when doing this kind of automatic writing oracle is not to think about it so much, but just be one with it. Rub the inscribed candle with vanilla oil and place in its holder on your temporary altar.

Next, hold the red candle in your hands and repeat the process, taking a few deep breaths in and out and focusing on your success. Merge with Oneness and write on the candle the first few words that come to mind. Dress the red candle with vanilla oil and place it in its holder. Add several more drops of the oil to the bath water. As you do this, chant:

Divine vision, blessed be!

Rinse any remaining oil off your hands in the bath water, then dry them. Light the green candle. Merge with the Goddess, focus on the lighthouse figurine and the way the candlelight illuminates it, and say this simple prayer:

Dear Goddess, you are a divine beacon of light. I pray you, please be my lighthouse and light my way. Help me to review my love goals and discover the most positive path on my journey to love. Dear Lady, please guide, bless, and protect me and those I love, now and forevermore. Blessed be the Lady!

Next, light the red candle. Merge with the God, focus on the lighthouse figurine, and say this simple prayer:

Dear God, you are a divine beacon of light. I pray you, please be my lighthouse and light my way. Help me to review my love goals and discover the most positive path on my journey to love. Dear Lord, please guide, bless, and protect me and those I love, now and forevermore. Blessed be the Lord!

Now immerse yourself in the bath and soak. Close your eyes, and in your mind's eye imagine you are sailing a boat on calm seas while gradually approaching your port of origin. It's a beautiful sunny day without a cloud in the sky. Ahead is a massive drawbridge that stands like a gate in the harbor. The bridge opens, and as you pass through its open gates, you sense an experience of celebration, knowing you have successfully navigated the steps of your love goals and come full circle. Returning to your home harbor, you feel empowered, joyful, and at one with yourself and the world.

Once you have safely navigated the drawbridge and entered the harbor, you spot a lighthouse ahead, its light guiding you safely into port. You sail toward the lighthouse beacon as you complete the last part of your voyage. The beacon streams across your boat and fills you and your vessel with bright light. It acts as a magical projector and shows you glimpses of your past, present, and future. In the light, you see yourself attaining your love goals. You review your process and bring those positive, empowering aspects forward into the present. You also see yourself setting new empowerment goals, planning them, and taking the steps to manifest them. As the beacon passes over your boat again, you feel as though you have been touched by the divine hands of the Goddess and God. Then the magical images disappear as quickly as they appeared.

You continue on your journey and when you dock, you secure your boat. You walk slowly through the harbor to your house. Once you are home, you sit back comfortably and begin assessing how well your voyage went in terms of the love in your life. Navigating successfully and manifesting your love goals has brought more love into your life. Now that you have completed your voyage, the time has come to reflect on your success. Think about what you have learned so your next voyage will be even more empowering and joyous. With the knowledge gained from your first voyage, you chart your second voyage. You realize that you have learned from your success and can now fine-tune your love life to make it all that you want it to be.

Take a deep breath in and out, and slowly open your eyes. Step carefully out of the tub and rub yourself dry with a soft towel. Sway back and forth from your right foot to your left foot, making an effort to evenly distribute your weight on both feet. Now sway from toe to heel until you feel balanced. Imagine a thick golden cord stretching down from your spine to the center of the earth. Become aware of the earth under your feet. The other end of the golden cord reaches up to the sky. Feel your spirit soar upward. Know that you are balanced between the two ends. You can feel yourself sink into the earth and reach upward to the sky. Once you have found your center, say this affirmation:

Today I envision my new love empowerment goals. With the help of the Goddess and God, my new goals come into clear focus, and I know the most positive path to take to manifest more love and joy in my life.

Repeat the affirmation several times a day for at least 28 days to get a clear vision of your new empowerment goals. Thank the Goddess and God, release the elements, and pull up the circle. Allow the candles to safely burn down. Put the lighthouse figurine in a conspicuous place where you will see it often. This will help remind you of your vision and keep you focused on your new love empowerment goals.

Be sure to record any insights from your experience in your empowerment journal. Refer to your notes as you set, plan, and begin taking the steps toward manifesting your new love empowerment goals.

Health

Within yourself, you know whether you are becoming healthier. You may be able to deceive everyone else, but you cannot deceive yourself. If you try, all is lost. You must be honest with yourself to improve your health. You must honestly answer the questions, "How is my health?

How can it be better? What parts of my health empowerment plans have been working? How can I move forward to better health and vitality?" When you answer these questions truthfully, you have taken another giant step toward health empowerment. In addition, you now have an idea of what you need to focus on, as well as what you need to let go of to become healthier.

Reflecting on Health

Add sandalwood incense, a crystal or stone, a small wind chime, a white candle, and a sea shell to your sacred healing altar. You will also need a mirror large enough to see your reflection in. Mirrors can act as magical doorways to other realms of knowledge. They also reflect the world of form around you.

Draw a magic circle and empower the elements. Put the crystal or stone in the north corner of the room, the small wind chime in the east corner, the candle in the south corner, and the sea shell in the west corner. In this way, the entire room becomes a sacred altar.

Once the room is set up as an altar, center your awareness. Take a few deep and complete breaths, breathing in white light and breathing out any stress, tension, or pain you may be feeling. Next, use the ballpoint pen to write in your empowerment journal and on the candle the first sentence or sequence of words that come to mind. The words don't need to make sense, just write them down. The important thing about automatic writing is to be one with it and allow the words to flow freely.

Now light the candle and incense. Dedicate them to your favorite God and Goddess of healing and good health. Stand where you can see your reflection in the mirror. Look into the mirror, merge with the divine, and say this prayer to your reflection, to the people on earth, to the God and Goddess, to Oneness:

Dear Lord and Lady, I pray you
May I never thirst and always thrive
May you never thirst and always thrive
Please grant me good health, now and always
And help all those who are need of healing.
Please guide, bless, and protect us all
In birth, life, death, and rebirth.

I ask this in the Lord and Lady's name
Blessed be! So be it!

Continue looking at yourself in the mirror and reflect on who you are. Ponder your inner and outer beauty for a few minutes. As you look at your reflection, chant over and over:

Inside out, outside in
Looking out, looking in.

Continue to gaze at yourself in the mirror and ponder all that you see, all that you feel, all that you sense, all that you create, all that you think about, all that you dream, and all that you find empowering about yourself. Look inside and outside yourself as you observe your reflection. Then say this healing affirmation:

Today and every day, I reflect divine health, shining within and shining without. Blessed be, I am now manifesting my vision for personal health empowerment.

Next, turn on some soft New Age music. Sit or recline comfortably where you can still see your reflection in the mirror. Gaze at your reflection and breathe in time to the music. As you do this, you become more and more peacefully relaxed, so peaceful and relaxed that your eyes naturally become heavier and heavier and eventually close on their own.

Now in your mind's eye, imagine floating into the corner of the ceiling and then out of the room. You float down a long hallway with several doors. Behind you are 11 doorways, and in front of you is a doorway that leads off to the left. Reaching the doorway, you push it open and float inside the room, which is dark except for a light shining on a mirror that is standing in the middle of the room.

The mirror is long and narrow, and as you approach it, the light around it seems to get brighter. It seems like a normal mirror until you get close to it, at which point magical images begin flashing across the glass. Initially, the images seem like a blur, but as you watch for a while, you realize that the images are reflections of your health empowerment goals. Like a movie, the mirror flashes the images of your empowerment process and how well you did overall. It mirrors the past, present, and future. You look for the positive and work from that point. The mirror helps you find and accentuate the positive aspects of your empowerment process.

Suddenly, the images in the mirror begin swirling around. Millions of multicolored dots of light begin circling one another until they finally blend as one. The image in the mirror reflects you as you prepare for your next empowerment process, decide on your health empowerment goals, and make your plans. You imagine yourself learning from your experiences, making your vision for greater health empowerment even more successful. You sense that with the help of the Goddess and God, and through your own efforts, you will continue to manifest your goals. You know you can make the changes you desire and be healthier and happier, now and in the future.

Now take a deep breath in and out, feeling refreshed and revitalized, knowing that you are a reflection of the divine, a reflection of the elements, a reflection of good health. Take another breath in and out, feeling renewed and alert, feeling healthy and empowered both within and without. As you breathe in and out again, move your toes and fingers and slowly open your eyes, coming back to the present time and place.

When you are done, thank the Goddess and God, bid farewell to the elements, and pull up the circle. Allow the candle to safely burn down. Also write down the insights from your experience in your empowerment journal. Refer to your notes as you set, plan, and begin taking the steps toward manifesting your new health empowerment goals. Also continue saying the healing affirmation several times a day for at least 28 days to help you envision, plan, and proceed toward empowered health.

Prosperity

Looking in your empowerment journal, survey your prosperity goals and plans. Ask yourself, "What goals have I achieved within my empowerment process? How has my life changed both day-by-day and as a whole? What have I learned?" Write down the answers to these questions on a new page in your empowerment journal. How close did you come to your prosperity empowerment goals? How can you make your next process even better? These are questions you need to answer before setting out on your next circle of empowerment.

Reflecting on Prosperity

Add a green candle, a jade plant, a compass, and sandalwood-scented oil to your sacred riches space. You will also need your wand, empowerment journal, and a ballpoint pen.

Begin by using the compass to determine the southeast corner of your home and the window closest to it. The southeast signifies good luck, prosperity, and wealth.

Next, draw a magic circle with your wand around the area in the southeast corner and empower the elements. Put the jade plant in the southeast corner within the magic circle of light you have just drawn, next to the window where it will get plenty of light. In Feng Shui, the ancient Chinese art of placement, the jade plant attracts prosperity, good luck, abundance, joy, and wealth.

Focus your awareness on the plant. With your wand in your power hand, gently tap the plant leaves with the wand tip three times and say:

May you ever thrive.

Gently tap the plant stem with the tip of your wand and repeat:

May you ever thrive.

Gently tap the base of the plant stem by the plant roots with your wand three times and repeat:

May you ever thrive.

Anoint the container the jade plant is in with a few drops of the sandalwood oil. Then anoint your hands, the bottoms of your feet, and the top of your head with the oil. Cradle your wand between your hands and take a deep, slow breath to center your awareness. Say the following prayer:

In this world and all worlds
At this time and all times
On this day and all days
I stand before the Goddess and God
I stand before all that is divine
And I pray for abundant empowerment.
Please grant me the vision and wisdom
To create an enriching and joyful life
Every moment of each day and every night.

I ask this in the Lady and Lord's name
Thank you dear friends, blessed be!

Put your wand down. Use the ballpoint pen to write in your empowerment journal and onto the green candle the first words or sentence that automatically come to mind. Just let the words flow out.

Dress the inscribed candle with sandalwood oil and wipe any remaining oil from your hands. Light the candle and say:

I dedicate this candle to the Goddess and God of prosperity. Blessed be the Lady and Lord of plenty! May you ever thrive!

Sit or recline comfortably where you can easily see the candle. Gaze at the candlelight and breathe in for three heartbeats, still your breath for three heartbeats, and then exhale for three heartbeats. Now close your eyes, and as you inhale, roll your eyes upward. As you exhale, roll your eyes downward. Do this several times.

Imagine the candle flame growing larger and large until it is a wide beam of bright blue light filling the room and completely surrounding your body. As it does so, you feel lighter than air, and you begin floating upward. Reaching the ceiling, you move right through it, up through the rooftop, and out into the sky, riding on a bright blue beam of light that carries you high into the sky. You feel yourself soaring higher and higher in the beam of light.

You hear the soft hum of a motor as you sense yourself being pulled up through a portal in the bottom of a spaceship. You move through it into a room that is completely lit. A being welcomes you and leads you into another room with panels on the wall that light up and occasionally beep and make other electronic noises. The being motions you to one side of the room where there is a giant screen, a screen that at the moment is glowing green.

As you approach the screen, it momentarily flickers before displaying the images of your life on Earth. At first, the images are of your life before beginning on your path to empowerment, then those images are replaced by images of you determining, planning, and taking the steps to manifest your prosperity empowerment goals. The screen shows you celebrating your success. The images then shift into future images of success, where you manifest everything that you envision. In an instant, all things become clear to you on the screen. Like the eternal cycle of the seasons, you understand that empowerment is a continuing process that must be planned, seeded, nurtured, reaped, and reseeded in order to be fully realized.

Now in your mind's eye, once again imagine the bright beam of blue light surrounding you and gently carrying you to Earth, through the sky, through the rooftop, through the ceiling, and back into your room. Take another deep breath in, feeling refreshed and revitalized, focused and aware. Begin to move your hands and feet and slowly open your eyes. Rub your hands briskly together several times and come fully back to your body.

Write your impressions of your experience in your empowerment journal. To affirm your experience, place your palms about two inches above the jade plant each day and repeat this affirmation:

Today and every day, I live an enriching life. I am focused, aware, and present. Blessed be!

Also make sure you tend and water the jade plant regularly so it thrives. This will attract more natural prosperity, wealth, and abundance into your home.

Appendix A

Empowering Goddesses and Gods

Adonis (Greek)   God of beauty, love, healing, fertility, and vegetation.

Aife (Celtic)   A powerful Scottish Queen and consort to the sea God Manannan.

Ailinn (Celtic)   Goddess of affection, romance, and love.

Aine (Celtic)   Goddess of earth and sun begotten by the spirits of night and fire. Sorceress and Faery Queen who is honored on Midsummer's Eve.

Airmed (Celtic)   Goddess of healing and herb and plant lore.

Akupera (Hindu)   Goddess of moonlight.

Alcmeme (Greek)   Goddess of the New Year, beauty, wisdom, and regal beauty.

Alcyone (Greek)   Sea Goddess of the moon, harmony, and tranquility.

Amaethon (Celtic)   Agriculture and harvest king associated with the fruits of the harvest and agricultural tools and farming equipment.

Anadyomene (Greek)   Sea-born Goddess of sexuality.

Andraste (Celtic)   Fertility Goddess associated with war, death, warriors, victory, and with sanctuaries in sacred woods like the one that existed on the Island of Mona (Anglesey).

Angus Og (Celtic)   God of love, youth, courtship, dreaming, and beauty. Angus is the healer of souls.

Anna Perenna (Roman)   Goddess of sexuality and fertility.

Annapurna (Hindu)   Great Mother Goddess of abundance and giver of plenty.

Anuket (Egyptian)   Goddess of the river and fertility.

Aphrodite (Greek)   Goddess of love, pleasure, passion, womanly beauty, flowers, and lovers.

Apollo (Greek)   Sun God of poetry, creative arts, music, healing, and divination.

Arianrhod (Celtic)   Powerful stellar and lunar Goddess of prosperity and keeper of the "Silver Wheel" or "Silver Disc." Her palace is the Corona Borealis, also called Caer Arianrhod (The Northern Crown).

Artemis (Greek)   Goddess of fruitful abundance, healing, creativity, the moon, love, shapeshifting, and nature.

Artio (Celtic)   Goddess of fertility, courage, and nature. She is portrayed as a bear.

Astarte (Assyro-Babylonia)   Great Mother Goddess associated with the planet Venus, astrology, love, fertility, victory, and sexual prowess.

Athena (Greek)   Goddess of wisdom and warriors in battle. She is associated with education, victory, and courage.

Atum (Egyptian)   Both female and male, she is complete, whole, and perfect. Mass without form, she is both everything and nothing at the same time.

Bacchus (Roman)   God of wisdom, inspiration, fertility, love, merriment, wine, and music.

Balder (Norse)   God of beauty, love, light, innocence, and rebirth.

Banba (Celtic)   Earth Goddess representing the sacred land.

Bast (Egyptian)   Cat Goddess of fertility, pleasure, dancing, music, and love.

Bel/Baal (Assyro-Babylonian)   Sky God of fertility and light.

Bel/Belenus (Celtic)   Sun God of light and healing, referred to as "The Shining One." He has a golden harp, golden curved sword, a golden spear, and the sun disc.

Belisama (Celtic)   Young fire Goddess associated with the rising sun whose name means "like unto flame" and "the bright and shining one."

Belisana (Celtic)   Goddess of healing, laughter, forests, and woodland plants and animals. She is warm like the sun.

Bhaga (Hindu)   God of marriage, fortune, and prosperity.

Bo Find (Celtic)   Goddess of fertility.

Boann (Celtic)   "She of the White Cow" and Mother of the herds. She is a river Goddess associated with fertility, prosperity, and inspiration.

Borvo (Celtic)   Healing God of unseen and concealed truth and inspiration through dreams. He is the golden God associated with healing hot springs, a flute, and a golden harp.

Bragi (Norse)   God of poetry.

Bran (Celtic)   God of music and prophecy, protector of bards and poets, associated with singing, the bard's harp, divination, and prosperity.

Branwen (Welsh)   Goddess of love and beauty, called the White-Bosomed One and Venus of the Northern Sea.

Bres (Celtic)   God of fertility and agriculture, one of the first kings of the Tuatha De Dannan.

Bridget (Celtic)   Fertility Goddess of the Sacred Fire, the sun, hearth and home. She is fire of fire, the bride Goddess of inspiration, poetry, medicine, healing, and smithcraft.

Brigantia (Celtic)   Goddess of nature and the sun, associated with the rivers, mountains, and valleys of the countryside.

Buddha (Buddhist)   The energy of knowledge and wisdom. He is all things and nothing, associated with healing, prosperity, mediation, dreaming, and spiritual love.

Caer (Celtic)   Swan maiden, shapeshifter, and Goddess of dreaming.

Cailleach (Pre-Celtic)   Goddess of earth, sky, moon, and sun. She controls the seasons and weather.

Calliope (Greek)   Muse of epic poetry.

Ceres (Roman)   Goddess of fertility, agriculture, crops, and farming.

Chandra (Hindu)   God of fertility and the moon.

Chango (African)   Powerful love God, drummer, dancer, and king.

Cherubim (Hebrew)   Goddess/God of sexuality and intercourse.

Clio (Greek)   The muse of history.

Cliodna (Celtic)   "Shapely One," Bird Goddess and Faery Queen associated with extraordinary beauty, shapeshifting, apples, sea gulls, and accompanied by three magical birds.

Concordia (Roman)   Goddess of peace, harmony, and tranquility.

Coventina (Celtic)   Goddess of the well and the womb of the earth, associated with healing springs, sacred wells, childbirth, renewal and the earth.

Creidne (Celtic)   Master Sword Maker named "The Bronze Worker," associated with smiths, wrights, metal-working, and craftspersons.

Cupid (Roman)   God of love.

Dagda (Celtic)   The "Good God" and "Good Hand." Chieftain Earth God of life, death, wisdom, prosperity, feasting, pleasure, abundance, and knowledge. He influences the seasons with the music from his harp.

Damona (Celtic)   Goddess of fertility, prosperity, and healing; her name means "divine cow."

Danu/Anu (Celtic)   Triple Goddess and All Mother. She is Goddess of love, creation, healing, wisdom, abundance, and prosperity. In stellar mythology, the constellation Cassiopeia honors her in its name, Llys Don, or Danu's House.

Demeter (Greek) Mother Goddess of fertility, marriage, agriculture, abundance, childbirth, and prosperity.

Devi (Hindu) The Goddess whose energy continues to protect the world from chaos.

Diana (Roman) Powerful moon and huntress Goddess.

Dianacht (Celtic) "God of Curing or Swift in Power," he is a God of herbal healing, medicine, and the physician to the Gods.

Dionysus (Greek) God of ecstasy, sex, revelry, and pleasure.

Dumiatis (Celtic) God of creative thought, story telling, and teaching.

Dwyane (Celtic) God of love, creativity, and mischief.

Edain (Celtic) Goddess of beauty, grace, and one of the "White Ladies" of the Faery. She has the powers of shapeshifting and transmigration (multiple births through time).

Eir (Norse) Goddess of herbal healing.

Epona (Celtic) Goddess of fertility, power, prosperity, and abundance, associated with horses.

Erato (Greek) The muse of love poetry, mimicry, and pantomime.

Eriu (Celtic) The triple mother Goddess. She is a shapeshifter and Goddess of the Sovereignty of the Land.

Eros (Greek) God of passionate love.

Eurynome (Greek) The mother of all pleasure, whose embodiment is the beautiful triplets, the Graces—splendor, abundance, and joyousness.

Euterpe (Greek) The muse of music and lyric poetry.

Fengi and Mengi (Norse) They were two magical giants, who in the time of the heroic Scandinavian King Frodi, worked a mill whose grindstone magically produced peace and prosperity.

Findabair (Celtic) Goddess of Connacht and the Otherworld, of beauty, grace, and love.

Fliodhas (Celtic) Goddess of the woodlands, protector of animals and forests, associated with the doe, abundance, and ancestral powers.

Flora (Roman) Goddess of fertility, sex, promiscuity, flowering plants, personal growth, and spring.

Forseti (Norse) God of justice, legal matters, and mediation.

Fortuna (Roman) Lady Luck, Goddess of love and sexuality.

Frey (Norse) God of fertility, joy, peace, prosperity, and happiness.

Freya (Norse) Goddess of Love, beauty, passion, and fertility.

Frigga (Norse) Mother Goddess of feminine arts and abundance.

Gaea (Greek) The Mother Goddess who embodies the earth and has existed before time began.

Gobannon (Celtic)   The Divine Smith and God of magic and craftspersons, also called "Gobban the Wright" and "Gobban Saer, The Master Mason."

Graces (Roman)   Three Goddesses embodying grace of manner—Thaleia (abundance), Aglaia (splendor and radiance), and Eurphrosyne (joy and happiness).

Gwalchmei (Celtic)   God of love and music and son of the Goddess Mei, also called the "Hawk or Falcon of May."

Gwydion (Celtic)   Shapeshifter and Celtic God of the creative arts, eloquence, kindness, healing, protection, prosperity, dreaming, and magic.

Harmonia (Greek)   Goddess of music, dance, and poetry.

Hathor (Egyptian)   Goddess of love, Mother of creation, and mistress of everything beautiful.

Heimdall (Norse)   God who guards the rainbow bridge, known for his incredible sight and hearing.

Heket (Egyptian) Frog Goddess of childbirth and creation.

Helen (Greek)   Moon Goddess of childbirth, love, and fertility.

Hellith (Celtic)   God of the setting sun and protector of souls of the dead.

Hera (Greek)   Goddess of women and their sexuality, including matrimony and motherhood.

Hermes (Greek)   God of flocks, communication, music, and business. He guides travelers and is the divine messenger.

Hertha (Celtic)   Goddess of fertility, spring, the earth, rebirth, and healing.

Hestia (Greek)   Goddess of the hearth fire and home.

Horae (Greek)   A group of Greek Goddesses representing the divine aspects of the natural order of the seasons.

Hypnos (Greek)   Mesmerizing God of sleep and dreams.

Inanna (Sumerian)   Mother Goddess who brought civilization to humankind.

Irene (Greek)   Goddess of peace.

Iris (Greek)   Divine messenger and Goddess of rainbows.

Ishtar (Babylonian)   Goddess of love, beauty, and war. She is associated with Venus, the morning star.

Isis (Egyptian)   All Mother Goddess, embodiment of femininity, associated with love, healing, and abundance.

Juno (Roman)   Mother Goddess of love, matrimony, and fertility, who rules over the entire reproductive cycle of women and the home.

Jupiter (Roman)   Powerful sky God and All Father.

Kama (Hindu)   God of love, called the "Seed of Desire."

Kernunnos/Cernunnos (Celtic)   Father God of virility, prowess, and nature, associated with love, culling, and prosperity.

Kerridwen/Cerridwyn (Celtic)   Powerful Goddess of knowledge, shapeshifting, and wisdom, who possesses the cauldron of inspiration.

Krishna (Hindu)   God of erotic delight, love, and ecstasy.

Kuan Yin (Oriental)   Goddess of compassion, love, healing, protection, and beauty.

Lakshmi (Hindu)   Goddess of beauty, prosperity, and good fortune.

Letha (Celtic)   Midsummer harvest Goddess of abundance and pros-perity.

Llyr (Celtic)   Sea God of music, shapeshifting, and King of the oceans.

Lugh (Celtic)   Champion of the Tuatha De Dannan, Sun God, and master of all arts. He is the God of prosperity, love, sex, romance, poets, bards, smiths, and warriors.

Maat (Egyptian)   Goddess of truth and balance.

Mabon (Celtic)   "The Divine Son" and "The Son of Light," God of sex, love, magic, prophesy, and power.

Maeve (Celtic)   Goddess of sexuality, fertility, and power.

Manannan Mac Llyr (Celtic)   Shapeshifter, teacher, God of magic, love, prosperity, the Otherworld, the sea, and travel.

Math (Celtic)   Son of Mathonwy, seasonal King and Welsh God of magic, wisdom, learning, prosperity, shapeshifting, enchantment, and sorcery.

Maya (Hindu)   Goddess of creativity.

Meditrina (Roman)   The Roman Goddess of medicine, wine, and health.

Mei (Celtic)   Mother Goddess, associated with the sun, earth, spring, green meadows, and growing things.

Mercury (Roman)   God of safe travel, communication, audio and visual production, creative arts, and writers.

Merlin (Celtic)   Woodland and nature God, associated with shapeshifting and sorcery.

Meskhenet (Egyptian)   Goddess of childbirth.

Mider (Celtic)   Faery King, God of the Underworld, bard, and expert chess player.

Min (Egyptian)   God of sex, fecundity, and crops.

Mitra (Hindu)   God of friendship.

Modrona (Celtic)   The Great Mother of Mabon (light).

Mokosh (Slavic)   The great Goddess of the earth.

Morgan Le Fey (Celtic)   Faery Queen, sorceress, shapeshifter, and beautiful enchantress.

Mother Mary (Hebrew)   Christian archetype of the Mother Goddess. She gives birth to the son of the divine through immaculate conception.

Nanna (Norse)   Goddess of fertility, the moon, earth, prosperity, and wealth.

Nantosuelta (Celtic)   River Goddess, associated with healing, protection, and prosperity.

Nemetona (Celtic)   Protectress of the sacred Drynemeton, Warrior Goddess of the oak groves, and patron of thermal springs.

Nephthys (Egyptian)   Goddess of dreams, divination, and hidden knowledge.

Nimue (Celtic)   Goddess of lakes, love, sovereignty, learning, and teaching.

Nodens (Celtic)   God of dreams and sleep.

Norns (Norse)   Three sisters, Urd/Verdandi/Sculd, who control the fate of everyone.

Nuada (Celtic)   The Good Father, powerful chieftain God of thunder, kingship, rebirth, war, treasure, and wealth.

Nwyvre (Celtic)   God of space, stars, universes, and the firmament.

Odin (Norse)   All Father God of wisdom, ancestry, love, healing, wealth, and inspiration. He is known by over 200 names.

Ogma (Celtic)   God of eloquence, invention, knowledge, public speaking, writing, and literature.

Omamama (Native American)   The Cree ancestral Goddess of beauty, fertility, gentleness, and love.

Oshun (African)   Goddess of love, pleasure, beauty, and dancing.

Osiris (Egyptian)   Father God of civilization and rebirth.

Ostara (Celtic)   Goddess of spring and fertility.

Pan (Greek)   Nature God of lust, love, play, and pleasure.

Parvati (Hindu)   Goddess of marital blessing.

Penelope (Greek)   Spring Goddess of fertility and sexuality.

Pi-Hsai Yuan-Chin (Chinese)   Goddess of childbirth who brings health and good fortune to the newborn and protection to the mother.

Polyhymnia (Greek)   The muse of hymns, mimic art, and harmony.

Psyche (Greek)   Goddess of love.

Ra (Egyptian)   Sun God and Father of all Gods. He has a detachable eye that can go off on its own.

Rhiannon (Celtic)   Queen Mother, associated with nobility, prosperity, poetry, the Otherworld, horses, birds, and travel.

Robur (Celtic)   Forest King and Monadic tree God of the forests, particularly oaks.

Rosemerta (Celtic)   Goddess of abundance, prosperity, fertility, beauty, and love.

Sadv (Celtic)   Ancient deer Goddess of the forests, nature, creativity, and ancestry.

Saga (Norse)   Goddess of poetry, story-telling, history, memory, and sagas.

Saturn (Roman)   God of agriculture, structure, patterns, and prosperity.

Selene (Greek/Roman)   Moon and love Goddess.

Shakti (Hindu)   Great Mother Goddess who embodies feminine energy.

Sheila na Gig (Celtic)   Goddess of sex, birth, passion, and laughter.

Shiva (Hindu)   God of creation who embodies masculine energy.

Silvanus (Roman)   God of the forests and agriculture, especially around woodland clearings.

Sulis (Celtic)   Goddess of healing and warm springs.

Taliesin (Celtic)   Son of Kerridwen, poet, prophet and bard.

Tarvos Trigaranos (Celtic)   God of vegetation, abundance, and virility.

Terpsichore (Greek)   The muse of dancing and music, especially the choral song.

Thalia (Greek)   The festive muse of comedy and idyllic poetry.

Thor (Norse)   God of thunder and protector from chaos and evil.

Thoth (Egyptian)   God of writing, math, music, medicine, drawing, astronomy, the moon, and magic.

Tlazolteotl (Peruvian)   Goddess of love.

Triana (Celtic)   The Triple Goddess—Sun-Ana, Earth-Ana, and Moon-Ana—of healing, knowledge, higher love, protocol, and wisdom.

Tyr (Norse)   God of justice, protection, courage, and the stars.

Uller (Norse)   God of glory whose name means "brilliant one."

Urania (Greek)   The muse of astronomy and poetry.

Var (Norse)   Love Goddess.

Venus (Roman)   Goddess of love and sexuality.

Vesta (Roman)   Goddess of fire, the hearth, home, and domestic matters.

Viviana (Celtic)   Goddess of love, birth, life, mothers, childbirth, and children.

Voluptas (Roman)   Goddess of pleasure and sensuality.

Voluspa (Norse)   Goddess who is known as a famous seer.

Zeus (Greek)   The powerful leader of the Gods of Olympus, associated with love, fertility, marriage, prosperity, hospitality, protection, and wealth.

Appendix B

Empowering Crystals and Gemstones

Love

Amethyst
Beryl
Carnelian
Clear Calcite
Clear Quartz
Diamond
Emerald
Fluorite
Garnet
Herkimer Diamond
Jade
Kunzite
Labradorite
Lapis Lazuli
Milky Quartz
Moonstone
Rhodochrosite
Rose Quartz
Ruby
Rutilated Quartz
Smithsonite
Sugilite
Topaz
Zircon

Health

Agate
Amazonite
Amethyst
Aquamarine
Aventurine
Azurite
Beryl
Bloodstone
Carnelian
Chrysocolla
Chrysophase
Citrine

Clear Quartz
Diamond
Emerald
Flint
Fluorite
Garnet
Gold Calcite
Hematite
Herkimer Diamond
Jade
Jasper
Kunzite
Labradorite
Lapis Lazuli
Lepidolite
Malachite
Moldavite
Moonstone
Obsidian
Opal
Peridot
Rhodochrosite
Rose Quartz
Ruby
Rutilated Quartz
Sapphire
Smithsonite
Smokey Quartz
Sodalite
Straurolite
Sugilite
Tanzanite
Tiger's Eye
Topaz
Tourmaline
Turquoise
Zircon

Prosperity

Amazonite
Apache Tear
Aventurine
Carnelian
Chrysophase
Citrine
Clear Quartz
Diamond
Emerald
Flint
Garnet
Gold
Jade
Jasper
Lapis Lazuli
Malachite
Milky Quartz
Moldavite
Moonstone
Onyx
Opal
Peridot
Pyrite
Ruby
Rutilated Quartz
Sapphire
Tiger's Eye

Appendix C

Empowering Magical Tools

Athame   A double-edge knife, associated with creative fire, used as a pointer to define space, for example, to cut the magic circle. Dull your athame's edges to avoid accidents. (Remember to keep all knives in a safe place away from children.)

Bell   Tool of the Goddess, a bell can be rung at the beginning and ending of a ritual. It is used to attract divine energies, as a fertility charm, and for protection against negativity.

Bowl   Tool corresponding to the earth element and north. A bowl can be ceramic, metal, wood, or glass.

Broom/Besom   Used for purification to clean your magic circle of unwanted energies, for protection, in handfastings (Wiccan marriages where vows of love are exchanged), and astral travel. Most often, besoms are made of straw or grass tied around a branch of pine, oak, fir, lavender, or rosemary.

Candles   Tools representing the fire element, used on the altar during mediation, prayer, and ritual. Excellent tools for focusing your mind and directing your thoughts. Beeswax candles can be returned to the earth.

Cauldron   Tool corresponding to water and signifying the womb of the Goddess. A three-legged pot, most often made of cast iron, with its opening smaller than its base.

Chalice/Cup   Tool of the Goddess, water, and the west (sometimes all directions), usually made of stone, glass, silver, lead-free pewter, or clay. It holds water, juice, or wine.

Cloak/Robe   Your magical skin donned when you do magic. Made of any fabric, any color, any design. You can wear a cloak or robe when you do rituals, or you can wear a tunic, cape, or your street clothes.

Color   All colors have unique energy signatures and meanings. In New Age Wicca, the traditional color correspondences are as follows:

> White: Divine guidance, power, purity, spiritual love, divination, motivation, peace, harmony, protection, Oneness
>
> Gold: Wealth, increase, creativity, power, ambition, security, solar energy
>
> Silver: Moon and star power, peace, dreaming, ancestral communication, insight, clairvoyance, astral travel, divination
>
> Gray: Mastery, balance, wisdom, merging, invention, discovery, protection
>
> Black: Banishing negative energies, ending negative relationships, the shadow self, dreaming
>
> Blue: Tranquility, purification, healing, divination, travel, loyalty, psychic protection, perception, directing magical energy, higher wisdom
>
> Purple: Psychic awareness, ancestral lore, sacredness, consecration, offensive protection, dreaming, spiritual healing, nobility, leadership
>
> Pink: Friendship, romance, love, children, kinship, kindness, compassion
>
> Rose: Harmony, divine love, enlightenment, romance
>
> Red: Strength, survival, action, passion, lust, sexuality, ambition, vitality, courage, focus, power, animation
>
> Orange: Business, joy, mirth, comfort, prosperity, plenty, home, friendship, happiness, meditation, justice
>
> Yellow: Attraction, persuasion, imagination, mental agility, understanding, comprehension, communication, perception
>
> Green: Fertility, creativity, birth, healing, prosperity, abundance, money, regeneration, growth, nature, good luck
>
> Brown: Grounding, stability, pets companions, nature, potential, nurturing, family, home, common sense

Cord   Can be used to draw a magic circle, a pentacle, or other magical symbol on the ground, symbolic of the cord of life. It measures nine feet with a knot at one end to anchor it to a stick, and it also has knots at 4.5 feet, 6.5 feet, and 7.5 feet.

Crystals/Gemstones   Energy magnifiers used for magic, especially healing, personal protection, and mental clarity. (Please refer to Appendix B for specific uses.)

Drum   Used for focusing, merging, communicating with ancestors, astral travel, and divination. Tool corresponding to the elements of air and earth.

Fetish   Divine tools, most often carved of stone, wood, or made of clay, in the shape of animals, the Goddess, the God, ancestors, or the sacred spirits. Used for focusing, for talismans, and amulets.

Incense and Censor   Tools corresponding to the fire and air elements, used to attract divine energies, for divine communication, mediation, and ritual. If you are sensitive to smoke, substitute essential oils and an aromatherapy diffuser or put a few drops of scented oil in a small pan of boiling water to scent your sacred space.

Pentacle   A five-pointed star (pentagram), surrounded by a circle, associated with the earth. It represents all elemental powers and the human microcosm. The pentacle is used for protection, to attract divine energies, and to manifest goals. Pentacles come in different shapes and sizes, from jewelry to bumper stickers and posters to altar tiles.

Staff   Associated with the earth element, representing authority, knowledge, and personal power, a staff is at least shoulder high and about 2.5 inches in diameter. The staff holds and focuses magical energy.

Sword   Tool of command corresponding to fire and the south, used to focus magical power, for protection, tapping into ancestral wisdom, and defining sacred space, for example, cutting a magic circle.

Talisman   Tool corresponding to the earth element, customarily made of metal, stone, or clay. It is empowered with specific energies and carried on your person or placed on the altar during rituals to set the tone or draw helpful energies to you.

Wand   Associated with the air element and east, the wand is made of wood and is a rod of authority and power, used to gather, direct, receive, and send energy. This most ancient of magical tools is an extension of you, usually no longer than the length of your forearm.

Appendix D

Empowering Herbs, Plants, Trees, and Flowers

Love

African Violet
Amber
Apple
Apricot
Aster
Avocado
Azalea
Bachelor's Buttons
Barley
Basil
Beet
Bleeding Heart
Brazil Nut

Caraway
Cardamon
Carrot
Catnip
Celery
Chamomile
Cherry
Chestnut
Chickweed
Chicory
Chili Pepper
Chrysanthemum
Cinnamon
Clove
Clover

Coconut
Columbine
Copal
Coriander
Crocus
Cucumber
Cumin
Cyclamen
Daffodil
Daisy
Damiana
Dandelion
Dill
Dragon's Blood
Elm

Endive
Fern
Fig
Gardenia
Geranium
Ginger
Gourd
Grape
Hemp
Hibiscus
Honeysuckle
Hyacinth
Jasmine
Lavender
Lemon
Lemon Balm
Lemon Grass
Lettuce
Licorice Root
Lilac
Lime
Magnolia
Mallow
Maple
Marigold
Marjoram
Meadowsweet
Mint
Mistletoe
Myrtle
Olive
Orange
Orchid
Pansy
Papaya
Patchouli
Peach

Pear
Periwinkle
Pineapple
Plum
Pomegranate
Primrose
Quince
Raspberry
Rice
Rose
Rye
Saffron
Sandalwood
Sesame
Strawberry
Sugar Cane
Sweet Pea
Vanilla
Vervain
Violet
Willow
Yarrow

Health

Acacia
Alfalfa
Allspice
Aloe
Alyssum
Amber
Anemone
Angelica
Anise
Apple
Arbutus
Ash

Aspen
Avocado
Azalea
Bamboo
Banana
Barley
Bay
Bee Pollen
Benzoin
Birch
Blackberry
Blessed Thistle
Bloodroot
Borage
Cabbage
Camphor
Carnation
Catnip
Cayenne
Cedar
Chamomile
Citrus
Clover
Comfrey
Cotton
Cucumber
Curry
Cypress
Dandelion
Dulse
Echinacea
Elder
Eucalyptus
Eyebright
Fennel
Fenugreek
Fern

Feverfew
Flax
Fleabane
Frankincense
Gardenia
Garlic
Gentian
Geranium
Ginger
Ginkgo
Ginseng
Goldenseal
Gotu Kola
Grape
Hemp
Henna
Hops
Hydrangea
Ivy
Juniper
Larkspur
Lavender
Licorice Root
Lotus
Mahogany
Mallow
Marjoram
Mint
Mugwort
Mulberry
Mullein
Mustard
Myrrh
Neroli
Nettle
Oak

Olive
Onion
Papaya
Parsley
Passion Flower
Pennyroyal
Peony
Peppermint
Persimmon
Pine
Plantain
Plum
Poppy
Potato
Radish
Red Clover
Rosemary
Rowan
Saffron
Sage
Sagebrush
Sandalwood
Sassafras
Shallot
Skullcap
Slippery Elm
Snapdragon
St. John's Wort
Stargazer Lily
Thyme
Tumeric
Valerian
Willow
Yarrow
Yerba Santa
Yucca

Prosperity

Alfalfa
Allspice
Almond
Apple
Apricot
Ash
Balsam Fir
Bamboo
Banana
Barley
Basil
Bay
Bean
Bee Pollen
Beech
Benzoin
Bergamot
Birch
Blackberry
Bluebell
Brazil Nut
Broom
Buckwheat
Cabbage
Camellia
Cashew
Cinnamon
Cinquefoil
Clove
Clover
Comfrey
Corn
Cotton
Daffodil

Daisy
Dill
Dogwood
Fenugreek
Fern
Flax
Garlic
Ginger
Goldenrod
Hazel
Heather
Holly
Huckleberry
Hyacinth
Iris
Lemon Balm
Lettuce
Mandrake Root
Maple
Moss
Myrtle
Nutmeg
Oak
Oats
Orange
Patchouli
Pea
Peach
Pecan
Persimmon
Pine
Pineapple
Pomegranate
Poplar
Poppy
Reed
Rice
Rowan

Saffron
Sesame
Straw
Sunflower
Vervain
Walnut
Wheat

Appendix E

Empowering Magical Symbols

Pentacle	The Triple Goddess	The Horned God	Altar

Earth	The Circle	Female	Male

New Moon	Waxing Moon	Full Moon	Waning Moon

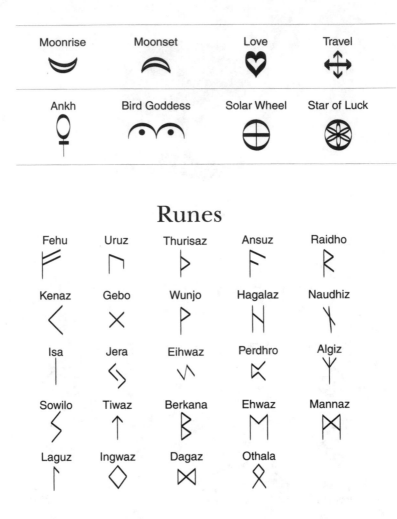

Moonrise	Moonset	Love	Travel

Ankh	Bird Goddess	Solar Wheel	Star of Luck

Runes

Fehu	Uruz	Thurisaz	Ansuz	Raidho

Kenaz	Gebo	Wunjo	Hagalaz	Naudhiz

Isa	Jera	Eihwaz	Perdhro	Algiz

Sowilo	Tiwaz	Berkana	Ehwaz	Mannaz

Laguz	Ingwaz	Dagaz	Othala

Bibliography

Armstrong, Lance. *It's Not About the Bike*. New York: Putnam Publishing Group, 2000.

Bacci, Ingrid. *The Art of Effortless Living*. Perigree, 2002.

Benson, Herbert, and Miriam Klipper. *The Relaxation Response*. New York: Avon, 1976.

Blair, Nancy. *Amulets of the Goddess*. Oakland, Calif.: Wingbow Press, 1993.

Bluestone, Sarvananda. *How to Read Signs and Omens in Everyday Life*. Rochester, Vt.: Destiny Books, 2002.

Bolen, Jean Shinoda, M.D. *Goddesses in Every Woman*. San Francisco: Harper & Row Publishers, 1984.

Borgman, Peggy Wynne. *Four Seasons of Inner and Outer Beauty*. New York: Broadway Books, 2000.

Broomfield, John. *Other Ways of Knowing*. Rochester, Vt.: Inner Traditions, 1997.

Buckland, Raymond. *Wicca For Life*. New York: Kensington Publishing Co., 2001.

Bulfinch, Thomas. *Bulfinch's Mythology*. Garden City, N.Y.: Garden City Publishing Co., Inc., 1938.

Canfield, Jack, and Mark Victor Hansen. *Chicken Soup for the Soul*. Deerfield Beach, Fla.: Health Communications, Inc., 1993.

Canfield, Jack, Mark Victor Hansen, and Les Hewitt. *The Power of Focus*. Deerfield Beach, Fla.: Health Communications, Inc., 2000.

Coffey, Lisa Marie. *Getting There With Grace*. Boston: Journey Editions, 2001.

Coghill, Roger. *The Healing Energies of Light*. Boston: Journey Editions, 2000.

Croce, Pat. *I Feel Great And You Will Too*. Philadelphia: Running Press, 2000.

Crosse, Joanna. *Encyclopedia of Mind, Body, Spirit, and Earth*. Boston: Element, 1998.

Cunningham, Scott. *The Complete Book of Incense, Oils, and Brews*. St. Paul, Minn.: Llewellyn Publications, 1989.

———. *Encyclopedia of Magical Herbs*. St. Paul, Minn: Llewellyn Publications, 1985.

———. *Living Wicca*. St. Paul, Minn: Llewellyn Publications, 1993.

Currot, Phyllis. *WitchCrafting*. New York: Broadway Books, 2001.

Davich, Victor. *The Best Guide to Meditation*. Los Angeles: Renaissance Books, 1998.

Dossey, Larry. *Recovering the Soul: A Scientific and Spiritual Search*. Bantam, 1989.

Emery, Marcia. *Power Hunch!* Hillsboro, Oreg.: Beyond Words Publishing, 2001.

Farrar, Janet, and Stewart Farrar. *The Witches' Way*. London: Robert Hale, 1984.

———. *A Witches' Bible Compleat*. New York: Magical Childe, 1984.

Gimbutas, Marija. *The Language of the Goddess*. San Francisco: Harper & Row, 1989.

———. *The Goddesses and Gods of Old Europe*. Berkeley: University of California Press, 1982.

Godwin, Malcolm. *The Lucid Dreamer*. New York: Simon & Schuster, 1994.

Green, Miranda J. *Dictionary of Celtic Myth and Legend*. New York: Thames and Hudson, 1997.

Griffin, Sally. *Wicca Wisdom Keepers*. Boston: Red Wheel/Weiser, 2002.

Grimal, Pierre (Editor). *Larousse World Mythology*. London: Paul Hamlyn, 1965.

Hammerman, David, and Lisa Lenard. *The Complete Idiot's Guide to Reincarnation*. Indianapolis: Alpha Books, 2000.

Hay, Louise. *You Can Heal Your Life*. Carson, Calif.: Hay House, 1984.

Jung, Carl G. *The Archetypes of the Collective Unconscious*. Princeton: Princeton University Press, 1990.

Kabat-Zinn, Jon. *Wherever You Go, There You Are*. New York: Hyperion, 1994.

Klein, Hailey. *The Way of Change*. Boston: Journey Editions, 2002.

Knight, Sirona. *A Witch Like Me*. Franklin Lakes, N.J.: New Page Books, 2001.

———. *Celtic Traditions*. New York: Citadel Press, 2000.

———. *Dream Magic: Night Spells and Rituals For Love, Prosperity, and Personal Power*. San Francisco: HarperSanFrancisco, 2000.

———. *Exploring Celtic Druidism*. Franklin Lakes, N.J.: New Page Books, 2001.

———. *Faery Magick*. Franklin Lakes, N.J.: New Page Books, 2002.

———. *Greenfire: Making Love with the Goddess*. St. Paul, Minn.: Llewellyn Publications, 1995.

———. *Goddess Bless!* Boston: Red Wheel, 2002.

———. *The Little Giant Encyclopedia of Runes*. New York: Sterling Publishing Co., 2000.

———. *Love, Sex, and Magick*. New York: Citadel Press, 1999.

———. *Moonflower: Erotic Dreaming with the Goddess*. St. Paul, Minn: Llewellyn Publications, 1996.

———. *The Pocket Guide to Celtic Spirituality*. Freedom, Calif.: Crossing Press, 1998.

———. *The Pocket Guide to Crystals and Gemstones*. Freedom, Calif.: Crossing Press, 1998.

———. *The Book of Reincarnation*. Hauppauge, N.Y.: Barron's, 2002.

Knight, Sirona, et al. *The Shapeshifter Tarot*. St. Paul, Minn.: Llewellyn Publications, 1998.

Leach, Maria (Editor). *Standard Dictionary of Folklore, Mythology, and Legend*. New York: Funk & Wagnalls Co., 1950.

Linn, Denise. *The Secret Language of Signs*. New York: Ballantine Book, 1996.

Lund, JoAnna. *String of Pearls*. New York: The Berkley Publishing Group, 2000.

Monaghan, Patricia. *The Book of Goddesses and Heroines*. St Paul, Minn.: Llewellyn Publications, 1990.

Oman, Maggie (Editor). *Prayers For Healing*. Berkeley, Calif.: Conari Press, 1997.

Rector-Page, Linda. *Healthy Healing*. Sonora, Calif.: Healthy Healing Publications, 1992.

Sabrina, Lady. *Exploring Wicca*. Franklin Lakes, N.J.: New Page Books, 2000.

Schiller, David, and Carol Schiller. *Aromatherapy Basics*. New York: Sterling Publishing Co., 1998.

Scully, Nicki. *Power Animal Meditations*. Rochester, Vt.: Bear & Company, 2001.

Shapiro, Debbie. *Your Body Speaks Your Mind*. Freedom, Calif.: Crossing Press, 1997.

Shapiro, Debbie, and Eddie Shapiro. *Peace Within the Stillness*. Freedom, Calif.: Crossing Press, 1998.

Shumsky, Susan. *Exploring Meditation*. Franklin Lakes, N.J.: New Page Books, 2002.

Simkins, C. Alexander, and Annellen Simkins. *Self-Hypnosis*. Boston: Journey Editions, 2000.

Simpson, Liz. *The Healing Energies of Earth*. Boston: Journey Editions, 2000.

Skafte, Dianne. *Listening To The Oracle*. New York: HarperSanFrancisco, 1997.

Spangler, David. *Blessing*. New York: Riverhead Books, 2001.

Starhawk. *The Spiral Dance*. San Francisco: HarperSanFrancisco, 1979.

Stewart, R. J. *Celtic Gods, Celtic Goddesses*. New York: Sterling Publishing Co., 1990.

Sunset New Western Garden Book. Menlo Park, Calif.: Lane Publishing Co., 1979.

Taub, Edward. *Seven Steps to Self-Healing*. New York: DK Publishing, Inc., 1996.

Telesco, Patricia. *FutureTelling*. Freedom, Calif.: Crossing Press, 1998.

Thomas, Richard (Editor). *It's a Miracle*. New York: Dell Publishing, 2002.

Thorsson, Edred. *Futhark: A Handbook of Rune Magic*. York Beach, Maine: Samuel Weiser, Inc., 1984.

Tuitean, Paul, and Estelle Daniels. *Pocket Guide To Wicca*. Freedom, Calif.: Crossing Press, 1998.

Valiente, Doreen. *Witchcraft for Tomorrow*. New York: St. Martin's Press, 1978.

Weinstein, Marion. *Earth Magic*. New York: Earth Magic Productions, 1998.

Williams, David, and Kate West. *Born In Albion*. Cheshire, England: Pagan Media, Ltd., 1996.

Worwood, Valerie. *The Complete Book of Essential Oils and Aromatherapy*. New York: New World Library, 1995.

Index

About the Author

Sirona Knight is a New Age Witch who lives in Northern California with her family: Michael, her husband of 27 years; Skylor, their 10-year-old son; four beagles; and a family of cats. Sirona's ancestors include James Smithson, founder of the Smithsonian Institute, and she comes from a long line of the Daughters of the American Revolution.

Sirona is a Third Degree Craftmaster and High Priestess of Celtic Druidism. She is also the award-winning creator and co-author of the best-selling tarot deck and book, *The Shapeshifter Tarot*. She is Contributing Editor for the international magazine, *Magical Blend* (www.magicalblend.com), and has interviewed notable Wiccans Phyllis Curott, Trish Telesco, Raymond Buckland, Raven Grimassi, and Silver RavenWolf; musicians Steve Vai, Brandon Boyd/Incubus, Chi Chong/Deftones, and Donovan; and New Age authors Mark Victor Hansen, James Redfield, Dr. John Gray, and Neale Donald Walsch. She also has a special Master's degree in stress management from California State University, Sacramento (with honors), and is a master hypnotherapist.

Sirona maintains strong Internet visibility (www.sironaknight.com), answering e-mail from fans and chatting on websites across the world. She also lectures and teaches workshops. She enjoys reading, spending time with her family, homeschooling her son, swimming, walking in the woods, watching classic movies, and tending her flower and vegetable gardens.